C000263413

SEEKING A CITY
WITH FOUNDATIONS

DAVID W. SMITH

SEEKING A CITY WITH FOUNDATIONS

THEOLOGY FOR AN URBAN WORLD

ivp

INTER-VARSITY PRESS
Norton Street, Nottingham NG7 3HR, England
Email: ivp@ivpbooks.com
Website: www.ivpbooks.com

© David W. Smith, 2011

David W. Smith has asserted his right under the Copyright, Designs and Patents Act, 1988, to be identified as Author of this work.

All rights reserved. No part of this publication may be reproduced, stored in a retrieval system, or transmitted, in any form or by any means, electronic, mechanical, photocopying, recording or otherwise, without the prior permission of the publisher or the Copyright Licensing Agency.

Unless otherwise stated, Scripture quotations are taken from the HOLY BIBLE, NEW INTERNATIONAL VERSION. Copyright © 1973, 1978, 1984 by International Bible Society. Used by permission of Hodder & Stoughton, a division of Hodder Headline Ltd. All rights reserved. 'NIV' is a trademark of International Bible Society. UK trademark number 1448790.

The quotation on page 29 is from T.S. Eliot, *The Rock*, 1934, permission requested from Faber & Faber.

First published 2011

British Library Cataloguing in Publication Data
A catalogue record for this book is available from the British Library.

ISBN: 978-1-84474-531-9

Set in Monotype Garamond 11/13pt
Typeset in Great Britain by Servis Filmsetting Ltd, Stockport, Cheshire
Printed in Great Britain by Ashford Colour Press Ltd, Gosport, Hampshire

Inter-Varsity Press publishes Christian books that are true to the Bible and that communicate the gospel, develop discipleship and strengthen the church for its mission in the world.

Inter-Varsity Press is closely linked with the Universities and Colleges Christian Fellowship, a student movement connecting Christian Unions in universities and colleges throughout Great Britain, and a member movement of the International Fellowship of Evangelical Students. Website: www.uccf.org.uk.

This book is dedicated to the memory of

TED HERBERT

Christian leader, biblical scholar and greatly-missed
friend, without whose encouragement and support it
would never have been begun.

CONTENTS

Preface   11
List of figures   14

1. **Introduction**   **17**
    The garden and the city   19
    The city of God   23
    The challenge for theology   24

PART ONE: THE URBAN WORLD

2. **The challenge of an urban world**   **29**
    The growth of an urban world   30
    Urbanization in Africa   31
    Cities of the rich, cities of the poor   34
    Understanding the urban world   39
    Agenda for an urban theology   42

3. **The birth and growth of the city**   **48**
    The sacred city   49
    The search for the good city   55

The fall and rise of urban cultures   58
The holy commonwealth   61
The city and the Industrial Revolution   64
Urban pathologies   69
Conclusion   74

4. **Urban visions, urban nightmares**   **76**
The garden city   78
The radiant city   79
Visions and nightmares   83
In the cities of the South   87
Storm clouds over the city   91
Back to the future?   94
The really big issue   102

5. **City skylines, city meanings**   **103**
From sacred centre to preserved monument   105
Moving down the hill   107
The forest of symbols   108
Visions of utopia   113
A city without meaning?   115

**PART TWO: BIBLICAL AND THEOLOGICAL
            PERSPECTIVES**

6. **The Bible and the city: from patriarchs to prophets**   **121**
In the beginning   124
Let my people go   128
The challenge of the cities of Canaan   133
Holy Zion: the promise and the failure   140
The prophetic perspective   147
The critique of urban religion   148
Love in the city   152
Lament for the city   155
Hope for an urban world   160
The promise of *shalom*   162
The cities of the world   165

7. **The Bible and the city: From Jesus to John of Patmos**   **171**
   Jesus and the city   172
   The tragedy of Jerusalem   186
   Death and resurrection   190
   Urban Christianity in the Roman Empire   192
   Romans: a letter to an urban church   197
   The new Jerusalem   205
   Conclusion   212

8. **Theology for an urban world**   **215**
   Idols of our time   217
   Theology and hope for the city   221
   The gospel for an urban world   225
   Pentecostalism, theology and the urban world   228
   The urban *ekklesia*: evangelical, emerging and catholic   231
   Here is your God!   237

Bibliography   **241**
   Social science perspectives   241
   Biblical/theological perspectives   248

   Index of names   257
   Index of Scripture references   261
   Index of subjects   265

PREFACE

In 2001 I received an invitation to move to Glasgow to lead a team at the International Christian College developing a programme of postgraduate studies in urban ministry. The vision was to enable experienced practitioners of ministry in an urban world to undertake critical reflection and research on their work by providing tools enabling the analysis of urban situations and fresh readings of the Bible in the light of urban realities, local and global. As I considered this move I cast my mind back over my own journey, searching for evidence that my career contained experience giving me some credibility should I relocate to Glasgow! I thought of the eleven years spent in pastoral ministry in Cambridge, but although this qualified as urban ministry, it did not involve exposure to the kind of realities my colleagues in Glasgow had in mind. It was service in Nigeria which in this, as in so much else, opened my eyes to life in the city as it is lived by millions of people today. I visited churches in the Muslim cities of the north, including Kano, as well as those built in colonial times in the south-east, such as Calabar and Port Harcourt. But above all there was Lagos! During an extended stay in this sprawling metropolis I first encountered the slums of the Global South, an experience which recurred later during a summer in the Philippines where I visited Christian congregations in shacks built on stilts just above the waterline in Manila.

These experiences of urban life left an indelible impression and prompted a series of questions to which I had no answers. How had it come about that so many people, my brothers and sisters, seemed condemned to live and die in such appalling situations? Nothing in my education, certainly not my theological education, had provided knowledge related to the causes of such urban poverty and destitution. But there were even more troubling questions: when asked to stand in front of a congregation of fellow believers in the slums and preach to them, what could I say? How did my understanding of the Bible connect with the circumstances of their lives? To this day I blush when I remember a message preached to a group of poor people whose circumstances triggered shock and anger within me, prompting a sermon in which I said the right things *to the wrong people*. In truth I was struggling to relate an inherited theology to a situation within which it would not fit, an experience which drove me back to the Bible with questions which had never entered my head in Cambridge.

I did make the move to Glasgow and have had the privilege of working there with a wonderful group of colleagues who, between them, possessed a wide range of expertise and shared a passionate commitment to the creation of an innovative programme of in-service studies in ministry in an urban world. I must thank Steven Chester, Darrell Cosden, Linda Dunnett, Neil Pratt, Tony Sargent and Ian Shaw for their fellowship during this process, and I especially honour the memory of Ted Herbert whose encouragement was crucial at every stage, and to whose memory this book is gratefully dedicated. The research undertaken during the past decade has provided me with a framework for the understanding of the growth of an urban world, while also compelling a re-reading of many biblical texts in the light of the urgent issues arising in this context. However, at least as important as these personal studies has been the ground-level experience of the students I have been privileged to engage with, members of international cohorts of practitioners of ministry in demanding city contexts from Aberdeen to Nairobi, and from Leipzig to Belfast. My sincere thanks are due to Proshanto Baroi, Henk Bouma, Philip Bowdler, Paul Ede, Mike Edwards, Andrew Elliott, Carl Lahr, Chris Martin, Richard Mayabi, Bos Menzies, John Merson, Patrick Mukholi, Steve Taylor, David Thompson and Alison Urie.

A book of this kind, drawing insights from a wide range of academic disciplines, involves considerable risks on the part of an author who is a specialist in none of these areas. That being so, I am grateful for the critical feedback provided by specialists who have read and commented on all or part of my manuscript: John Goldingay, Pekka Pitkänen, Andrew Smith, Colin Smith and Eldin Villafañe. My colleague Wes White has offered me his perceptive insights, pointed out some key resources which I had overlooked, while always being an enthusiastic supporter of this project. More than anyone I know, Wes exemplifies the meaning of the phrase, a 'reflective practitioner', and I am profoundly grateful for his friendship. However, despite the advice mentioned here, there are places in this text where I skate on very thin ice, so making it more than ever necessary to absolve all of the above friends of responsibility for my mistakes; for these I alone must take the blame. Finally, I cannot imagine a better editor than Phil Duce at IVP; he has chased me when necessary, raised questions about dubious statements, been wonderfully patient and, above all, has given unstinting encouragement and support from start to finish.

David Smith
Glasgow, November 2010

LIST OF FIGURES

1.1 'The situation of the Garden of Eden', from the 'Breeches Bible' of 1560.   20

1.2 Reconstruction of the city of Lachish.   22

2.1 Recent and projected trends in urbanization.   31

2.2 Urbanization in Africa in the twentieth century.   33

2.3 The growth of cities in independent Africa.   35

3.1 The dawn of urbanization: cities of Ancient Mesopotamia.   51

3.2 The city of Babylon.   52

3.3 Contrasts between urban and rural in 'bi-polar moralist' urban models.   71

5.1 Glasgow: old and new.   117

7.1 Excavations at the site of the city of Sepphoris.   176

New York, New York. Photograph © Stacey Whitaker.

1. INTRODUCTION

> Future historians will record the twentieth century as the century in which the whole
> world became one immense city (Cox 1968b: 101).

This claim, made by one of the best known urban theologians, may appear to
be an over-statement. After all, even if the percentage of the world's population residing in cities has reached the tipping point of 50% for the first time
in human history, that still leaves practically half the people on this planet
living in rural locations. Despite the undeniable and explosive growth of cities
throughout the world, vast tracts of the earth's surface remain 'undeveloped'
and sparsely populated. How can these areas, and the peoples who dwell in
them, be classified as belonging to an 'urban' world? And do we not run the
risk of completely misreading the varied contexts in which human beings
exist and live their lives if we ignore the reality of the persistence of traditional
societies in rural situations?

The question raised here is an important one and it is closely related to
long-standing tensions between the urban and rural contexts, between the
'garden' and the city. However, before we dismiss Cox's claim we must reflect
on how 'urbanization' is to be defined. If we understand it to relate simply
to the growth in the number of people living in cities then, although this is
in itself a development of enormous historical significance, it would clearly
not justify the claim that the entire world has become a single city. However,

'urbanization' may be taken to have a broader meaning if it is understood to indicate the social, geographical, economic and cultural impact of cities far beyond the physical area which they occupy on the earth's surface. Geographers refer to a city's 'ecological footprint', meaning the area beyond the boundary of a particular city which is affected by its existence. As Andrew Davey points out, city footprints often stretch far beyond both regional and national boundaries and in the case of a megalopolis like London extends to 125 times its surface area 'and nearly equivalent to the total of Britain's productive land' (Davey 2001: 17).

Or again, consider the cultural impact of cities. The sociologist Manuel Castells observes that 'urbanization' can refer both to the 'spatial concentration of a population on the basis of certain limits of dimension and density' *and* the 'diffusion of the system of values, attitudes and behaviour called "urban culture"' (Castells 2002: 21). Values, practices and aspirations that originate within the city become widely diffused beyond the city and, especially in the age of electronic means of communication, undermine more rural, traditional ways of life. Urbanization in this second sense has a long history, as can immediately be recognized simply by the mention of cities like Babylon, Athens, Rome and Constantinople. For better or for worse, such urban settlements spread their influence over vast areas beyond their walls, and this suggests that the unprecedented physical expansion of cities at the present time will leave very few parts of the world unaffected by 'urbanization' in this second sense.

Not long ago I found myself in a queue in a supermarket in the city of Nairobi, Kenya. As I waited my turn I glanced up at the TV screen above the checkout in front of me which was relaying a European football game, just in time to see a replay of a goal scored by my home city team of Watford, England! A few days before this I had been in the huge slum of Kibera and walked past a shack christened 'Stamford Bridge' in which football games from the English Premier League were being relayed. The connections between the urban centres of the world, and the cultural impact of those cities across vast areas, is hugely increased by comparison with the ancient cities mentioned above as the result of the power of modern electronic means of communication. Manuel Castells has made the study of the emergence of a networked society the key to his urban sociology, and this phenomenon would suggest that urban culture is indeed pervasive across the world today.

Consider another scenario. A small-scale society struggling to defend traditional values and practices exists on a remote atoll in the Pacific Ocean. This might be described as an 'island paradise', and indeed, it could well be so identified in a Western tourist brochure. Here, surely, Cox's claim that the 'whole world' has become an 'immense city' must seem absurd? However, the very existence of this community is under threat as sea levels rise and the garbage thrown overboard from ships transporting goods along international sea lanes washes ashore on the beaches on every incoming tide. Some of this rubbish is toxic and threatens both human well-being and the previously abundant sea life in the surrounding ocean. What is more, visitors to this island paradise, fleeing the cities of Europe and America, bring with them a distinctly urban culture and display a way of life that threatens to erode what remains of traditional values, especially among the young. 'Urbanization' begins to feel like something in the atmosphere; less a location, more like a change in the climate, or perhaps even a virus.

The garden and the city

It is well known that the story told in the Bible begins in a garden and ends in a city. The world as created by God is a rural paradise in which complete harmony exists between human beings and their Maker, and between people and all other created beings. God himself is said to have looked on this scene and to have declared that it was 'very good' (Gen. 1:31). But in the final chapter of the Bible, after the long and complex story that has unfolded since Adam and Eve were expelled from the Garden of Eden, it is a city that comes into view as the ultimate goal and hope of human history. In this vision the glory of God is no longer displayed in a natural wilderness, but rather shines with great brilliance in a vast and holy city (Rev. 21:10–11).

This transition from the garden to the city has been interpreted in contrasting ways throughout history. On the one hand, an awareness of the personal and social costs of living 'east of Eden' has frequently stimulated a longing for a 'return to paradise' in which primal, rural values are treated as normative and essential to human well-being.

Seen in this light, the expulsion from the garden and the loss of the original harmony with the natural world, together with the beginnings of human culture, including of course, the building of cities, may be viewed as a disaster. Civilization comes with burdensome 'discontents' and to exist outside of Eden is to live under the curse of God. This anti-urban reading of the biblical narrative overlaps in surprising ways with the conclusions reached by some historians and sociologists who have repeatedly drawn attention to what are called 'urban pathologies'. Lewis Mumford, perhaps the best-known historian of the city, argued that the earliest cities, 'as distinct from the village community', were organized 'for the satisfaction of a dominant minority: no longer a community of humble families living by mutual aid' (Mumford 1966:

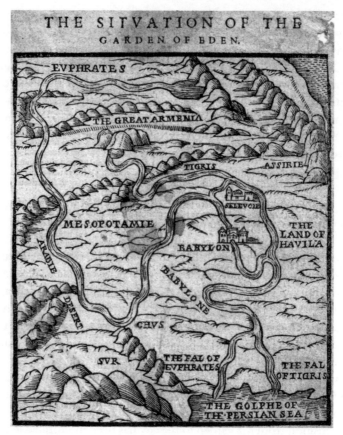

Figure 1.1: 'The situation of the Garden of Eden', from the 'Breeches Bible' of 1560

50). This sounds very much like a 'fall' from a condition of primitive simplicity in which life was originally shared in community. The picture painted by Mumford grows darker yet when he asserts: 'Throughout the greater part of history, enslavement, forced labour, and destruction have accompanied – and penalized – the growth of urban civilization' (ibid.: 56).

Mumford's negative verdict on the earliest cities to appear on the face of the earth is echoed, and indeed amplified, by many of the sociologists who attempted to understand the impact of the Industrial Revolution and the appearance of cities of unprecedented size and influence. The urban settlement had by this time metamorphosed from a location within a predominantly agrarian and rural society, to become the dominant source of all human values and cultural meanings. As Krishnan Kumar observes, theorists who examined the growth of urban centres in the early modern period were concerned not simply with the impact of the massing of population within the cities, but with the 'absolute predominance' that the city established over the life of society:

> The pre-industrial city had often been of great commercial, cultural and political importance. But it had existed within, usually parasitic upon, the body of the society as a whole, which in large segments could display attitudes and activities barely touched by urban life. Now in industrializing societies, whatever the purely quantitative size of the urban sector, the city had emerged from its encapsulated state and come to provide the economic, cultural and political framework of the whole society. . . . The city had become society itself (Kumar 1986: 68).

If that was the case in nineteenth-century Europe, then the consequences of the spread of vast cities around the globe – of the emergence of Cox's world which has become 'one immense city' – will be of enormous significance. It is perhaps not surprising that this urban explosion and the threat it is perceived to pose both to human well-being and to the very survival of the planet, should stimulate a fresh longing for a 'return to Paradise'. Indeed, the revolt against modernism has given birth to an even grimmer view of urban civilization than that expounded by Mumford fifty years ago. One may now discover analyses which claim that humankind has suffered from a 'collective psychosis' for 6,000 years. That is to say, from the point at which historians generally recognize the emergence of civilized societies in ancient Egypt and Sumer, postmodern writers see 'little more than a catalogue of endless wars' and successive invasions, designed to gain fresh territory and 'increase the glory of the empire' (Taylor 2005: 13). While not derived from the biblical narrative, this view of human civilization clearly posits something like the 'fall' of humankind and connects this directly to the growth of the great *urban* cultures of the ancient world. The spread of violence and the appearance of new forms of economic and social stratification are related to the appearance of cities between the Tigris and the Euphrates rivers around 2,500 BC and it is observed that these ancient urban settlements shaped the form of the city through the erection of huge city walls and new military technologies.

As we shall see, the narrative of the Bible unfolds within the context of the growth of the earliest urban cultures, so that Israel's lawgivers, sages and prophets were bound to respond to the challenges presented by this newly urbanized world. Did they, like some modern historians and cultural commentators, react with a simple anti-urbanism and a romantic longing for a return to paradise? Or did they possess a faith which offered grounds for hope that cities might become places which would enable human flourishing?

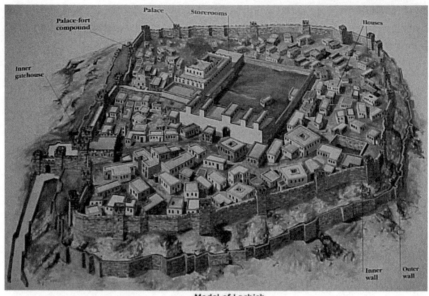

Model of Lachish

Figure 1.2. Reconstruction of the city of Lachish. Its upper walls were 6 m (20 ft) thick, the lower ones 4 m (13 ft) thick. The city was conquered and burned by Nebuchadnezzar in 589 BC

Whether nostalgia for a pre-fall state comes from a particular reading of the biblical narrative or from a postmodern quest for the recovery of a 'spiritual' and more egalitarian way of life, it frequently results in a deep-seated anti-urbanism, as city-building comes to be viewed as the action of alienated people whose creative activities, despite revealing great skill and resulting in impressive achievements, produce human settlements characterized by injustice, greed and violence. In theology and across a range of academic disciplines concerned with the understanding of the phenomenon of urbanization, we will therefore encounter profoundly anti-urban traditions which present the city in almost wholly negative terms. It becomes a 'parasite', or 'like a vampire'; it preys on the created world and is depicted as 'an enormous man-eater'. The garden and the city come to be set against each other, as in a famous line from the eighteenth century poet William Cowper (to whom we shall return): 'God made the country, and man made the town.'

The city of God

It is of course possible to interpret the biblical story, and the move from the garden to the city, in a quite different manner. The great narrative which starts in Eden and finishes in New Jerusalem can, so to speak, be read *backwards*. The purpose of human existence and the meaning of history are disclosed, not by reflection on origins, but through the hoped-for outcomes that are the stuff of eschatology. To approach the biblical narrative in this way is to discover a very different perspective on the urban condition, one that is the antithesis of the romantic longing for a return to paradise. The future – God's future – is urban, and since the final image in the Bible is of a city whose proportions far exceed those of any existing megalopolis, the transition from rural innocence to urban civilization is granted the divine stamp of approval. On this reading the Bible turns out to be a pro-urban book after all and life in the city can be celebrated as the context within which the appearance and growth of the reign of God is to be expected.

Moreover, just as the desire to recover paradise has its secular parallels, leading to anti-urbanism, so also the city has often been celebrated by secular writers as the instrument of human liberation. Karl Marx could speak dismissively of 'the idiocy of rural life', anticipating a human future shaped by the emergent urban world which, once its dazzling energy had been tamed and harnessed in the service of human freedom, would result in utopia. The headlong rush toward industrialization in the former Soviet Union, and a similar movement now being played out in the nominally Communist society in China, were (and are) underpinned by faith in the processes of modernization and urbanization and by an accompanying hope that the trek from the garden to the city will result in a golden era of human well-being and happiness.

What we have briefly sketched here are the two ends of a spectrum of approaches to the understanding of the urban process:

- the city is the concrete expression of the human fall from grace, a physical embodiment of man's independence and alienation and an environment that undermines community and creates lonely people;

or
- it is the instrument of human liberation, opening up previously unknown possibilities of freedom and creativity and promising the arrival of the kingdom of God on earth, or of utopia.

The contrast between the garden and the city, between a rural paradise and urban life and culture, has recently undergone a striking change in which these two seemingly conflicting contexts have been fused together. Paradisal conditions may now be recreated within secular urban settings so that the city can become *a new kind of paradise*. For those people who have access to it, this new urban existence offers peace and security, and a way of life combining access to the natural world with the availability of the most advanced forms of modern technology. The Palm Jumeirah development in Dubai, for example, has been promoted as the 'eighth wonder of the world', a vast offshore creation built of sand and rock, providing multi-million-dollar homes for the world's elite where hi-tech living can be enjoyed in surroundings in which imported bottle-nosed dolphins play in an eleven-acre lagoon.

However, vast financial resources are required to gain access to this urban paradise and the human costs involved in creating and maintaining the new Eden cast a long shadow across it. The 30,000 labourers, mainly from India and Bangladesh, who built and maintain Palm Jumeirah live in a camp in the desert ten miles away in prefabricated blocks in which twelve men share each room. The average wage for these workers is £25 per week and many are in debt to the agents who arranged and paid for their passages (Booth 2008: 7). Clearly, 'paradise' is being redefined here and, noting the somewhat sinister inversion of language involved, Mike Davis comments,

> On a planet where more than 2 billion people subsist on two dollars or less a day, these dreamworlds enflame desires – for infinite consumption, total social exclusion and physical security, and architectural monumentality – that are clearly incompatible with the ecological and moral survival of humanity (Davis & Monk 2007: xv).

The challenge for theology

Davis's recognition that certain contemporary urban developments threaten the 'ecological and moral survival of humanity' surely cries out for a theological response. And yet theologians have been strangely indifferent to the issues and challenges posed by the growth of an urban world. By contrast, in the fifth century, faced with the collapse of Rome, Augustine made the city the central theme of his theological reflection and produced work of such depth and wisdom that it shaped Christian thinking for centuries to come. His was, like ours, an age of crisis in which 'civilization' appeared to be under threat. Faced with this situation Augustine refused to adopt an anti-urban stance but developed his famous model of two contrasting cities, one of which was dysfunctional and doomed, while the other promised an urban future characterized by love, justice and community:

We also must know first our captivity, then our liberation: we must know Babylon and Jerusalem. . . . These two cities as a matter of historical fact, were two cities recorded in the Bible. . . . They were founded, at precise moments, to crystallize in symbolic form, the reality of these two 'cities' that had begun in the remote past, and that will continue to the end of the world (quoted in Brown 1969: 314).

Augustine derives from the Bible the insight that there are radically different urban forms. The city can be organized without reference to love and justice, and as such it threatens human well-being and is unsustainable; but there is the city characterized by love, beauty and holiness which will last, and brings joy to the heart. *This* is the city for which Christians should 'pine', according to Augustine: 'By pining, we are already there; we have already cast our hope, like an anchor, on that coast.' This 'ideal' city is yet to be revealed but it is the focal point of hope and causes the heart to sing: 'The citizens of Babylon hear the sound of the flesh, the Founder of Jerusalem hears the tune of our heart' (ibid.: 315).

At a time when, to repeat Cox's phrase again, the whole world has become 'one immense city', theology surely risks the complete loss of whatever credibility it still retains if it fails to meet this central challenge of our times. This being so we shall obviously need to return to the project of developing urban theology later in this book, but for now I want simply to indicate two themes connected to the movement from the garden to the city which are foundational to this task. The first of these concerns the doctrine of *creation*. We have already noted the Creator's delight in the cosmos and in a pristine earth teeming with an abundant variety of new forms of life, so that God himself pronounces the created world 'very good' (Gen. 1:31). That declaration must remain as the bedrock of theology in an urban world, not to justify a romantic flight from the city to some pre-civilizational paradise, but as a constant reminder of the material basis upon which all human and non-human life depends.

This book is being written in the Scottish city of Glasgow, one of the earliest industrial cities with, as we shall see, a history that has considerable significance both for urban studies and Christian mission. When I turn on a tap and clean water flows out, it is easy to forget the source from which it comes. Fifty miles to the north of the city is the beautiful Loch Katrine, set amid the mountains for which this country is famous. There is a direct connection between this particular 'garden' and life in the city because during the Victorian era the Glasgow city fathers fought a long political battle to create and fund a scheme by which the waters from the loch would become the source of clean drinking water in every home in the city of Glasgow. In the urban environment, especially where little space has been left for reminders of the created world, it is easy to forget our dependence upon the earth for the basic necessities which sustain human life. However, the recognition of the createdness of the world, of our position as stewards rather than lords of that creation, and of the need to live within the necessary limits imposed by our dependence upon the material basis of all life, is the foundation and starting point for a biblical urban theology.

The second theme to notice here relates to the eschatological vision of the new Jerusalem, which forms the culminating point of the Bible's narrative. This is indeed an urban paradise in which the glories of the original Eden are surpassed in the appearance of 'trees of life', which bear multiple crops and provide leaves which bring healing 'for the nations of the world' (Rev. 22:2). We shall return to this seminal vision later, but notice that, while it stands in stark contrast to the terrifying picture of the dysfunctional urban form represented by Babylon in Revelation 18, it also challenges those who are tempted to flee the city in a vain attempt to build some private paradise of their own. The future promised by God is an urban future in which creation and civilization are reconciled. In this holy city human beings will know and accept their createdness, and will exercise the gifts and abilities with which their Maker has endowed them, so reflecting his 'image and likeness'. Such a city has never yet been seen on earth, but the vision of it must shape Christian theological reflection on the urban form in the present, even as it sustains Christian hope for the eventual arrival of a city where love, justice and holiness will reign. As Augustine said, there will be peace 'full and eternal' in this city: 'Brethren, when I speak of that city, and especially when scandals grow great here, I just cannot bring myself to stop' (Brown 1969: 312).

PART ONE: THE URBAN WORLD

Bangkok, Thailand, promoted as 'City of Life'. Photography © David W. Smith

2. THE CHALLENGE OF AN URBAN WORLD

> Contemporary Western society seems to have lost its moral bearings, except for
> uneasy faith in market forces, while other forms of fundamentalism appear to be
> consolidating elsewhere. . . . If ever there was a need for public debate on moral issues,
> this is the time. Otherwise humankind risks losing any residual grip on the meaning of
> the good life, any capacity to recognise and challenge evil (Smith, 2000: vii).

Reflecting on the growth of cities in the wake of the industrial revolution, the
poet T. S. Eliot wrote lines which must still haunt people who devote themselves to the serious study of urbanization and, in particular, theologians who
reflect on the response of Christianity to the city.

> When the Stranger says: 'What is the meaning of this city?
> Do you huddle close together because you love each other?'
> What will you answer? 'We all dwell together
> To make money from each other'? or 'This is a community'? (Eliot 1961: 106)

The question posed by Eliot, and the radically contrasting answers to it, have
lost none of their relevance and power across time. Indeed, if the whole world
is becoming 'one immense city', then the Stranger's concern with the *meaning*
of this development becomes more urgent than ever before. The options
provided in these memorable lines suggest that the city *either* constitutes an

environment within which human community will flourish, resulting in a new freedom and wholeness for the human family, *or* its impact is profoundly negative in that it sets people against each other, destroying the very foundations of communal life and leading to social fragmentation, individual loneliness and human despair.

However, might it be the case that *both* of these things may happen within the city at one and the same time? Might urban life be the context for a struggle between forces that work for human liberation, on the one hand, and those that result in dehumanization, on the other? A case can be made for the view that cities make possible entirely new forms of community, transcending the limitations of tribes and clans. Indeed, as Philip Bess points out, prior to the Industrial Revolution and the spread of the urban squalor which came to dominate the imagery of urban life,

> . . . it was the city that was the moral center, the locale of privileges, civil rights, and liberties; undomesticated nature – the wilderness, the home of beast and brigand – was the domain of danger and chaos (Bess 2006: 93).

At the same time, historical and sociological evidence also suggests that there are forces at work in the city, and especially in the urban forms of today, which destroy the traditional bonds of kinship and, instead of replacing them with broader, richer forms of community, create a terrible sense of anomie, leaving individuals to find their way alone in unrelenting competition with their neighbours. We might say that cities have become the sites on which the drama of the destiny of humankind is being played out as competing forces strive for control and dominance. The critical issue then becomes one of discovering the factors which determine whether people flourish in the urban setting or whether they become enslaved. Clearly there are no simple solutions here, because to ask such questions inevitably requires that we explore the complex web of social, political, economic, religious and structural forces which are involved in determining the nature and shape of urban environments.

The growth of an urban world

According to Andrew Davey, 'being urban will be the challenge of the twenty-first century' (Davey 2008: 27). This claim is based on evidence drawn from a wide range of academic disciplines which converges toward the conclusion that we are witnessing the emergence of an urban world on a scale never seen before in human history. As we noticed in the previous chapter, cities have

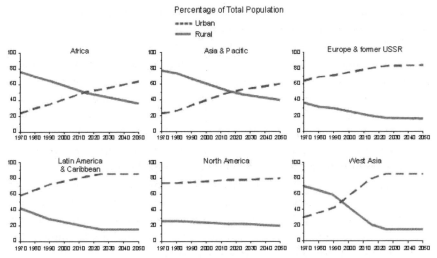

Figure 2.1: Recent and projected trends in urbanization, based on UNEP's unpublished *Global Environmental Outlook* (1997)

existed since ancient times, but what David Clark calls the 'wholesale transition to urban living' taking place across the whole world today is unprecedented. Clark does not exaggerate when he claims that the present movement of peoples toward the cities constitutes 'the largest shift of population ever recorded' (Clark 2003a: 4). The percentage of the world population living in cities has leapt from a mere 2% in 1700 to 50% and rising at the present time.

The magnitude of this change can be illustrated in various ways. In 1997 the United Nations Environmental Project (UNEP) tracked recent and projected trends in the growth of urban populations across six regions of the world, and everywhere the move toward the cities was accelerating (see Figure 2.1 above). In Europe, North and South America, and West Asia, urban populations had exceeded 50% of the total inhabitants of those regions for decades and were anticipated to reach an astonishing 80% by 2020. By contrast, in Africa, Asia and the Pacific, urbanization had begun late in comparison with other continents, but was now increasing sharply and would cross the 50% mark early in the twenty-first century.

Urbanization in Africa

In the chapters that follow we will pay particular attention to the forms that the city has taken historically and will identify some of the lessons to be learned from previous experience, as well as seeking to identify the critical issues demanding urgent attention in relation to the culture of cities today. Philip Bess echoes the language of Augustine when he comments on the present condition of the cities of Europe and North America: 'The more architects and planners have turned their attention to building up the City of Man apart from some vision of the City of God, the meaner and uglier the City of Man has become' (Bess 2006: 94). His words only serve to highlight the perils which lie in wait elsewhere in the world where new cities are expanding across vast landscapes, often shaped by the very ideas and concepts of the city that are now found to be failing in the developed world.

The enormity of the social, ethical and environmental challenges created by rapid urbanization can be illustrated by considering the impact of the growth of the cities of Africa. Until well into the twentieth century this continent remained overwhelmingly rural, with the result that traditional cultures and values remained strong (see Figure 2.2 opposite).

When African Christian theology began to emerge during the second half of the twentieth century it reflected this predominantly rural context in that one of its major concerns was with the issue of *identity* – how might Christianity on this continent be related to the African *past* in such a manner that it would be possible to affirm an identity that was both faithfully Christian and authentically African? African Christian theologians thus sought to relate the gospel to the primal worldviews which remained living religions for millions of Africans but which had too often been treated as having no point of contact with Christ.

Significantly a somewhat different emphasis was to be found in South Africa where the issue of apartheid created a different theological agenda in which the primary concern was less with the *past*, and more with the loss of identity as the outcome of *present* patterns of domination and oppression. What is more, the oppressive system which created such concerns made its deepest impact in *urban* contexts, including Johannesburg, which in the late 1960s remained the only city south of the Sahara with a population exceeding one million people. African theology in this setting was concerned with the liberation of the African peoples from systems of domination and oppression and it took an overtly political form in the quest for dignity and freedom in the present.

However, with the end of colonialism and the rise of independent African states the move toward the cities across the continent was swift and massive. Urban settlements like Lagos, Kampala, Nairobi and Salisbury, built as administrative centres during colonial rule and dominated by European officials and settlers, were now opened to the African population by the leaders of

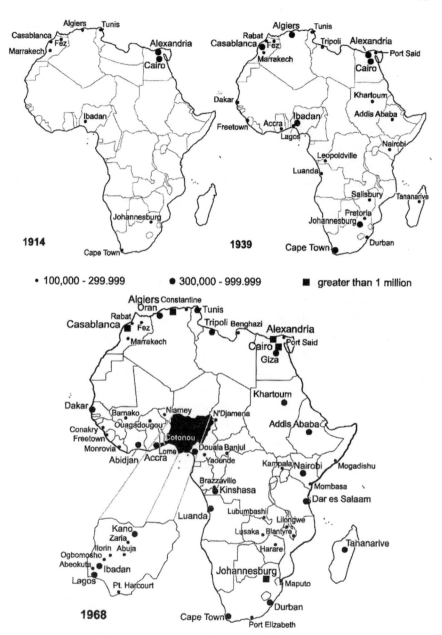

Figure 2.2: Urbanization in Africa in the twentieth century. Used by permission of Africa World Press, Trenton, NJ

newly independent states. Cities which had been carefully constructed on
European models to ensure the maintenance of a privileged way of life were
now engulfed by a tidal wave of migrants sensing the opportunity of sharing
the economic prosperity so ostentatiously displayed by their former colonial masters. In the space of less than fifty years the population of cities like
Khartoum, Lagos, Kinshasa and Johannesburg leapt above five million souls,
while elsewhere throughout Africa thousands of formerly small market towns
expanded almost overnight into cities (see Figure 2.3). The problems created
by such rapid growth are obvious and serve to illustrate the conflicting forces
at work in the city mentioned at the beginning of this chapter. On the one
hand, the African city could appear to incomers as a place of freedom, offering
an escape from the restrictions of village life in a traditional community. But,
on the other hand, the erosion of traditional social structures connected to
the extended family created a vacuum which, in the absence of new, inclusive
social networks, undermined social cohesion.

Johannesburg has been described as sub-Saharan Africa's one genuine,
so-called, 'World City', a fact recognized in the awarding of the 2010 soccer
World Cup finals to the city. Yet the post-apartheid dream of a new South
Africa, expressed in the African National Congress's 1994 Reconstruction
and Development Programme, quickly faded, resulting in an image of
Johannesburg 'as Africa's capital of glitz and conspicuous consumption,
rather than as a laboratory for social justice' (Bond 2007: 115). Perhaps, after
all, the work done by African theologians on the fundamental issue of *identity* in relation to the deeply communal traditions of the *past* provides a vital
resource for Africa's urban *future*, charting a new-old way of living together
within the burgeoning cities across the continent.

Cities of the rich, cities of the poor

If we move from the continent of Africa, we can observe the contrasting
forms that the city is taking in a globalized world today. This is obviously
a vast field of study and we are limited here to two 'snapshots' of cities
which have experienced explosive growth within a very short period of time.
Consider first, the city of Dubai, to which brief reference was made in the
previous chapter. It has been described as 'the new capital of the world', a
mushrooming city which has almost literally risen out of nothing and now
boasts, amid a forest of huge skyscrapers, the tallest building on earth.
Everything about this city is massive: it will possess the two largest shopping
malls on earth, between them covering 22 million square feet. It has been

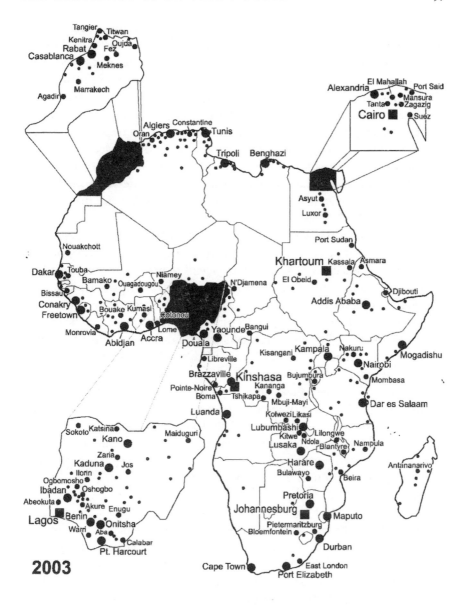

Figure 2.3: The growth of cities in independent Africa. Used by permission of Africa World Press, Trenton, NJ

estimated that $100 billion will have been invested in the construction of this extraordinary city, including its two massive airports and a vast port complex. The state-owned airline, Emirates, has expanded its routes across the globe, a growth made possible by the biggest order for new aircraft ever placed with the Boeing Corporation, worth $9.7 billion. The vision fuelling this extraordinary development is one that sees Dubai as the fulcrum between East and West, a shining, hi-tech, well-serviced business, entertainment, gambling and tourist centre built astride the 'strategic routeway of the modern world'. It is intended that Dubai will become the connecting point between China and India to the East, and Europe and North America in the West, providing a city meticulously planned to provide 'the best life of any city that has ever been created' (Nicholson 2006: 9).

And yet, what is the *meaning* of this city? According to George Katodrytis, Dubai 'thrives on newness and bigness, in an act of ongoing self-stylization and fantasy'. It is a city where 'everything seems to point to the twin towers of consumerism and tourism', and Katodrytis regards it as a prototype of urban development for the twenty-first century, a city which 'creates appetites rather than solves problems' (Katodrytis 2005). Yet problems there are: the opulent hotels, the luxury villas and apartments which house the world's super-rich, have a dark underside in that the labour force required to build and maintain this strange 'paradise' has been recruited from areas marked by great poverty across Asia. As we have already noted, the construction of this city has been 'carried on the shoulders of an army of poorly paid Pakistanis and Indians working twelve-hour shifts, six-and-a-half days a week, in the asphalt melting desert heat' (Davis 2007: 64). It has been reported that one hundred migrant workers committed suicide in the Emirates in 2006 and, despite severe restrictions on political protest, unrest among indentured labourers has become increasingly visible.

One is reminded of Fritz Lang's famous movie, *Metropolis,* in which the shining city of light, rising into the skies in a dazzling display of human creativity, is contrasted with the pathetic lot of the army of enslaved people who labour deep underground, keeping the city operating by supplying its power and removing its garbage. Dubai is *Metropolis* made real; the film maker's fantasy has become historical reality.

It can be argued that this city is but the most high-profile example of a form of urban development which can be observed today in many rapidly growing cities around the world. The spectacular growth and apparent success of Dubai is already spawning copycat developments in the oil-rich states of the Gulf, including Madinat al-Harar, or 'Silk City', in Kuwait, where a reported £132 billion is being invested in a spectacular metropolis designed by London-based architects and expected to be complete in 2023 (Bowcott 2008). Many contemporary urban developments across the world reflect similar patterns which, despite promises to the contrary, fail to address deep-seated social and economic injustices and throw into sharp relief the apparently unbridgeable gulf between the rich and the poor. For example, Anne-Marie Broudehoux describes Beijing as 'a city without urbanity' where iconic buildings created by celebrity architects are erected 'on the ashes of an organic urban fabric'. It is reported that two-thirds of Beijing's traditional courtyard houses were demolished as the Chinese Communist Party spent $40 million reshaping the city as a modern, prosperous venue for the 2008 Olympics. Such postmodern cities, whether newly constructed or emerging on the ruins of the urban forms they replace, reflect 'an increasingly individualist society that wilfully sacrifices a more cohesive one, where a predatory elite of private entrepreneurs, technocrats, and party members preys on a disenfranchised and vulnerable populace' (Broudehoux 2007: 101). If we listen to the Stranger's question as to the *meaning* of these mushrooming urban forms, it seems clear that they are purpose-built to conform to his first option: *We dwell together to make money from each other.*[1]

Our second example takes us further east to the city of Chongqing in China. Unlike Dubai this city has not attracted worldwide attention, in fact it is probable that it remains largely unknown beyond the borders of China. And yet, if anything, the growth of this city is even more significant than that of Dubai, both because it represents the extraordinary move toward the cities in China in general, and because the explosion of the urban population in this city is more rapid and extensive than anywhere else on the planet. The municipality of Chongqing has an estimated population of 31 million people, with thousands of peasants continuing to migrate from the countryside every year. Carolyn Steel describes this vast city as 'blanketed in a choking smog that causes thousands of premature deaths every year' and notes that none of its 3,500 tonnes of daily waste is recycled, but is emptied into a huge landfill site that swallows a volume of garbage the size of two Albert Halls every week.

---

1. The description of Dubai here was drafted before the global economic crisis created by 'sub-prime' loans created a crisis for this city's continuing development. However, all the signs are that the response of world leaders to that crisis involves discovering a way of returning to 'business as usual' rather than addressing the fundamental issue of the values underlying the global economic system. In which case, the critical issues raised here are likely to remain relevant in the future.

Chongqing, she concludes, is churning out cars and electrical goods as if there were no tomorrow, 'which, if cities like this are to be the urban future, there probably won't be' (Steel 2008: 290).

Across China the annual growth of the urban population amounts to an astonishing 8.5 million people, and while the significance of cities like Hong Kong, Shanghai and Beijing is well known, what is often overlooked is the fact that at least ninety Chinese cities have more than a million inhabitants. Urbanization on this scale is historically unprecedented and unmatched any-where on earth today. As in Africa, this rapid urbanization is related to the push-pull factors of the decline of the rural economy and the prospects of greater economic stability within the city. Jonathan Watts reports his con-versation with a newly arrived peasant farmer in Chongquing who told him: 'I used to be a farmer, but I could not afford to raise my two children. So we left them behind with relatives. I see them two or three times a year' (Watts 2006: 9).

This brief survey of some of the key sites of contemporary urbanization enables us to define one of the crucial questions arising today: does the urban world of the twenty-first century offer hope of the emergence of a new way of being a human family, or are vast numbers of that family doomed to live in squalor and terrible poverty? The possibility that the urban future, so clearly beneficial to some, will condemn millions of people to a tragic existence is highlighted by a 2003 United Nations report which warned that, if present trends continue, one third of the world's population will be living in urban slums within thirty years. Already at that time, 940 million people worldwide were said to be urban slum dwellers, existing in unhealthy conditions without clean water, sanitation, public services or legal security (Vidal 2003). The increasing concentration of conspicuous wealth and grinding poverty within urban areas led Douglas Massey, president of the Population Association of America, to issue a warning that is worth citing at length:

> In the coming century, the fundamental condition that enabled social order
> to be maintained in the past – the occurrence of affluence and poverty at low
> geographic densities – will no longer hold. In the future, most of the world's
> impoverished people will live in urban areas, and within these places they will inhabit
> neighborhoods characterized by extreme poverty. A small stratum of rich families
> meanwhile will cluster in enclaves of affluence, creating an unprecedented spatial
> intensification of both privilege and poverty.
>
> The juxtaposition of geographically concentrated wealth and poverty will cause
> an acute sense of relative deprivation among the poor and heightened fears among
> the rich, resulting in a rising social tension and a growing conflict between the haves

and the have-nots. . . . [W]e have entered a new age of inequality in which class lines will grow more rigid as they are amplified and reinforced by a powerful process of geographic concentration (Massey 1996: 395).

Massey's disturbing analysis was delivered as long ago as 1996 and since then we have witnessed the increasing rise of cities, or privileged parts of cities, of glass and steel alongside slums, or 'informal settlements', so that the privileged and wealthy are, as Massey predicted, in sight of the poor and their way of life is placarded from billboards and TV screens as that to which everyone must aspire. At the same time, the rich attempt to retreat from the life of the rest of the city, protected by ever higher walls and sophisticated electronic security systems and wilfully ignorant, like the inhabitants of *Metropolis*, of the sub-human conditions in which an army of labouring people must live their lives.

How has the human family managed to arrive at this stage of urbanization? Can we gain insights into the urban condition by examining previous experience, both before and during the era of industrialization? And, from the theological perspective, what response must Christians make to this urban world as those who are guided both by a belief in creation and by a vision of another kind of city, inhabited by people of all nations, in which there are no tears because 'the old order of things has passed away' (Rev. 21:4)?

Understanding the urban world

The complexity of the city and the vastly different range of experiences which it provides for those who dwell in it, or are affected by it, has given rise to very different, often diametrically opposed, views concerning the process of urbanization. The city has been the object of serious academic and scholarly study on the part of historians, archaeologists, geographers, architects, sociologists, philosophers and psychologists. Theology, as we have noticed, has often been slow to recognize the significance of the urban phenomenon, although there is a considerable literature dealing with the practice of *mission* in the city. In addition, writers, artists and film makers have produced important literary and visual commentaries on the urban experience. We have already made several references to Fritz Lang's landmark movie, *Metropolis,* and the mention of the novels of Charles Dickens is enough to further illustrate the role the arts have played in depicting urban life.

Clearly then, the study of the city, and of the 'urban world' we have briefly described, demands a cross-disciplinary approach in which the wisdom and

insights from a very broad range of sources are utilized. We will seek to draw
on some of these resources in the following chapters. However, even with
such an approach we will confront the problem of the existence of a diversity
of views concerning the merits of urban life and culture. As Gary Bridge and
Sophie Watson put it, there have always been 'two opposing imaginaries of
the city' which have become 'embedded within pro- and anti-urbanist movements'. They continue:

> Cities are places which enable the realization of the self, or conversely, cities separate
> the self from creativity and imagination in spaces of alienation and estrangement.
> There is a long Western tradition of representing cities as both dystopia or
> hell – Sodom the city of corruption – or utopia or heaven – Athens the city of
> enlightenment, democracy and reason. Literature and more recently film play a crucial
> part in forming dominant representations of the city (Bridge & Watson 2002: 3).

If we substitute the cities of Sodom and Athens in this statement with those of
Babylon and Jerusalem, we identify a tension between two 'opposing imaginaries' of the city that runs through the narrative of the Bible. There are *two*
representative cities, one is corrupt and evil, a place of violence and oppression which is constantly threatened with judgment and destruction; the other
is the city of God, shaped by a radically alternative vision of urban life and
possibility, and the object of faith and hope. The presence within the Bible of
these contrasting pictures helps to explain why Christians can read the same
Bible and come to radically different conclusions concerning the place of the
city within the purposes of God.

In 1785 the poet and hymn writer William Cowper wrote a long and very
popular work entitled 'The Task'. Cowper lived in the village of Olney in
Buckinghamshire and was a close friend and colleague of John Newton. He
reflects on the growth of the city of London in language that may seem distinctly anti-urban:

> Thither flow as to a common and most noisome sewer
> The dregs and feculence of every land.
> In cities foul example on most minds
> Begets its likeness. Rank abundance breeds
> In gross and pampered cities sloth and lust,
> And wantonness and gluttonous excess.

Cowper acknowledges the external glory of London, 'the fairest capital in all
the world', but then requests his readers to 'mark a spot or two':

It is not seemly or of good report,

That she is slack in discipline; more prompt

To avenge than to prevent the breach of the law;

That she is rigid in denouncing death

On petty robbers, and indulges life

And liberty, and oftentimes honour too,

To peculators of the public gold;

That thieves at home must hang, but he that puts

Into his overgorged and bloated purse

The wealth of Indian provinces, escapes (Cowper n.d.: 234–235).

The poet proceeds to notice what may be called the secularizing tendency of the city as the practice of worship descends into 'unrespected forms/And knees and hassocks are well nigh divorced'. Then comes the famous line, 'God made the country, and man made the town', which seems to confirm this as a thoroughly reactionary, anti-urban position. However, notice what Cowper objects to: within a few lines he has managed to critique the corruption of the judiciary, attack the growing obsession with wealth and acquisition, and connect the economic success of London with the rape of colonial possessions on the other side of the world. We might even suggest that this is the beginning of a theological critique of the political and economic expansion of Europe, since Cowper realizes that the glory and wealth of the metropolitan city is only possible at the expense of peoples who are being exploited elsewhere in the world. Cowper may not be anti-urban so much as a perceptive critic of the particular form that London was taking at this time; he was after all, a witness to the shift away from *community* and toward the unrestrained pursuit of wealth for its own sake.

In approaching the task of constructing an urban theology for the twenty-first century, we will have need of precisely the kind of discernment and prophetic courage shown by this early evangelical poet. We should be under no illusions about the difficulty and the challenges of gaining real understanding of the contemporary urban context and of then bringing the word of God to bear upon it. Cowper's passion was fired by an ethical and moral vision which convinced him that 'urban man' in the eighteenth century was in danger of taking a fundamentally wrong turn, one that was capable of destroying human community and leading toward social chaos and individual misery.

This voice from the past finds perhaps surprising echoes today in the analyses of the urban condition provided by academics across a range of disciplines. To Douglas Massey's voice, which we heard above, we may add that of the geographer, David M. Smith, writing about the problems facing post-apartheid cities in South Africa. Smith insists that the fundamental issue to be faced today concerns foundational ethics:

> A way of life which inevitably excludes a substantial majority of a society's population is hard to defend from a moral point of view. It is clearly inadequate to conceive of development merely in (re)distributive terms, racial or otherwise, in the context of the prevailing way of life of the affluent minority. An alternative conception of the good life is therefore required, to replace the possessive individual materialism which prevails among the well-to-do here, and elsewhere, in the contemporary world (Smith 2000: 168–169).

Agenda for an urban theology

Unfortunately, Christian reflection on the urban challenge has often jumped far too quickly to the *practice* of mission within the city, and so has lacked adequate research and understanding of the nature of the urban context. The reasons for this are understandable: the clamant needs of cities cry out for action, and people driven by the love of Christ and by compassion for the deprived and needy cannot indulge in ivory tower, theoretical reflection as a precondition for active service and ministry. Many of the outstanding Christian activists of the nineteenth century plunged into ministries of compassion and mercy in the appalling conditions of the slums of the Victorian cities and only later came to ask serious questions regarding the impact exerted by structural factors on the creation and maintenance of those conditions. In the urban world of today, however, activism divorced from serious reflection runs the grave risk of misunderstanding the social and cultural context within which our work is done, and it may end up appearing to support an unjust status quo in a manner that discredits the gospel in the eyes of suffering people. If this were to happen the consequence could well be that millions of oppressed people around the world will turn elsewhere in the search for liberation and freedom and the much-vaunted growth of Christianity in the southern hemisphere will prove to have been a brief, passing interlude.

One of the lessons we derive from the history of the missionary movement from the West over the past two centuries is that time taken to enter and understand a strange new cultural world was not wasted time. Indeed, the more thorough the preparation and the deeper the insights gained into the new worlds which missionaries entered, the greater their long-term effectiveness both in communicating the message of the gospel and acting as catalysts for positive social and cultural transformation. So today, the staggering growth in urban populations and the rapidity with which urban cultures are changing, demand a theological foundation built on profound biblical reflection, engagement in dialogue with a wide range of relevant disciplines, and a spirituality that recognizes both the true nature of the struggle in which we are engaged and the spiritual resources available to those committed to it.

So then, where will we find the resources we need to engage in this task? First, we will need to draw on the rich, but often neglected, traditions of *theological reflection in urban settings throughout the history of the Christian movement*. We have already noticed the importance of the work of Augustine of Hippo, who made the city the object of profound and prayerful study. Aware of the deeply ambivalent nature of the city, Augustine saw the Christian calling as involving the creation of a community that would live within an urban world guided by a vision of 'another city'. He describes the earthly city as a society 'not based on faith' and so limiting the agreement of its citizens 'to the establishment of a kind of compromise between human wills about the things relevant to mortal life'. This is a remarkable insight which anticipates by more than 1,500 years theories later developed by urban sociologists to explain the ways in which urban life alters human relationships. Augustine insists that the heavenly city 'knows only one God as the object of worship' and so is a *community* which is 'on pilgrimage in this world'. This radically alternative community 'calls out citizens from all the nations and collects a society of aliens, speaking all languages'. Insights like these have enormous relevance and are capable of providing a world church, now drawn even more comprehensively from all nations than Augustine could have imagined, with a vision of its calling to model an alternative way of being human in an urban world.

There are many other examples of such historical resources, including the struggles of the Protestant Reformers to apply the gospel to an emerging urban culture at the dawn of the modern world, and the reflections of evangelicals throughout the period of industrialization and urbanization in nineteenth-century Europe. We shall return to these periods later in the book.

Second, urban theology will have to be done *in dialogue with scholars working in a range of academic disciplines*. The challenge of the city is too great for urban theology to operate in isolation and we cannot afford the luxury of ignoring the rich insights available to us in the work of geographers, historians, sociologists, planners and architects. We have already discovered some of the ways in which the research of geographers and sociologists provides us with the raw materials which enable us to gain a proper and accurate understanding of the urban world. In the chapters that follow we shall pursue this cross-disciplinary dialogue at many points.

Third, in the urban world of today we will need the experience, wisdom and insights of Christians across the world, but *especially that provided by those who live in conditions of poverty and suffering in the slums*. Much attention has been given in recent years to what has been called the 'shift in the centre of gravity' of world Christianity, and it has been noticed that the decline of the churches of the West (especially in Europe) has occurred as Christianity has been growing almost everywhere else. What has sometimes been overlooked however, is the fact that the new 'centre of gravity' is to a considerable degree located globally in areas of urban poverty, so that the church emerging in the twenty-first century looks very different from one it replaces, having few of the privileges, wealth and power of the old Christendom. The contribution to be made to theology in an urban world from this context will not be detached, abstracted from reality and theoretical, but is likely to be characterized by the urgency, passion and righteous anger of those who know at first hand the struggle for life and dignity in cities that continue to be shaped by structural evil.

The need for Western theology to listen and learn from the experience of a world church is further highlighted by the fact that scholars within the academic disciplines most directly concerned with understanding our urban world increasingly recognize that the theoretical models developed to understand the growth of cities in the industrialized world do not possess universal, trans-cultural validity. The urban experience of the peoples of the Global South is, as we have already seen in the case of Africa, profoundly shaped by the experience of colonialism, with the result that the southern continents are dotted with *post-colonial cities*. Their physical shape, political and economic structures, and cultural and social problems are related to the colonial experience in ways that mean that urban theory developed at the metropolitan heart of colonial empires will be, to state it mildly, of limited value in such contexts. As Jennifer Robinson puts it, a situation in which urban theory 'framed in a western context parades as universally relevant knowledge while ignoring the urban experiences of most of the world', is unacceptable (Robinson 2004: 571).

As we have already discovered, one of the supreme challenges posed by the city concerns its apparent tendency to erode community and, especially in a postmodern world, to expand on the back of the spread of a possessive individualism that, in the end, endangers the very meaning of human existence. Precisely in this context we have heard the urban geographer, David M. Smith, arguing for the recovery of normative ethical language. What is even more striking is Smith's recognition that the 'alternative conception of the good life' so desperately needed today *might come from African tradition*. He cites a Xhosa proverb which says, *umuntu gumuntu ngabantu* ('a person is a person through persons'), and suggests that the traditional African sense of group solidarity could prove to be fertile ground in the search for a fresh concept of the 'good life' in urban settings. Indeed, Smith notes the way in which the African Initiated Churches (AIC) have been remarkably successful at preserving and nurturing a profound sense of community in the urban slums and have contributed significantly toward social and economic development in such contexts. Smith cites G. Oostuizen who says,

> *Ubuntu* is the name given to the ethos of mutual support whereby individualism is harmonized with social responsibility, which underlies the fabric of traditional African society. But in the AICs, *ubuntu* finds a complement in Christianity: not the secularized Christianity that has become a feature of the developed world, but the mutualism and communal sharing which was a characteristic of the early Christian church (Smith 2000: 170).

While the AIC have emerged alongside mission-originated churches as local expressions of Christianity in the cities of Africa, an even more widespread form of Christianity found both there, and in the slums and *favellas* of Asia and Latin America, is global Pentecostalism. The scope and impact of this movement has astonished many observers, including urban sociologist Mike Davis, who comments that in the new 'cities of poverty' described in the UN-HABITAT 2003 *Global Report on Human Settlements,* it looks as if Karl Marx 'has yielded the historical stage to Muhammed and the Holy Ghost'. Surveying what he describes as a 'planet of slums', Davis comments: 'If God died in the cities of the industrial revolution, he has risen again in the postindustrial cities of the developing world' and he credits Pentecostalism with refusing to accept 'the inhuman destiny of the Third World city' described in the UN Report. Pentecostalism, says Davis, is 'the first major world religion to have grown up almost entirely in the soil of the modern urban slum' (Davis 2004: 11).

Let me underline the point being made here: if urban geographers, sociologists and other academics are recognizing the social significance of the churches of the poor in the cities of the South, and if they detect within such communities the seeds of hope for an alternative future for those cities – a future which may also offer the prospect of the moral renewal of the spiritually impoverished cities of the West – then these 'signs of the kingdom' must become key components in the development of a Christian theology in an urban world.

Fourth, we will have to listen afresh to the Bible and *pay particular attention to the response of the biblical writers to the rise and influence of the great imperial cities of the ancient world.* Existing urban theologies have, of course, sought to ground their

analyses on the Bible, but (as we shall see later) this has too often involved a
proof-texting approach in which favoured passages have been extracted from
the flow of the biblical narrative as a whole and have been forced to serve as
justification for a particular argument concerning the 'biblical view' of the city.

The Old Testament scholar Walter Brueggemann has pointed out that
ancient Israel existed 'always in the shadow of empire'. He traces this history
in relation to the dominating cultural, religious and economic influence of
the successive empires of Egypt, Assyria, Babylon and Persia and comments
that it was within these contexts that Israel struggled 'to maintain its distinct
identity and to protect space for its liberated imagination and, consequently,
for its distinctive covenantal ethic' (Brueggemann 2000a: 74). This observation becomes directly relevant to our concerns here when we add that each of
these empires were centred on imperial *cities* – Memphis, Heliopolis, Nineveh,
Babylon, Susa. The very cities which, according to archaeologists and historians, represent the first era of urbanization in world history, provide the broad
context within which the story of biblical Israel unfolds. This being so, it was
inevitable that her rulers, wise men and prophets responded to the challenge
presented by these urban civilizations. What is more, if we extend this rea-
soning forward into the New Testament, the principle holds good since the
drama of redemption unfolds there against a background dominated by the
ultimate urban empire, that of Rome.

What this means is that a biblical theology of the city cannot be made to
rest on isolated texts, but will emerge from a process of extended reflection
on the message of the patriarchs and prophets of Israel, and of Jesus and his
apostles, against the background of the cities which played such a significant
part in shaping the context within which their ministries took place. This will
prove to be a far more demanding and complex task than creating a 'biblical
view of the city' from a few pre-selected proof-texts, but it promises to yield
an understanding of the place of the city within the Bible, and within the purposes of God, capable of providing a solid foundation for a credible urban
theology. If that enables us to 'protect space' for a 'liberated imagination' and
a 'distinctive covenantal ethic' in our urban world of today, then the resultant
theology is likely to have resonance well beyond the confines of the church.

Finally, *we must travel in hope*. The problems confronting the urban world of
today are immense and attempts at their solution seem to be blocked again
and again by resistance and opposition from enormously powerful vested
interests. One notices constantly a spirit of resignation on the part of many
well-intended scholars who offer excellent analyses of urban problems, only
to despair of the possibility of real change and transformation. It is precisely
at this point that a *theological* perspective becomes so important. The prophet

Isaiah caught sight of a vision of a transformed city which would become a global centre of light and truth, resulting in all nations settling their disputes and destroying their weapons. Of course, when the vision was over nothing had actually changed in the empirical world of the prophet's time! The actual city in which he lived remained as corrupt and violent as before. And yet, there was a difference, a revolutionary change *within the prophet's own imagination.* The vision of God had convinced him, against all the odds, that the present arrangements were not final, so that he summoned his followers: 'Come, O house of Jacob, let us walk in the light of the LORD' (Isa. 2:5). That is to say, for biblical faith the promise of *what will be* determines and shapes the life and practice of the believing community in relation to the world *as it now is.* Such a vision is always precarious, and in no way should it lead us to underestimate or minimize the seriousness of the challenges we face, but faith can humbly confess the knowledge that our 'labour in the Lord is not in vain' (1 Cor. 15:58).

3. THE BIRTH AND GROWTH OF THE CITY

Some have praised the city as an oasis of civilization in a desert of intellectual darkness and rigid custom. Others have condemned it for breeding instability, alienation, licentiousness and crime. As a social phenomenon, the city in history has been all of these and more (Berleant 2005: 41).

As we noticed briefly in the previous chapter, the earliest cities to appear in human history can be traced back thousands of years, having come into existence and played a crucial role in the human story long before the modern age and the emergence of the social sciences. The remains of such cities can be found in many parts of the world, but the key sites for the understanding of this remarkable early flowering of urban cultures are those related to the empires which flourished beside the rivers Nile, Tigris and Euphrates in biblical times. In fact, the first cities to have appeared in Mesopotamia pre-date the stories of the patriarchs in the Bible by some two thousand years, so that when Abram made the long trek up the Euphrates valley from Ur to Haran, and then turned southward toward Canaan, he was traversing territory in which walled cities had already existed for more than two millennia.

Clearly, it is vital that we seek to understand the factors that resulted in the emergence of these cities. Why did people begin to move from the countryside into the city? What was the significance of the city wall, and of the central buildings, the palace and the temple, which are characteristic of these earliest urban settlements? And, given that the ancient urban empires form such a crucial aspect of the context within which the entire biblical story unfolds, what was the attitude of the patriarchs and prophets, and later, of Jesus and his apostles, to these impressive and powerful cities?

A knowledge of the factors which resulted in the creation of these ancient cities is important not just for biblical and theological studies, but also in relation to urban history and sociology. The challenges and problems presented by the contemporary urban world which we have outlined in the previous chapter, compel us to ask whether we can find insights into our own urban condition through the study of the appearance of the first cities on earth. If 'history begins at Sumer', then despite the obvious and huge contrasts between those ancient cities and our urban world, these sites are of vital importance for us. To reflect on what happened, for example, at Uruk around 3,500 BC, and in the subsequent wave of city-building across the region, is to trace and seek to understand our own urban beginnings.

The sacred city

Cities appear very early in the story told in the Bible. In the creation narratives in Genesis, no sooner have human beings been banished 'east of Eden' than we come across a pregnant sentence informing us that 'Cain was then building a city' (Gen. 4:17). A few chapters later we discover an extraordinary 'table of nations', an unparalleled geographical and ethnic survey of the known world in which some of the cities destined to play a central role in the history that follows appear for the first time: Babylon, Nineveh, Sodom and Gomorrah (Gen. 10:10–12, 19). Then comes the familiar story of the building of the Tower of Babel, the effort of the people who had settled in Babylon to 'build ourselves a city' with an architectural feature that would 'reach to the heavens' (a phrase that anticipates our word 'skyscraper'), symbolizing the boasted supremacy and dominance of this urban settlement (Gen. 11:1–4).

I have before me as I write an aerial photograph of the site of the Tower of Babel, located some ninety kilometres south of the city of Baghdad in modern Iraq. The original ziggurat was destroyed by Alexander the Great in the fourth century BC, but in 1913 the site was rediscovered and excavated. This was clearly an immense structure, with each of its sides stretching 91 metres. It has been estimated that when Nabupolassar and Nebuchadnezzar II restored this tower between 625 and 563 BC, the work required thirty-two million bricks and took more than forty years to complete. This is but one example of the spectacular ruins of ancient cities that dot the often barren landscapes of modern Syria, Iraq and Iran.

The oldest of all the cities of which evidence remains in Mesopotamia is believed to be that of Uruk, once located on the banks of the Euphrates. When the course of the river shifted westwards in the fourth century AD, cutting Uruk adrift from the source of its life and sending it into terminal decline, an uninterrupted tradition of urban settlement stretching back at least 4,000 years came to an end. Michael Müller-Karpe comments that Uruk can claim a history which, with regard to its antiquity, is unmatched by any city on earth and he notes that as early as the third millennium BC it had grown to a size never equalled by any European city in the Middle Ages (Müller-Karpe 2003: 320).[1]

If we ask the fundamental question highlighted in the previous chapter concerning the *meaning* of these ancient cities, this will lead us in various directions. One way of answering the question involves listening to the accounts which the inhabitants themselves have left us concerning their understanding of the origin and purpose of their cities. This of course takes us directly into the spheres of religion and myth since these are, without exception, *sacred* cities in which the most prominent buildings – the palace and the temple – fulfilled religious functions. It hardly needs to be said that religion at this stage was not separated from the rest of the life of the city; on the contrary, it was foundational to the city's identity and permeated the whole of its life.

Exactly what was involved in the rituals enacted within the 'sacred spaces' of these ancient cities and the content of the mythical beliefs underlying them, became clear more than a century ago with the discovery of the great library of Ashurbanipal (669–633 BC) at the site of the city of Nineveh. Among the thousands of texts discovered and deciphered were works like the Babylonian poem *The Epic of Gilgamesh*, containing deeply moving reflections on life, death and the problem of human suffering. Alexander Heidel has said that this work, which he describes as 'the *Odyssey* of the Babylonians', must rank 'among the great literary masterpieces of mankind' (Heidel 1949: 1).

What this means is that within the walls of these earliest cities we find the beginnings of what may be called 'traditions of wisdom'; the reflections of thoughtful – and often troubled – people who first asked the fundamental

---

1. Recent reports have suggested that when it becomes possible to resume archaeological investigations in this troubled region, evidence may well support the claim that the true origin of urbanization actually lies some considerable distance north of Uruk at two sites within Syria (Lawton 2004: 33).

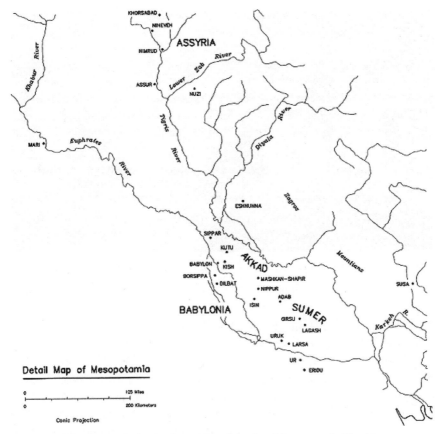

Figure 3.1: The dawn of urbanization: cities of Ancient Mesopotamia. Used by permission of the Oriental Institute, Chicago

questions concerning the meaning and purpose of human existence. Was this a *consequence* of life within the walls of the sacred city? Did urban experience, even in its earliest phases, actually give rise to this kind of questioning and, if so, was this the result of the cultural developments which took place when people first abandoned the village and moved to the city? Such questions cannot be answered with any certainty but they are worth pondering.

What we do know is that by about 1,000 BC an elaborate mythology had developed in which the older Mesopotamian deities ceded their roles and authority to a supreme Babylonian god named Marduk. The source of our knowledge here is another of the texts discovered in Ashurbanipal's extraordinary library, entitled *Enuma Elish*. This provides an account of the origins and order of the cosmos, but its principal purpose is, in Heidel's words, 'to

Figure 3.2: The city of Babylon, in a nineteen-century artist's impression, from a
Victorian book

offer cosmological reasons for Marduk's advancement from the position of
chief god of Babylon to that of head of the entire Babylonian pantheon'. What
is of particular interest to us is the fact that this elevation of Marduk by the
Babylonian priesthood responsible for the composition of the epic is paralleled by the praising of the *city* of Babylon, the dwelling place of Marduk and
the site at which rituals honouring him were enacted. *Enuma Elish* thus had a
politico-religious purpose and functioned as a means to strengthen the claim
of the city of Babylon 'to supremacy over all the cities of the land' (Heidel
1951: 11). Rex Mason summarizes the myth as follows:

> It tells how the god Marduk championed the cause of the other gods in battle against
> Tiamat, the dragon symbolizing the chaos ocean, slew her and, tearing her body in
> pieces, formed out of them the earth below and the firmament above. As a reward
> the gods decide to have a palace/temple . . . built for Marduk. And where is that
> temple to be built? It is hardly a breathtaking surprise to learn that it is to be built in
> Babylon (Mason 1997: 8).

The events described in this myth of origin were annually re-enacted in
Babylon at the New Year festival, when the king played the central role in the
drama, so renewing the original victory of Marduk over the forces of chaos.
The king was thus himself a sacred person and his ritual actions were essential
to ensure the maintenance of order and the fertility of the land in the year

ahead. Fertility religions based on similar mythologies were common throughout the ancient world, including in the city states of the land of Canaan. As
Mason says, the Canaanite kings

> ruled from fortified cities and were responsible for establishing 'order' in their realm,
> food and water for the people and defence against the attacks of enemies who always
> threatened to reduce the order of the realm to chaos (ibid.: 10).

We are now in a position to answer the question as to how the inhabitants
of these cities, or perhaps we should rather say, the rulers and religious specialists within them, understood their *meaning*. The city was a sacred sphere, an
enclosed and protected area chosen by the gods and, provided the occupants
were faithful in their ritual obligations, guaranteed security from destructive
forces – human, animal and spiritual – which threatened those who dwelt
beyond the encircling walls. Lewis Mumford observed that the walls of
ancient cities acted as 'physical ramparts' for defensive purposes under pressure of 'the new institution of war' and functioned as 'a spiritual boundary of
even greater significance, for it preserved those within from the chaos and
formless evil that encompassed them'. Mumford concludes: 'Without the
sacred powers that were contained within the palace and the temple precinct,
the ancient city would have been purposeless and meaningless' (Mumford
1966: 48).

At this point we need to ask whether there were *alternative* ways of understanding the meaning of the ancient city? In particular, what happened when
the myths of the origins of the gods and their cities came to be questioned? I
do not wish to run ahead here by discussing in detail the understanding of the
city to be found in the Bible, but we are bound to notice that the prophetic
perspective of the Old Testament resulted in an inevitable clash of worldviews at precisely this point. According to the author of the book of Hebrews,
Abram abandoned Ur and later moved on from Haran, wandering as a landless pilgrim across the ancient world because 'he was looking forward to the
city with foundations, whose architect and builder is God' (Heb. 11:10). Does
this imply that the patriarch had come to doubt the mythical foundations of
the cities in which he grew up? Did he question the ability of the pagan cities
to provide the promised human security and well-being? Did the reality of
human suffering cause him to react like Gilgamesh who said: 'I became fright-
ened and became afraid of death, so that I now roam over the steppe' (Heidel
1949: 75)?

These questions are largely speculative and we are unable to answer them.
What can be said however, is that precisely such critical questions were asked

within the prophetic tradition of Israel, enabling the claims of the ancient cities to be subjected to the most searching critique. Bernhard Anderson observes that the religion of biblical Israel stands out 'as a unique phenomenon – indeed, a revolutionary development' in this context. For Israel the decisive move was not one that took them *back* into mythical time, but one that thrust them *forward* in historical time to discover the reality of God 'in the realm of the profane, the secular, the historical'. The saving power of Israel's God was revealed, not by means of mythical battle, but through historical events such as the exodus in which an enslaved and oppressed people were delivered from bondage and granted freedom and dignity. What is more, when God is known through such saving actions in history then 'the realm of nature, which ancient people regarded as sacred, was desacralized, or emptied of divinity' (Anderson 1967: 30–31).

It will be remembered that the cities of the ancient world with which we are dealing here were at the heart of a series of urban *empires*. The mythical understanding of the city as a sacred enclosure, fenced off from the realms of darkness and barbarity which surround it, leads with a terrible logic to a sense of imperial mission in which that darkness must be overcome through the spread of the light. These cities thus became the bases from which civilizing empires spread through military conquests in ever-widening circles across the ancient world. Rex Mason observes that by advancing across the known world and bringing more and more peoples under the control of the empires, sacred kings saw themselves as once again 'bringing order out of chaos'. With regard to Assyria, he comments that Nineveh came to be seen as 'the centre of civilized order . . . of processed goods, of wealth, culture and all truly noble human achievement'. He concludes, 'It is the role of others to supply the raw material, the tax and the tribute and, where appropriate, the manual labour, by which this superior civilization can be fed and may flourish' (Mason 1997: 20).

There is a final point concerning the myths which justified the founding and expansion of these cities, and this concerns the role of *violence* in their accounts of creation. As we note from the description of the *Enuma Elish* above, the gods struggled to overcome the destructive forces of chaos and only succeeded because they were able to call on superior force in the cosmic battle. Violence is thus written back into the pre-historical, mythical realm and, since order was achieved in the heavens through the exercise of such power, violence becomes justified and sanctified when used by sacred kings to extend the realm of civilization into the surrounding darkness of the world. This aspect of ancient belief has come to be known as the *myth of redemptive violence* and, since it remains alive and well in various guises in the modern world, we shall return to it at a later stage.

The conclusion to which this discussion leads us is that while the founders and rulers of these cities understood them to have come into being as the result of a sacred calling, believing that the ritual re-enactment of events that had occurred in mythical time secured the blessing of the gods and assured peace and fertility, those who belonged outside such a system, who possessed what Brueggemann has called a 'liberated imagination', were able to challenge such ideas and to suggest that what was paraded as sacred knowledge was in fact *propaganda*. There is a lesson here that is of abiding importance when evaluating the claims that are made for cities, ancient and modern. While there is a vast difference between the cities of the ancient world which we have discussed here, and the contemporary situation described in the previous chapter, we should not underestimate the abiding power of *mythology* and the ways in which it can be deployed to screen out uncomfortable aspects of urban reality. The real *meaning* of a city may be rather different from the perceptions of those who promote its public image, and urban theology will need to discern what lies beneath the surface when this image is wrongly presented as 'the whole picture'.

The search for the good city

The era of the great urban empires reached its culminating point in the rise to world dominance of Rome, centred on a city which both in its size and glory exceeded any urban settlement previously seen on the earth. This too was a 'sacred city' in that it came to be viewed as the outcome of prophecies which placed Rome at the centre of the purposes of the gods. Virgil's *Aeneid*, for example, linked the founding of the city of Rome to ancient prophecies in which Jupiter is heard announcing: 'To Romans I set no boundary in space or time. I have granted them dominion and it shall have no end' (Mason 1997: 3). The message of the *Aeneid* thus provided a basis for the myth of 'eternal Rome', giving religious justification for Roman domination of the world. This city, this empire, are divinely appointed to bring peace and civilization to the earth, to be the agents of the *salvation* of the world.

What is more, Rome was an urban empire not just in the sense that the greatest city then known to the world lay at its heart, but also because it understood its civilizing role within history in terms of a policy of establishing cities across the empire. As Justo Gonzalez points out:

> Rome saw itself as the great city, the great builder of cities, the great 'cityfier' – or, as we would say today, civilizer. The Roman vision was that of a world dotted with

cities, all patterned after Rome and all submissive to Rome. Where ancient cities already existed, they were rebuilt, embellished, often granted special privileges. Where there were no cities, the Romans built new ones. This was their great pride, so that when Aelius Aristides, the famous orator from Smyrna, visited Rome and sought to praise her for her achievements, he did so by boasting that 'the coasts and interiors have been filled with cities' (Gonzalez 1999: 106).

All the elements we have discussed above in relation to earlier urban empires are also present in Rome, but they now become magnified to an enormous extent, with the result that the impact of this particular city on human history continues to be felt to this day. Lewis Mumford believed that, from the perspective of urban studies, ancient Rome provides a significant lesson 'of what to avoid' because 'its history presents a series of classic danger signals to warn one when life is moving in the wrong direction' (Mumford 1966: 280). However, since this urban empire forms a central aspect of the context of both the life and ministry of Jesus, and the spread of the early Christian movement, and since the *meaning* of this urban phenomenon is addressed explicitly within the writings we know as the New Testament, we will defer further discussion of this subject to a later chapter.

If the history of the city begins in Mesopotamia and finds its first climax in Rome, it also moves by way of Athens and the great outburst of Greek philosophical reflection associated with Plato and Aristotle. While we have not yet arrived at the age of 'social science', these thinkers are rightly viewed as precursors of such studies and have been described as the first people to systematically address fundamental issues concerning the problems of social life within cities. J. H. Abraham suggests that there have been two periods in pre-modern history in which societies experiencing violent change produced brilliant intellectuals able to reflect on the structures of social life: the first of these was in Athens in the time of Plato (427–347 BC) and Aristotle (384–322 BC), and the second was in North Africa when Ibn Khaldun (1332–1406) formulated 'the most brilliant and original' theory of social change 'ever conceived by a writer' (Abraham 1973: 29).

The Greek philosophers are especially important to this study since they were concerned with the fundamental question: what constitutes a 'good' city? It was axiomatic to them that human beings are social animals and are to be defined by the fact that they exist within a society. Aristotle put it like this:

Not being self-sufficient when they are isolated, all individuals are so many parts all equally depending on the whole (which alone can bring about self-sufficiency). The man who is isolated – who is unable to share in the benefits of political association, or has no need to share because he is already self-sufficient – is no part of the *polis* and must therefore be either a beast or a god (Aristotle 1973: 37).

To be human is then to exist within society, to be part of a community, a *polis*. It is simply inconceivable that people can exist alone since this would imply either that they operate by pure instinct, and so have a merely animal existence, or that they possess the super-human qualities that belong to the gods. Aristotle is clear that the isolated individual is in danger of descending into a sub-human way of life: 'Man, when perfected, is the best of animals; but if he be isolated from law and justice he is the worst of all' (ibid.). Human beings exist within communities in order to 'serve the purposes of moral prudence and virtue', but if they lose their way and abandon those moral ends for which they are made, then man 'is a most unholy and savage being, and worse than all others in the indulgence of lust and gluttony'.

The mention of law and justice highlights those ethical and moral norms which determine whether or not a society, a city, may be rightly described as 'good'. Aristotle believed that the knowledge of right and wrong is innate within human persons, so that a moral sense is another of the defining marks of humankind:

> It is the peculiarity of man, in comparison with the rest of the animal world, that he alone possesses a perception of good and evil, of the just and the unjust, and of other similar qualities; and it is association in (a common perception of) these things which makes a family and a *polis* (ibid.: 36).

For Plato and Aristotle then, the fundamental question concerned the *purpose* of the city: for what *end* does it exist, and what is required for it to fulfil this objective? The answer was related to the understanding of what constituted 'goodness' and, while this might be the subject of legitimate discussion, it was clear that a good society would be one in which the citizens flourished as members together of a virtuous community. Such a community, according to Aristotle, 'depends on friendship; and when there is enmity instead of friendship, men will not even share the same path'. For friendship, love and community to flourish it is necessary to avoid economic extremes and it is 'the greatest of blessings for a state that its members should possess a moderate and adequate property' (ibid.: 39).

We are surely struck here by the contrast between the ethical language of the Greek philosophers and our own inability to define what a 'good city' might look like. In the previous chapter we noticed the claim that Dubai has been designed to provide 'the best life of any city that has ever been created'.

The Greek philosophers would want to ask: in what sense is 'the good life' being defined here? And for whom is this *polis* being built? What human community will it enable to flourish? It is, of course, too easy to set up Dubai, or Las Vegas, as easy targets for criticism (although, in truth, one imagines that Aristotle would simply be unable to comprehend such developments), but what is far more worrying is the fact that across the world we witness the growth of cities, or districts within cities, which are constructed, or renovated, without the fundamental questions concerning their ultimate purpose ever being asked. Tragically, at a time in history when we are most in need of the kind of ethical language employed by the Greeks, we appear to have lost their ability to ask questions concerning the meaning of our cities. As a result, we multiply urban settlements which too often seem to be designed to stimulate the very desires and appetites which the philosophers believed would destroy human society if they went unchecked by the power of an enlightened reason.

The fall and rise of urban cultures

It is not possible here to do more than offer a brief summary of the history of the city between the collapse of Rome and the emergence of the modern world. We have already noticed the powerful theology of history developed by Augustine in the fourth century at precisely the point at which Roman power was seeping away. Over the following centuries his vision of the ideal, transcendent City of God, was to exert a significant influence on European society. Describing the impact of this religious vision in the context of the vacuum created by the fall of Rome, Lewis Mumford observed:

> By renouncing all that the pagan world had coveted and striven for, the Christian took the first steps towards building up a new fabric out of the wreckage. Christian Rome found a new capital, the Heavenly City; and a new civic bond, the communion of the saints. Here was the invisible prototype of the new city (Mumford 1966: 282).

It should be remembered that for many centuries the empire of Byzantium, centred on the great city of Constantinople, remained as a bulwark of Christianity when Western Europe was collapsing into chaos. In the Western Middle Ages the urban cultures of antiquity disappeared, replaced by rural and deeply traditional ways of life that were governed 'by the rhythms of sowing and reaping' rather than those of production (Moeller 1979: 261). As a consequence the urban character of the early church gave way to new forms of Christianity which were profoundly shaped by an agrarian culture, and this transformation was to have enormous significance for the future of the church. Meantime, the 'holy city' of Constantinople became the base for a vigorous missionary expansion as the Christian faith spread northwards into Russia and the Slavic lands and shaped the cities built there, including Moscow, understood as the 'Third Rome', with a destiny to model to the world what the city might become when filled with the light of the 'true faith'. Later in this chapter when we encounter a famous Russian author appalled by a visit to the modern city of London, we should remember the historical and cultural heritage of 'Holy Russia'. Byzantium thus played a vital, often overlooked, role in the transmission of faith through the dark ages and 'when urban civilization had all but disappeared from the rest of Europe' it remained possible to 'look "to The City", *eis tēn polin*, or as the Turks pronounced it, *Istanbul*' (Kishlansky *et al.*1993: 195).

The mention of Istanbul serves to remind us of the significance of the rise of Islam with regard to urban history. Joel Kotkin points out that while Constantinople survived during the West's 'dark ages', it was 'the only European city among the twenty largest in the world; almost all the rest were part of the Oriental world, either in China or within the Dar-al-Islam' (Kotkin 2005: 43). From its beginnings Islam was a profoundly urban religion, bearing a vision for social and political life shaped by the reign of God. Kotkin regards the Muslim era as 'a new beginning in urban history' and describes its distinctive character between the seventh and ninth centuries as follows:

> Islam broke dramatically with the long-standing traditions of classical urbanism, which, as Socrates saw it, found 'people in the city' as a primary source of knowledge. Islam would foster a sophisticated urban culture *but did not worship the city for its own sake*; religious concerns, the integration of the daily lives of men with a transcendent God, overshadowed those of municipal affairs (ibid.: 46, emphasis added).

This new vision was to have an enormous impact as Islam spread both East and West; its insistence that a place of prayer should replace the classical civic buildings at the heart of the city transformed both the physical layout and the social life of the city and underlay the glory which was to be successively displayed in cities such as Damascus, Baghdad and Cairo. By the thirteenth century an urban system integrated by monotheistic faith covered a vast area of the known world, from Spain to Delhi, and into Africa as far as Mombasa in the east and Timbuktu and Kano in the west. This extraordinary spread of a faith-based urban system was unprecedented and, as we shall see later, has significant implications in relation to our search for models of the sustainable, humane city today.

During the eleventh and twelfth centuries the population of Europe increased and this, combined with a growth in agricultural productivity, created a context within which urban culture underwent renewal in the West. As we have seen, prior to the eleventh century cities were a 'negligible presence' in Europe, but with a steadily increasing population and booming trade they expanded until by the end of the thirteenth century Venice, London, Ghent, Bruges and Cologne were all approaching populations of 100,000. Paris was the largest of them all, with double that number and, along with Bologna, it became a major centre of learning, laying the foundations of the university system of education which was soon to be replicated in many other emerging cities. Students travelled across Europe to these new centres of intellectual enquiry and they exercised tremendous power, controlling the appointment of staff and dictating 'the exact length of professors' lectures' (Kishlansky *et al.* 1993: 267). However, we should remember that, as Theodore Rabb notes, the entire urban population of Europe at this time did not exceed 10% of the total, so that the continent remained 'overwhelmingly rural' (Rabb 2006: 8–9).

Besides the university, the other institution which played a central role in the development of urban culture was the monastery. The monastic movement developed models of community life involving a deliberate renunciation of the very things that had been fundamentally important in previous urban cultures: property, prestige and power. Monasteries thus 'kept alive the image of the Heavenly City' and shaped both the physical and social form of new urban communities in ways that can still be recognized by those who wander around the medieval towns of Europe (Mumford 1966: 287). Maria Caterina Cifatte describes monasteries and convents as 'a kind of small town, ideal and far from the world of war and power struggles; in fact they were considered to be secure refuges and oases of peace'. She continues:

> They were frequently flanked by vegetable gardens and fields cultivated for the use of monks and nuns, but also for itinerant strangers, the communities often providing accommodation for pilgrims. The service of care and support was carried out, regardless of gender, both in monasteries and convents (Cifatte 2008: 46).

Of particular significance was the emergence of the new monastic orders of the Franciscans and the Dominicans, both of which must be understood as a 'response to the social and cultural needs of the new urbanized, monetized European culture' (Kishlansky 1993: 269). As is well known, the response of Francis of Assisi (1182–1226) involved a life of radical poverty and a complete rejection of the luxury and material excess increasingly evident in the cities.

The charisma and example of this extraordinary man attracted huge numbers of followers, many of whom came from the Italian cities. By contrast, Dominic (1170–1221) adopted a different strategy, devising new methods of preaching *within* the cities and seeking to relate faith to the realities of urban life. The Dominicans

> gravitated toward the cities of Western Europe and especially toward its great
> universities. These new orders of preachers, highly educated, enthusiastic and
> eloquent, began to formulate for the urban laity of Europe a new vision of Christian
> society, a society not only of peasants, lords and monks, but also of merchants, craft
> workers, and professionals (Mumford 1966: 271).

The holy commonwealth

During the fourteenth century Europe suffered a series of terrible disasters in the shape of famines and plagues which devastated its peoples, leaving some parts of the continent with population levels reduced by half. Aidan Southall described this century as calamitous for Europe, pointing out that the combination of the Black Death, seemingly endless warfare, and a series of 'urban uprisings' created a multitude of 'displaced persons' who formed militant groups traversing the continent and laying waste the districts through which they passed (Southall 2000: 116).

However, at the dawn of the Protestant Reformation the population of Europe was growing rapidly and the continent experienced a new age of expansion in trade, invention, exploration and ideas. It was also a new era of urbanization as cities were again growing both in size and influence. In some areas, for example Saxony (which was to be fertile territory for the Reformation), towns were attracting significant numbers of people, while the populations of cities like London, Paris, Florence, Venice and Naples all grew beyond 100,000 by the end of the sixteenth century. Steven Ozment comments that while cities still housed only a fraction of Europe's total population, 'they were then, as they have always been in Western history, the sites of creative change'. In particular, as Ozment notes, the Reformation came to birth and grew in these urban contexts.

> Although the Protestant Reformation appealed to educated and uneducated alike,
> it presupposed for its success a literate urban culture and seems particularly to have
> attracted rising urban groups who had either experienced or were determined to
> come into a new political and economic importance (Ozment 1980: 191–192).

Protestant piety and teaching, especially as it developed in Geneva under the influence of John Calvin, has been described as a distinctly urban form of theology, reflecting the values of city dwellers, especially 'their egalitarianism and sense of communal solidarity', and attempting to shape those values by the application of the Bible to the ethical and moral issues arising in this context.

The city of Geneva is of particular interest to us both because it was the site of a remarkable experiment in urban social transformation, but also because it became a model for Protestant leaders elsewhere who were striving to relate the Bible to a range of ethical challenges arising within other expanding cities. Ozment comments that the distinguishing feature of the Calvinist Reformation was 'the enforcement of a high standard of individual and social sanctification' (ibid.: 356). Calvin's deep conviction that faith and works belong together, and that this demands that Christians live the whole of life, public and private, for the glory of God, is nowhere more vividly illustrated than in a statement he issued on his return to Geneva in 1537:

> I consider the principal enemies of the Gospel to be, not the Pontiff of Rome, nor heretics, nor seducers, nor tyrants, *but bad Christians*. . . . Of what use is a dead faith without good works? Of what importance is even truth itself, where a wicked life belies it *and actions make words blush?* (ibid.: 366, emphases added).

It was the genius of Calvinist theology that it confronted the reality of a rapidly shifting culture in which traditional models of social and economic life were breaking down under the impact of new forms of economic power and sought to direct and control this economic revolution through a re-reading of Scripture within this context. Calvin's passionate insistence on the necessity of good works as the evidence of genuine faith did not restrict such works to the realm of private piety, but included economic and political actions within the public sphere. This is nowhere more evident than in his sermons which 'do not speak very much of another world and happiness there' but 'cry scorn against all injustice, whether it be ecclesiastical, bureaucratic, legal, or in the marketplace' (Graham 1978: 19). Thus, Calvin recognized the work of a new type of capitalist as legitimate, seeing this as a valid calling which could – and must – be pursued for the glory of God, and his sermons identify clear ethical guidelines for the merchants and bankers in his congregation. Here he is on the practice of hoarding wheat in order to make a killing when the price rises:

> There will be those who would rather that the wheat spoil in the granary so that it will be eaten by vermin, so that it can be sold when there is want (for they only wish to starve the poor people). . . . See the wheat collected; how well our Lord has poured

out his grace and his benediction so that the poor world would be nourished. . . .
How true it is that the Lord is mocked by those who want to have much profit. . . .
These people entomb the grace of God, as if they warred against his bounty and
against the paternal love which he displays toward everyone (ibid.: 56).

Preaching of this kind was clearly radical and would today be described as 'holistic', but Calvin went beyond this with his insistence that social righteousness
required both such teaching, and a system of ecclesiastical discipline designed
to enforce the practice of Christian ethics in economic, political and social life.
R. H. Tawney memorably described Calvinism in the following words: 'Having
overthrown monasticism, its aim was to turn the secular world into a gigantic
monastery, and at Geneva, for a short time, it almost succeeded' (Tawney 1936:
115). We should add that historians have used similar language to describe the
impact of the Reformation on cities elsewhere, as is clear from Lee Palmer
Wandel's description of Huldrych Zwingli's preaching in Zurich which turned
that city into 'a kind of monastery'. Wandel connects the social reforms in
Reformation Zurich with the preaching of 'a social Christ' and concludes that,
'In caring for its poor, the community of Zurich mirrored Christ, as he reached
out to the wretched in body and the poor in spirit' (Wandel 1990: 177).

Someone who witnessed the Reformation in Geneva, and clearly believed
that it *did* succeed, was the Scottish reformer, John Knox, who famously
described this city as 'the most perfect school of Christ that ever was on
earth since the days of the Apostles'. Other citizens, especially those on the
receiving end of Reformed discipline, saw Geneva in a rather different light,
and like other revolutionary movements, religious and secular, the Calvinist
Reformation did, over time, become legalist and oppressive under what has
been called 'the dictatorship of the ministry'. Nonetheless, like many of the
refugees who resided in Geneva during Calvin's time, Knox carried the vision
of the city as a 'holy commonwealth' back with him to his homeland, with
significant consequences for the social and cultural history of Scotland, the
fruits of which can still be recognized in cities like Edinburgh and Glasgow.
As Tawney observed,

In the sixteenth century . . . the claim of Calvinist Churches is everywhere to exercise
a collective responsibility for the moral conduct of their members in all the various
relations of life, and to do so, not least, in the sphere of economic transactions, which
offer peculiarly insidious temptations to lapse into immorality (ibid.: 125).

The original Calvinist vision of the city as a 'holy commonwealth' may yet be
discovered to have surprising relevance in relation to the ethical and moral

issues arising in a globalized urban world and it certainly offers guidance to those who search for an urban theology in that world.

The city and the Industrial Revolution

While theologians like Calvin re-read the Bible in a search for the fresh insights which might make it possible to harness the revolutionary powers unleashed by the new learning of the Renaissance in the service of the kingdom of God, other Christians reacted to the passing of the old, familiar world with fear and pessimism. In the Brancacci Chapel of the Santa Maria del Carmine in the city of Florence there are a series of frescos painted in the first half of the fifteenth century by the artist known to us as Massacio, a nickname which translates as either 'Sloppy Tom', or perhaps 'Mad Tom'. The most remarkable of these paintings depicts 'The Expulsion from Paradise', a strikingly realistic representation of the biblical scene in which Adam covers his face with his hands, while Eve simply throws her head back and wails in agony, releasing what has been called 'the first scream in Western art'.

Massacio's picture is significant for two reasons. First, it reflects profound insight in his reading of the biblical narrative and, in doing so, deepens our understanding of the meaning of the loss of innocence and its consequences within that story. For example, Massacio shows that Adam's terrible shame is the outcome, not of a sexual act (as so often implied in art), but of a rebellious assertion of human independence in the realm of the mind and the will. It is his head, not his penis, which is covered in shame!

Secondly, this extraordinary picture reflects something concerning the artist's own times as the Renaissance assertion of human independence seemed to challenge the fundamental axioms of Christendom upon which social life had rested for centuries. For very many people at the time this new cultural movement was simply cause for celebration, and many of Massacio's contemporaries gave uninhibited expression to this mood. But for this artist there was a dark side to the changes through which he found himself living; the gains of the coming new age had to be set against very serious losses, including the sense of being thrust into a world in which human beings would find themselves radically alone and spiritually and psychologically troubled. The freedoms opened up by the explosion of fresh learning and knowledge, and the spectacular scientific and technical achievements that this knowledge would make possible, would involve the heavy cost of a deepening sense of existential isolation. In other words, for Massacio (and perhaps this was why his optimistic contemporaries regarded him as 'mad'), it seemed as though the story of the expulsion from Eden was being replayed in his own lifetime. The biblical narrative was far from being a redundant myth, and, precisely because it provided a description of a universal human condition, it powerfully illuminated contemporary reality.

The world from which Massacio felt that he, and modern people in general, were being expelled was that of medieval Christendom. Let us be clear about what is being said here: the world that was being lost was no latter-day paradise in which the values of the gospel had permeated the entire society and created an urban heaven on earth. Christendom has far too many skeletons in its cupboards to allow us to accept such a romanticizing of the past; nor should we minimize the huge benefits that flowed from the revolutionary changes brought about by the Renaissance. What Massacio realized however, was that 'progress' is not an unmixed blessing and that the huge cultural transition through which he was living carried with it the danger of losing things that were vital to human well-being, so creating new types of societies cut off from contact with transcendent realities. As Etienne Gilson has said,

> The difference between the Renaissance and the Middle Ages was not a difference by addition but by subtraction. The Renaissance . . . was not the Middle Ages plus man, but the Middle Ages minus God, and the tragedy is that in losing God the Renaissance was losing man himself (quoted in Donskis 1996: 58–59).

As we have seen above, the Protestant Reformers recognized the clear dangers posed by the revolutionary changes that were taking place in Europe. Their attempt to move beyond the ethical systems of the medieval church was motivated by the desire to ensure that the new social and economic powers being unleashed in the cities would be governed by ethical norms derived from the gospel. However, some Protestant artists, including Hans Holbein, shared the doubt and unease of Massacio and worried that the revolutionary forces at work in the world might result, not in social harmony and human flourishing, but in a destructive individualism and a terrifying erosion of the meaning of human existence.

Fast forward for a moment to 1893. We said that Massacio's Eve utters the first scream in the history of Western art; it was not, alas, to be the last. In this year Edvard Munch painted his famous work *The Scream*, in which a barely human figure utters an even more terrifying wail than that of Eve as a protest against the meaninglessness and emptiness of the world. Munch's own description of the circumstances in which he painted this iconic picture is worth quoting:

One evening I was walking along a path, *the city was on one side* and the fjord below. I
felt tired and ill. I stopped and looked out over the fjord – the sun was setting and
clouds turning blood red. I sensed a scream passing through nature: it seemed to me
that I heard the scream (Hodin 1972: 48, emphasis added).

This painting is often understood as a generalized depiction of the existential
crisis associated with modern culture, but notice that Munch makes explicit
mention of *the city*. The sense of terror, of dislocation, in this picture, as in
another painted a year later entitled *Anxiety*, in which a group of people are
seen on the same bridge, staring out at the viewer as though traumatized
and devoid of all normal human emotions – all of this is related by the artist
to the urban context and its impact upon the natural world. Munch has left us with
unforgettable artistic images of the very people who were showing up in ever
greater numbers in the clinics in Paris and Berlin complaining of a variety of
phobias and seemingly irrational fears, which compelled psychologists and
urban theorists to ask why life had become so problematic for these inhabitants of the modern metropolis. As Anthony Vidler has said,

> The rapid growth of big European cities toward the end of the nineteenth century,
> the transformation of the traditional city into what became known as *die Grossstadt*
> or metropolis, engendered . . . a culture of interpretation dedicated to the study
> and explanation of these new urban phenomena and their social effects, supported
> by the emerging new disciplines of sociology, psychology, political geography, and
> psychoanalysis. The pathology of the city . . . gained new and apparently scientific
> validation in the last quarter of the nineteenth century (Vidler 2001: 25).

In the period between Massacio and Munch, the time between the 'two
screams', European culture underwent precisely the kind of massive changes
anticipated by visionary artists. The Protestant Reformation resulted in revolutionary religious developments which, if Max Weber (1864–1920) is to be
believed, created the conditions in which the modern, capitalist system could
take off. According to Weber, the Protestant emphasis on the priesthood of all
believers, combined with a religiously-inspired passion to work at one's calling
for 'the glory of God', released a tremendous social and economic dynamism
which resulted in increased prosperity. But over time the power unleashed
by this movement proved too great to be controlled by traditional Christian
ethics and so broke free from the restraints on personal acquisition that had
been taken for granted for centuries during the era of Christendom. When
the medieval vision of the 'heavenly city' finally disappeared from public
view during the Enlightenment, replaced by the secular 'city of man', capital-

ism shook itself entirely free from the control of Christian ethics, becoming instead the *source* of cultural values. As a result, modern people inhabiting the growing industrial cities of Europe came to be 'dominated by the making of money, by acquisition as the ultimate purpose' of life (Weber 1985: 53). The asceticism once displayed in the monasteries had been transferred by the Reformers and Puritans into the sphere of everyday life and played a crucial role in 'building the tremendous cosmos of the modern economic order', but once this became established it cut loose from its religious origins and 'the technical and economic conditions of machine production' came to 'determine the lives of all the individuals who are born into this mechanism, not only those directly concerned with economic acquisition, with irresistible force' (ibid.: 181).

Weber's study of the relationship between Protestantism and the modern economic system has been criticized at many points, but the broad thesis remains convincing and serves to identify a number of serious challenges for urban theology. In particular, at the end of his study, Weber wonders whether there is a possibility that eventually 'entirely new prophets will arise' and, breaking free from the dominant ideology, will offer an alternative vision of the human future; or whether, in fact, religion is now destined to remain confined to the private sphere, so that the future will involve 'mechanized petrification, embellished with a sort of convulsive self-importance' (ibid.: 182). Here the gauntlet was thrown down and I suggest that the urban world still waits for evidence that genuine prophecy is possible when the acquisitiveness Weber had witnessed spreading across Europe has now become a global phenomenon.

The growth of urbanization in the nineteenth century, particularly in the wake of the Industrial Revolution in Britain, was completely unprecedented in its speed and extent. For example, in the middle of the eighteenth century there were only *two* cities in Britain with populations exceeding 50,000 people: Bristol (60,000) and London (750,000). A century later 38% of the entire population had shifted into the cities, and when Queen Victoria died in 1901 this had risen to 75%. A city like Glasgow (which we shall examine in detail in a later chapter) was virtually created by the Industrial Revolution, growing from a small town clustered around its cathedral to the 'Second City of Empire' with astonishing speed. Edinburgh, Manchester, Sheffield, Liverpool, Birmingham and Leeds experienced similar patterns of growth, so transforming society as a whole to an extent that, as we have already noticed, the city became 'society itself' (Kumar 1986: 68).

In the twenty-first century we have become so familiar with huge cities that we may easily overlook how recent this development has been and how astonishing such urban centres appeared to people who encountered them for the first time. A revealing example can be found in the experience of the great Russian author Fydor Dostoevsky, who arrived in London in 1862 during the euphoria surrounding the great World's Fair at the Crystal Palace. Wandering around the city by day and night, Dostoevsky noted the stark contrast between 'magnificent parks and squares' and the 'terrifying streets of a section like Whitechapel, with its half-naked, wild and starving population'. He watched in amazement on Saturday evenings as 'half-a-million workers, with their wives and children, swarmed through the downtown streets to celebrate the beginning of their one day of leisure'. The celebration ended with thousands of people hopelessly drunk, but Dostoevsky observed, 'without gaiety, with a sad drunkenness, sullen, gloomy, strangely silent'. These sights, and the thousands of prostitutes he saw in the Haymarket, tormented him for days afterwards.

When Dostoevsky came to publish his reflections on the London visit he gave them a pregnant, one-word title: 'Baal!' It seemed to him that the ancient pagan deity was an appropriate symbol for the gross materialism that appeared to hold London in a vice-like grip. And where others viewed the Crystal Palace as a sacred space, even as the signal of the arrival of the kingdom of God, for the Russian writer it was the ultimate expression of 'the unholy spirit of modernity that brooded malevolently over London'. Watching the incessant stream of visitors who poured into the exhibition he commented:

> This is some sort of biblical illustration, some prophecy of the Apocalypse fulfilled before your eyes. You feel that one must have perpetual spiritual resistance and negation so as not to surrender, not to submit to the impression, not to bow the knee before the fact and deify Baal, that is, not to accept the existing as one's ideal (quoted in Frank 1986: 239).

We are reminded again of the Stranger's fundamental question regarding the *meaning* of this growing urban world. Max Weber described it as a world that was now *disenchanted*, by which he meant that religious beliefs, which previously played such a crucial role in creating urban communities, had become marginalized by the new 'sacreds' embodied in the institutions of market capitalism. At the very end of *The Protestant Ethic and the Spirit of Capitalism* Weber says that modern people are, 'even with the best will, unable to give religious ideas a significance for culture and national character which they deserve' (Weber 1985: 183). If that were true (and it is a claim open to debate), then an absolutely vital question follows: where would the new city-builders, now operating within the 'cosmos of the new economic order', find a vision capable of guiding their planning and the shaping of the urban forms of the modern world? Clearly, Augustine's vision of the 'City of God' had been eclipsed, but Weber observed that even the 'rosy blush of the Enlightenment' was by this time 'irretrievably fading'.

To be bereft of any vision at the point at which cities were about to expand as never before would open up the terrible prospect that the emergent urban world would take forms dictated by the purely pragmatic interests of those who held power within the market system. This would then result in the growth of urbanized areas in which the ideal of the city as a community united by the pursuit of a social life that could be described as 'good' would be abandoned, replaced by urban forms designed in the interests of the pursuit of maximized profits. Thus, when Ernest Burgess attempted to produce an explanatory model of the growth of American cities, he assumed the existence of a 'central business district' at the core of the modern city and argued that urban expansion would involve 'a process of distribution . . . which sifts and sorts and relocates individuals and groups by residence and occupation' (Burgess 2002: 247). We are struck by the absence of any vision of what a city might be in this model; it is simply a description of how a city evolves when its development is left to the forces of market capitalism. Lewis Mumford could well have had such models in mind when he wrote:

> At the very moment that cities were multiplying in numbers and increasing in size all through Western civilization, the nature and purpose of the city had been completely forgotten: forms for social life that the most intelligent no longer understood, the most ignorant were prepared to build (Mumford 1966: 478).

Urban pathologies

Not surprisingly given this context, the pioneers of urban sociology concentrated their attention on a range of pathologies which seemed to be associated with social and individual life in the capitalist city. David Clark observes that the classic commentaries on the nineteenth-century city 'expressed astonishment, perplexity, and often a pronounced concern over the developing conditions of modern urban life'. He suggests that the pioneering scholars who first attempted to analyse these changes experienced life in the modern city as 'nothing less than a fundamental and unnatural mutation of the human species' (Clark 2003b: 78–79). We should keep these comments in mind when reading the following description of the work of some of these key sociological thinkers.

Ferdinand Tonnies (1855–1936) drew a sharp contrast between traditional forms of 'community' and the new type of 'society' which came into being in the industrial city. In his 1887 study, *Gemeinschaft und Gesellschaft,* Tonnies compared older, traditional communities, which were small-scale, characterized by intimate relationships of kinship, friendship and neighbourliness, with the new forms of 'society' (or perhaps 'association') in which individuals related to each other in a merely functional way. The older societal structures Tonnies described as 'living organisms', whereas urban associations for the purposes of business, politics (or even, under urban conditions, religion), were 'a mechanical aggregate and artefact'. While he recognized *Gesellschaft*, 'society', as an inevitable outcome of the development of a modern, capitalist system, Tonnies was troubled by the evidence that this involved the loss of forms of genuine community without which life might soon be reduced to the war of 'all against all'. He has been described as the first sociologist to have taken an uncompromising stand against the new industrial order, believing that unless it 'retained some of the elements of the old it was irretrievably lost' (Abraham 1973: 205). However, it was almost impossible to see how these necessary components of community could be retained, because a modern, capitalist system actually demanded that the 'natural relations of human beings to each other must be excluded'. Tonnies saw the essence of modern society as follows:

> In *Gesellschaft* every person strives for that which is to his own advantage and affirms the action of others only in so far and as long as they can further his interest. Before and outside of convention and also before and outside of each special contract, the relation of all to all may therefore be conceived as potential hostility or latent war. ... This conception is the only one which does justice to all the facts of business and trade where the rights and duties can be reduced to mere value and definitions of ability to deliver (Tonnies 1973: 263).

The concerns of scholars like Ferdinand Tonnies with the loss of community, and their linking of this with urban life, has drawn considerable criticism from those who detect an anti-urban bias underlying such conclusions. Tonnies' views have been classified as a 'Bipolar Moralistic Model' of urban studies in which a long list of characteristics associated with traditional *rural* life come to be set against another list said to be symptomatic of urban living, with the clear implication that the one is positive and the other negative (see Figure 3.3, opposite). John Gulick, for example, objects to 'the uncritical, unempirical manner in which these terms have too often been applied' and says that they 'represent moralistic biases and emotions that seem essentially to be feelings about the human condition generally, not about cities in particu-lar'. He points out that 'a correlate of city anonymity is freedom from personal surveillance as opposed to the social constraints of small town or rural life'. On the other hand, Gulick cites research undertaken in American cities which revealed 'the reality of closely knit, small-scale, localized support systems in large industrial cities' which led scholars to begin talking about 'urban villages' (Gulick 1989: 9–10). Similar evidence can be found in the slums of cities in the southern hemisphere today, so that doubt is cast on Tonnies' conclusions with regard to both *Gemeinschaft* and *Gesellschaft*.

Rural	Urban
Communal	Individual
Natural	Artificial
Tribal society	Mass society
Moral traditions	Moral uncertainty
Face-to-face	Anonymous
Integrated	Fragmented
Sacred	Secular
Primitive	Civilized
Homogenous	Heterogenous
Gemeinschaft	*Gesellschaft*

Figure 3.3: Contrasts between urban and rural in 'Bipolar Moralist' urban models

At the same time, the interconnectedness of capitalism and modern urbaniza-tion, together with the more recent development of globalization, demand that we continue to ask critical questions about the way in which these partic-ular movements, and the ideologies underpinning them, do shape urban areas and impact human lives and communities in ways that are often profoundly negative. To raise these issues is not to adopt a 'bipolar moralistic model' of the city, but it is to ask entirely valid questions about the way the city is being envisioned at any particular time and place.

Among other early sociological studies of modern urban life, the work of Georg Simmel (1858–1918) focused on the ways in which life in the city affected *human consciousness*. For the city-dweller, life consists of endless encounters with people who are 'strangers', so that the individual is subject to a vastly increased number of impressions and meetings and finds his senses bombarded by these encounters. In a 1903 essay entitled 'The Metropolis and Mental Life', Simmel argued that urban life posed a new set of psychological challenges to people as the result of 'the intensification of emotional life due to the swift and continuous shift of external and internal stimuli' (Simmel 2002: 11). In traditional societies there is a 'slower, more habitual, more smoothly flowing rhythm' to one's experience of life, especially in regard to person-to-person encounters, but the metropolis increases the whole tempo of life so that one must come to terms with the growth in contacts with other people, mostly unknown strangers. In this situation people undergo a transformation in mental attitudes which is essential for their survival:

> The mental attitude of the people of the metropolis to one another may be designated formally as one of reserve. If the unceasing external contact of numbers of persons in the city should be met by the same number of inner reactions as in the small town, in which one knows almost every person he meets and to each of whom he has a positive relationship, one would be completely atomized internally and would fall into an unthinkable mental condition. Partly this psychological circumstance and partly the privilege of suspicion which we have in the face of the elements of metropolitan life . . . necessitates in us that reserve, in consequence of which we do not know by sight neighbours of years standing and which permits us to appear to small-town folk so often as cold and uncongenial (ibid.: 15).

Like Weber, Simmel also recognized the significance of the growth in the power of money and its role in human relationships within the metropolis. The city 'has always been the seat of money economy' because the concentration of commercial economy has 'given the medium of exchange an importance which it could not have acquired in the commercial aspects of rural life'. But in a 'complete money economy' the distance between people, the reserve with which they treat each other, is increased as individuals develop a matter-of-fact attitude 'in which a formal justice is often combined with an unrelenting hardness' (ibid.: 12).

The extent to which this 'unrelenting hardness' seeped into the business dealings of people who appeared to be devout Christians became a matter of serious concern to theologians who reflected critically on the changes they observed taking place within Christianity in the course of the nineteenth century. Simmel himself warned of this danger, commenting that modern culture prioritized the 'objective spirit over the subjective', with the result that a massive increase in external comforts and institutions was not matched by what would today be called 'personal growth'. In other words, economic and material progress was far outstripping the progress of the human spirit and there had been 'a regression of the culture of the individual with reference to spirituality, delicacy and idealism' (ibid.: 18).

The urban pathologies identified thus far, and others such as the increase in mental disorders and suicide, and what Emile Durkheim described as the incidence of anomie, related largely to the experience of the growing middle classes. These are the disorders of people who, by and large, actually benefited materially from the growth of the industrial city. If one looks closely at Edvard Munch's painting *Anxiety*, the individuals depicted in such anguish are certainly not poor people, but represent prosperous, respectable society. In the first half of the twentieth century the American artist Edward Hopper, whose 1942 painting *Nighthawks* is possibly the best known of all artistic images of the modern city, painted numerous urban scenes depicting people who, despite obvious material wealth, struggled to communicate with each other. Hopper described his painting *Approaching A City*, in which two sets of rail tracks lead into a dark subway tunnel, as expressing the 'interest, curiosity, fear' one feels when entering a strange city by train for the first time (Kranzfelder 1998: 119). Paintings like these serve as visual illustrations of the middle-class urban pathologies described by Simmel and later amplified in Louis Wirth's 1938 essay, 'Urbanism as a Way of Life'.

There were other painters of the city, however, whose attention was focused on the plight of large numbers of people without access to money, seemingly locked into conditions of extreme poverty, and facing constant illness and hunger. For example, the German artist Käthe Kollwitz devoted her very considerable gifts to depicting the urban poor, especially women, in a manner that highlighted both the tragedy of their existence and their extraordinary dignity. Her deeply moving depictions of a revolt by Silesian weavers in the 1840s has been described as 'a landmark of class-conscious art' which broke new ground by representing 'the plight of the worker and his age-long struggle to better his position' (Zigrosser 1969: ix). When these prints were nominated for a gold award at an exhibition in Berlin in 1898, the decision was vetoed by the Emperor who denounced Kollwitz's work as 'gutter art'.

This realization that the industrial city not only created a new type of society and led to changes in human psychology, but that it also increased class divisions and undermined traditional forms of economic activity which had enabled families to retain their independence and dignity, also shaped urban sociology. Friedrich Engels, for example, provided an influential description of slum conditions, holding up a mirror to the back alleys of London and Manchester and concluding that the 'narrow-minded egotism' that had become a leading feature of society, was blatantly obvious 'in the frantic bustle of the great city':

> The disintegration of society into individuals, each guided by his private principles and each pursuing his own aims has been pushed to its furthest limits in London. Here indeed human society has been split into its component atoms (Engels 2007: 69).

Conclusion

It may appear from the foregoing discussion that the classical urban sociologists were preoccupied with social *problems* which appeared to be related
directly to the emergence of the industrial city. This can be interpreted, as we
have seen, as implying an anti-urban bias on their part. Western intellectuals have frequently been accused of just such bias and of creating an ethos
which glorifies rural virtues. However, in defence of this body of work we
may say, first, that these sociologists were not unaware of the positive aspects
of contemporary urbanization. For example, Emile Durkheim contributed
to the analysis of the urban pathologies we have described while profess-
ing an unambiguous belief that 'great cities are the uncontested homes of
progress'. Durkheim was not alone in believing that cities were the contexts
within which positive change and development would take place. Innovations
which result in the enhancement of human life are likely to be welcomed in
the city, and those responsible for them will enjoy prestige there, in contrast
to the conservatism of rural societies in which proposals for change continue
to meet stout resistance in cultures which sanctify tradition and honour the
ancestors. And yet, like many of his contemporaries, Durkheim was 'torn
between the admiration he felt for the undoubted progress' of Western civilization, and 'the deep concern and anxiety he felt for the future of society in its
headlong rush towards what nobody could tell' (Abraham 1973: 101).

Second, the unease and anxiety which can be detected in the work to which
we have referred was generally the result of the realization that the changes
taking place in modern societies were truly revolutionary. Marx and Engels
famously described these changes as involving the abolition of all 'fixed,
fast-frozen relations' and the creation of a way of life in which 'all that is
solid melts into air' and 'all that is holy is profaned'. While the progress witnessed in industrial cities was not ignored or minimized, these were difficult
times in which to live and what troubled many of the scholars who wrestled
with the task of understanding this age was the uncertainty about just where
the juggernaut of social change was headed. The cultural marginalization of
religious beliefs and values, the growth of an instrumental rationality and an
impersonal bureaucracy, the increasing erosion of normative ethical language,
and an ever-encroaching individualism and acquisitiveness, these aspects of
modern culture were what troubled the early sociologists, rather than antip-
athy toward the city as such. Lewis Mumford, who has himself been accused
of anti-urbanism, explained the underlying reasons for his apprehension concerning the forms the modern city was taking with characteristic clarity: from
the nineteenth century onwards, he wrote, the city 'was treated not as a public

institution, but a private commercial venture to be carved up in any fashion that might increase the turnover and further the rise in land values' (Mumford 1966: 486).

By the end of the nineteenth century then, it had become very difficult to respond to the Stranger's question as to *the meaning of the city*. Earlier sources of inspiration which related city-building to transcendent models had been forgotten, and the humanist ideal of a new, utopian City of Man was now in danger of being overwhelmed by the seemingly uncontrollable power of the market economy. Within a generation or two warfare would unleash unprecedented levels of violence in which the newly industrialized nations would bomb each others' cities to smithereens. All of which created a tremendous vacuum which, in the absence of the creation of a new meaning for the city, was likely to be filled by architects, planners and builders whose work, whether by intention or not, would likely result in the reappearance of Babylon. The situation cried out for fresh visions which, as we shall see in the next chapter, were not long in arriving.

4. URBAN VISIONS, URBAN NIGHTMARES

> Cities have become extraordinarily intricate, and for this, difficult to generalize. We can no longer even agree on what counts as a city. . . . The city is everywhere and in everything. . . . The traditional divide between the city and the countryside has been perforated (Amin & Thrift 2002: 1).

As we saw at the conclusion of the previous chapter, the beginning of the twentieth century was characterized by a mood of considerable uncertainty and anxiety across the Western world; much of this focused on the problems arising in industrial cities. Officially, pride in the achievements of civilization remained undimmed and it was widely assumed that the blessings associated with science and technology would bring freedom and progress around the globe. However, many doubted these claims and worried about the prospects for human well-being if the experience of London, Paris, Berlin and New York really did presage the future for the whole human race.

This spirit of anxiety was expressed by both writers and artists. The painter George Frederick Watts, for example, once known as England's Michelangelo, reacted to the social problems of London in much the same way as Dostoevsky, only in this case the spirit animating the city was represented by a horrific depiction of Mammon as an evil beast crushing human beings, including children, beneath his giant hands and feet. The critic John Ruskin published *Unto This Last* in which he argued that modern political and economic theories were turning urban dwellers into 'covetous machines' and warned that if this trend could not be arrested it would result in deep structural inequalities between peoples and would eventually bring complete destruction to the natural world. The system that now dominated capitalist society, Ruskin said, brought wealth to a segment of the population while leading to the pauperization of many other people. With remarkable insight, Ruskin argued that the rising standard of living enjoyed by some people at the urban heart of the Empire was related to economic devastation at its periphery. More seriously still so far as this study is concerned, Ruskin saw Victorian Christianity as complicit in social and cultural developments that were entirely at odds with the teaching of the Bible:

> The writings which we (verbally) esteem as divine, not only denounce the love of money as the source of all evil, as an idolatry abhorred by the Deity, but declare mammon service to be the accurate and irreconcilable opposite of God's service . . . and declare woe to the rich and blessing to the poor. . . . Whereupon we forthwith investigate a science of becoming rich, as the shortest road to national prosperity (Ruskin 1997: 341).

The sense of cultural crisis so clearly reflected in statements like these increased and deepened after the slaughter of the First World War, and as sociologists, planners and architects wrestled with the immense challenge of creating urban environments in which human beings might flourish, they inevitably began to search for fresh models. At the end of the war, Walter Gropius, the influential director of the Bauhaus school of design in Germany, which has been called 'the incubator' of architectural modernism, summed up the sense of an ending that many of his contemporaries experienced:

> Today's artist lives in an era of dissolution without guidance. He stands alone. The old forms are in ruins, the benumbed world is shaken up, the old human spirit is invalidated and in flux toward a new form. We float in space and cannot perceive the new order (quoted in Pearman 2006: 22).

In this situation two options were open to city builders: either they returned to the past and explored ways of applying and adapting the principles and values that had underpinned much earlier urban visions, or they began, so to speak, from ground zero, developing an entirely fresh urban blueprint and attempting to build a new type of city from the bottom up. We will briefly notice the two outstanding examples of these apparently diverse approaches.

The garden city

In 1898 a London civil servant named Ebenezer Howard, deeply concerned about the problems of overcrowding in the inner city, and equally worried by current reactions to this in the shape of a growing suburban flight from the city, published a pamphlet with the title *Tomorrow: A Peaceful Path to Real Reform*. The title suggests that Howard shared the concern of many of his contemporaries that unless something was done, there was a real prospect of violent revolution. His proposals were intended to offer a realistic way of limiting the apparently endless expansion of cities like London and involved a return to some of the fundamental values which had underpinned much earlier urban visions. For example, Howard accepted the idea, developed by the Greek philosophers, that since there was a natural limit to the growth of an organism it was essential to restrict urban expansion if cities were to be environments within which human communities might flourish and relate in a sustainable way to the natural world. It was deplorable, Howard said, that people 'continue to stream into already overcrowded cities'.

Howard's initial ideas, which were shaped by utopian visions from the time of Thomas More onwards, were fleshed out in *Garden Cities of Tomorrow*, published in 1902. Carolyn Steel summarizes the book's proposals as follows: it envisioned a city in which the built environment and cultivated land would be inextricably linked together, so that a thriving agricultural sector would have a guaranteed market for its produce, while the waste from the city would be used to increase the soil's fertility.

> Crucially, all land would be owned by the community and held in trust on its behalf, with all rents going to run the city and fund public works. This would mean that as land values rose, it would be the city, and not individual landowners, that would get rich (Steel 2008: 300).

This was obviously a bold, utopian vision which involved an explicit challenge to one of the fundamental principles of the market economy. Peter Hall, who regards Howard as the most important theorist and visionary in the entire history of urban planning, suggests that his proposals offered a kind of third way between the extremes of Victorian capitalism and a bureaucratic and centralized socialism. Remarkably, within two years the vision outlined in *Garden Cities*, or at least a significant part of it, became reality with the building of Letchworth, later to be followed by Welwyn Garden City. Howard's ideas attracted the financial support of philanthropic industrialists like Lord Leverhulme, Joseph Rowntree and the Cadburys, all of whom had established their own experimental communities with the provision of adequate housing and services for their workforces. Howard's concept of a cluster of cities, limited in size (although large enough to ensure the creation of 'a decent orchestra'), was intended to ensure that the population would enjoy the benefits of urban life combined with 'all the fresh delights of the country'. According to Mumford, Howard's vision 'affected the pattern of housing and city-building in many areas, from Scotland to India' (Mumford 1966: 594), and it is possible to trace a connection between his theory and the New Towns Act of 1946, with the subsequent creation of a series of cities guarded by green belts, including most recently, Milton Keynes. Yet certain aspects of Howard's original ideas, crucial to the fulfilment of his vision, were never carried out; those who held power in Letchworth 'reneged on the intended transfer of funds to the municipality, while the residents, instead of bonding with one another and cooking communal meals, kept mostly to themselves and commuted to a nearby corset factory for work' (Steel 2008: 302).

The radiant city

It will be noticed that Howard's vision was developed before the outbreak of the Great War. In the aftermath of that terrible conflict the atmosphere in Europe changed dramatically and in the 1920s urban sociologists, psychologists and architects despaired of the inheritance from the past and felt compelled to seek new directions. Modernist architects in the inter-war period desired a clean break with the past and set about 'scraping away the traces of history and the styles of bygone eras', replacing them with new designs using glass, steel and concrete (Pearman 2006: 22).

We have already noticed the appearance from the 1870s onward of a range of phobias which seemed to be associated with urban living in the huge, and ever increasing, cities of Europe. Anthony Vidler describes how the great city – the metropolis – came to be viewed as sheltering 'a nervous and feverish population', and he comments that the *space* of the city was subjected to growing study and analysis as the possible cause of the psychological alienation of many metropolitan individuals (Vidler 2001: 25). Discussing the pathological conditions which 'became an almost obsessive part of clinical practice' at the turn of the century, Vidler identifies no less than twelve such phobias, before adding that there were 'multitudes of others'. In the atmosphere of dejection and despair that followed the war, the stage was thus set for the radically fresh ideas of modernist architects and planners:

The pathologies of agoraphobia and claustrophobia, joined if not caused by their common site in metropolis, provided ready arguments for modernist architects who were eager to reconstruct the very foundations of urban space. Arguing that urban phobias were precisely the product of urban environments, and that their cure was dependent on the erasure of the old city in its entirety, modernist architects from the early 1920s projected images of a city restored to a natural state, within which the dispersed institutions of the new society would be scattered like pavilions in a landscape garden (ibid.: 51).

The key figure here was the Swiss/French urban planner and architect, Le Corbusier (1877–1969). He made no secret of his contempt for existing cities, regarding them as beyond renewal or renovation and as the source of the maladies that oppressed so many contemporary people. He felt particular hostility toward what had, until then, been a central feature of all cities – the street. Urban streets, Le Corbusier wrote, were cut off from the open skies and were forever 'plunged in eternal twilight'. No matter how long one lives in a city, the 'enclosing walls' of the street always oppress the human heart, and the dangers that confront us on the street, whether from people or traffic, leave us disgusted with this urban space.

The solution seemed simple: *destroy the street!* The city must be entirely reconceived in a way that would forever abolish the kind of interactions that occur on the streets. Le Corbusier had twice visited the Parthenon in Athens and while there had experienced what sounds like a 'secular epiphany' in which he discovered what he called 'ineffable space'. The trouble with the ghastly cities bequeathed to us by history is that they are cramped, confused and completely lacking in rational design; they must be razed to the ground so that on their ruins visionary planners and architects can then erect open, light-filled cities. Le Corbusier knew that he had a fight on his hands: existing cities were like 'BEASTS' (the capitals are his), but the beast must be confronted and destroyed: '. . . we can take control and decide in what direction the coming battle is to be waged. For the desire to rebuild any great city in a modern way is to engage in a formidable battle' (Le Corbusier 2002).

In 1933 Le Corbusier published *La Ville Radieuse* ('The Radiant City') which has been described as 'the gospel of modern urbanism'. It enunciated the fundamental principles which were to shape both modern architecture and town planning and was intended to be a definitive guide for the construction of all future cities. The idea was to eliminate once and for all confusion, chaos, uncertainty; the city of the future would be rationally planned to the last detail, a shining, light-filled metropolis rising into the sky, and made transparent by the creative use of steel, glass and concrete. For Le Corbusier city building involved a struggle against nature in which she must be undermined; the architect and planner need to 'hack at nature' and take a position in which they oppose her.

Very few such cities were ever built, one exception being Brasilia which was 'a paradise for the modernist architect'.[1] Nonetheless, Le Corbusier's influence was immense and lingers still wherever there are city planners determined to erase the remains of older urban forms, or where eight-lane expressways are built to keep the traffic moving, or where tower blocks reach into the clouds. Ironically, while the vision of the 'Radiant City' emerged as a reaction to the phobias and disorders blamed on inherited urban forms, the only city ever built in accord with Le Corbusier's principles gave birth to a new phobia which came to be known as 'brasilitis'. The causes of this condition were 'the absence of crowds ... the anonymity of places and the facelessness of human figures, and a numbing monotony of an environment devoid of anything to puzzle, perplex or excite' (Bauman 1998: 44).

Le Corbusier's ideas were first presented at the *Congrès Internationaux d'Architecture Moderne* (CIAM) in 1933 and quickly became very influential in Europe and, especially, in the United States. Much of the urban development in the USA in the course of the twentieth century reflects Le Corbusier's influence, and his fundamental approach to urban architecture and planning became known as the 'International Style'. Kathryn Milun comments that in the past fifty years this style has stencilled 'European architectural modernism on cities around the world', so that 'ubiquitous, gigantic glass-and-steel structures and vast concomitant networks of urban freeways so typical of the International Style' have mushroomed across the globe and have come to symbolize 'modernization' (Milun 2007: 124). The social and human costs of such developments may yet prove to be immense given that where the vision of the radiant city has been implemented, however partially, it has created fresh nightmares and problems. Indeed, in a classic study of the history of urban planning, Peter Hall observes that the influence of Le Corbusier's ideas on urban development in the twentieth century has been 'incalculably great', with results which were 'at best questionable, at worst catastrophic' (Hall 1996: 203).

---

1. The Nigerian Federal Capital, Abuja, was modelled on Brasilia and is twinned with it. Designed by American planners and architects it was envisaged as a 'Radiant City' at the heart of this vast country and a contrast to the chaos of Lagos. See Murray 2008.

We may pause here for a moment to reflect on the curious fact that these twentieth-century urban visions contain striking echoes of the biblical narrative of creation. The concept of the 'garden city' clearly recalls the loss of Eden, while also representing a significant attempt to envisage a type of city that would relate far more closely and directly to the created world than was possible in a megalopolis like London. But equally, the even more radical notion of the 'radiant city' cannot fail to remind readers of the Bible of the first words recorded there as spoken directly by God himself: 'Let there be light' (Gen. 1:3). What is more, both these themes reappear in striking ways in the final vision of the Bible, in which the new Jerusalem is discovered to contain a 'tree of life' which comes into fruit every month with twelve different fruits, while this vast city is suffused with light, the source of which is to be found in the presence of God himself within it (Rev. 22:1–5).

Given the loss of the earlier visions of sacred cities, the ending of the monopolistic power of Christendom, and the privatization of Protestant faith, it seems remarkable that such biblical themes should reappear and occupy such prominence in the work of secular urban planners and architects. We have noticed how the biblical writers reacted to the sacred cities of the ancient world with prophetic criticism, insisting that the God of Israel was revealed as a liberating deity whose saving activity was displayed within human history. Furthermore, it is striking that the new Jerusalem glimpsed by John of Patmos contains 'no temple', it is in fact, a *de-sacralized city*. Does this suggest that the desire of modern planners to discover urban forms transcending the patterns of the past, so creating environments in which human beings might at last be truly free, are not so distant from the kind of city that God intends? Perhaps so, but we are bound to notice that in the new Jerusalem the temple is redundant only because God himself dwells within this city, eliminating forever by his presence the sacred/secular divide. The crucial question then becomes whether the tendency of modernist urban dreams to turn to dust and ashes is the result of the hubris that imagines light to be a human creation, rather than the gift of the Creator-God who is its ultimate source?[2]

---

2. Speaking in June 1955 at the dedication of his chapel of *Notre Dame Du Haut* (a building now visited by 100,000 people every year), Le Corbusier said: 'In building this chapel, I wished to create a place of silence, of prayer, of peace, of spiritual joy' (*The Guardian,* 2007).

Visions and nightmares

Nowhere were the principles of modernist architecture and city planning more extensively applied to an existing city than in the reshaping of New York. Robert Moses, who designed and built the city's urban freeways, employed ideas taken straight from Le Corbusier when he said, 'When you operate in an overbuilt metropolis, you have to hack your way with a meat ax'. Faced with local opposition to plans that involved the razing of entire neighbourhoods, Moses invoked the French architect's concept of battle when warning local people, 'I'm just going to keep right on building. You do the best you can to stop it.' Marshall Berman, who recalls weeping for his neighbourhood when the Cross-Bronx Expressway was driven clean through it in 1953, says that when Moses set about demolishing the old city and creating the new, 'no temporal or spiritual power could block his way' (Berman 1983: 292). Berman concludes:

> Moses' great construction in and around New York in the 1920s and 30s served as a rehearsal for the infinitely greater reconstruction of the whole fabric of America after World War Two. The motive forces in this reconstruction were the multibillion-dollar Federal Highway Program and the vast suburban housing initiatives of the Federal Housing Administration. This new order integrated the whole nation into a unified flow whose lifeblood was the automobile. It conceived of cities principally as obstructions to the flow of traffic, and as junkyards of substandard housing and decaying neighborhoods from which Americans should be given every chance to escape (ibid.: 307).

Someone who attended a meeting in New York to protest at Moses' plans to destroy yet another existing square in the city to make way for an access road to the lower Manhattan Expressway was the young Jane Jacobs, who was later to publish the influential study *The Death and Life of Great American Cities* (1993). Interviewed not long before her death at the age of 89, Jacobs recalled Moses' anger at needing to justify his urban reconstruction plans. Before walking out of the meeting he had shouted, 'There is nobody against this – NOBODY, NOBODY, NOBODY – but a bunch of, a bunch of mothers!' (Kunstler 2001).

Moses had his way in New York, while elsewhere across the United States city planners with similarly radical visions flattened existing urban forms to make way for the creations of modernist architects. In the interview cited above, Jacobs described how another leading planner, Ed Logue, told her in all seriousness that the best thing that could happen to San Francisco would

be a second earthquake like that of 1904! If the city were to be destroyed
by such an 'act of God', it would create the space for a rationally designed
metropolis.

The post-Second World War shaping of American cities thus owed much
to the modernist visions of Le Corbusier, whose ideas took off as they did
because they meshed with certain basic features of American culture.[3] A negative view of the past did not arise in the USA as a reaction to the First World
War; it was present in the 'New World' from the beginning as a response to
the perceived backwardness and repression of old Europe and so became
deeply embedded within the American psyche. But in addition, the mass
production of the motor car, combined with the vast extent of open, physical space across the continent, made possible the expression of individual
freedom and the choice of 'lifestyles' in ever-expanding suburbs. In the words
of Philip Bess, suburban development in the USA seems to have been 'an
expression of the increasing dominance of emotivist cultural tendencies
inherent in American democracy from its origins' and resulted in the migration of much of the middle class from urban centres to the now-familiar 'edge
cities' (Bess 2006: 21).

The physical growth of American cities as the result of suburban sprawl
has resulted in a situation in which, as Amin and Thrift say in the quotation
at the head of this chapter, it is no longer clear 'what counts as a city'. For
example, when a city like Atlanta has increased by incorporating roughly 500
acres of land for fresh suburban development every week, the traditional
notion of an urban 'centre' becomes virtually meaningless. A metro region
that registers 2.5 million motor cars annually and removes 190,000 acres of
tree cover in a ten-year period is the very antithesis of the garden city! Urban
settlements on this scale are inevitably de-centred and the services needed
by their populations will be scattered across a variety of sites separated by
great distances. Such cities are no longer confined within clearly identifiable

---

3. Rem Koolhaas has, however, pointed out the ambivalence of Le Corbusier's
   response to New York from the time of his first visit in the mid-1930s. Clearly,
   this was the modernist's dream made real, but it failed to meet the criteria of the
   radiant city because its skyscrapers were erected without a fully rational master plan
   and they left the despised street intact! Koolhaas says that Le Corbusier viewed
   the inhabitants of 'this grotesque congregation of architectural cripples' with pity
   and he quotes him as saying: 'In the age of speed the [American] skyscraper has
   re-established the pedestrian, him alone . . . He moves anxiously near the bottom
   of the skyscraper, louse at the foot of the tower . . .' (Koolhaas 1994: 251).

spaces, but become chains of settlements linked by networks of communication, so that, as Amin and Thrift say, the city is now 'everywhere and in everything'.

This physical, geographical expansion of cities has been accompanied by a significant cultural change in which human beings have come to be defined as *consumers*. The *polis* is no longer understood as a community united by the pursuit of virtue, but is judged to be successful in terms of its ability to stimulate and satisfy an ever-growing range of human desires. Even in suburbs in which significant numbers of people profess allegiance to a religious worldview, it is the economic sphere which provides 'the ordinary-language terms and expressions that we use to give meaning' to daily life, with the consequence that people in an urban world perceive themselves as 'competitors driven by motives of wanting, having, choosing – never by need, by the wish to share, or by altruism' (Collier & Esteban 1998: 16, 21).

The concrete symbol of this cultural shift is the hypermarket, or shopping mall. David Clark quotes Baudrillard as saying that in the early development of consumerism, with the now-redundant department store at its 'cultural and commercial zenith', the city retained its traditional form, but the postmodern city is '*satellized* by the hyper-market or *shopping center*' and so expands to become a 'metropolitan area' (Clark 2003b: 95). The 'Mall of America', opened in 1992 outside Minneapolis in a blaze of patriotic pride, boasts that it is five times larger than Red Square, twenty times the size of St Peter's in Rome, and required twice as much steel as the Eiffel Tower. However, one observer comments that the arrows on well-lit store maps signalling YOU ARE HERE 'are more inclined to raise existential angst than to offer directional comfort' (Milun 2007: 194).

It is time to recall our earlier comments about the need to ask critical questions concerning urban myths. In a brilliant study of contemporary urban pathologies, Kathryn Milun points out that beneath the Mall of America, out of sight and sound of the consumers who throng its light-filled arcades, disabled workers wearing face masks staff a recycling station in which they sift garbage passing on a conveyer belt. The waste management corporation can apparently pay disabled people less than the standard minimum wage, with the result that, yet again, Fritz Lang's prescient movie comes to life and the line dividing fantasy from reality disappears. But, as Milun observes, problems are not confined to the basement because all is not well upstairs in the Mall:

> There is no social contract to ensure that the public's interests are served in these sites. Unlike the city's streets, groups and individuals do not get permission to speak

or stage demonstrations in mall atriums unless their message is inoffensive to mall management and to shopping culture in general (ibid.: 195).

What is more, the mention of 'existential angst' alerts us to the re-appearance of the very phobias and fears that the modernist city was designed to eliminate. However, whereas nineteenth-century urban pathologies were experienced largely by men, and were triggered by the vast open spaces of central city squares built to celebrate imperial glory, these same disorders now appear to be suffered mainly by women, and the triggers are to be found in the urban freeway systems and shopping malls so characteristic of the modernist city. This has led feminist theorists to argue that modern urban space is *gendered* space. In the words of Leonie Sandercock,

> The spatial order of the modern industrial city came to be seen as a profoundly
> patriarchal spatial order . . . an arrangement of space in which the domination of men
> over women was written into the architecture, urban design, and form of the city.
> Cities . . . confined women to the suburbs, to the home, to the private sphere, and
> then, having segregated them, doubly disadvantaged them by not recognizing that
> their needs in the city were different from those of men, based as they were around
> home, neighbourhood, and caring for children and the elderly (Sandercock 1998: 18).

The mention of children and the elderly prompts the question as to whether the modern city constitutes a hostile environment for them. The British journal *The Economist* ran an editorial in 1998 in which it argued that children constitute a 'negative externality' in public places and that, like cigarettes and mobile phones, they should be tightly controlled. Governments were said to respond to such 'market failures' either by making polluters pay for their 'anti-social behaviour', or by banning them from public spaces. Either of these solutions 'might work for children' (quoted in Milun 2007: 210). As to the elderly, Jeremy Seabrook describes the experience of a seventy-nine-year-old woman who, having fallen on her face in a city street recalled hearing a young woman say, 'Poor old thing' and thinking afterwards, 'Yes, love, you were right three times. I am poor. I am old. And, above all, I am a thing. That's how they look at you.' Seabrook poses a critical question which echoes yet again that asked by Eliot's Stranger, as quoted at the start of chapter 2:

> Is the creation of ever more wealth synonymous with the betterment of human
> lives? Is the well-being of vulnerable people really dependent upon perpetually
> rising incomes, or does the creation of wealth itself militate against social cohesion,
> belonging and solidarity? (Seabrook 2003: 51)

As far as women's experience of the modern city is concerned, they would seem to have three options:

- they may become socialized, or acculturated, into the urban ethos of late modernity, fulfilling their allotted role as consumers. This will demand the suppression of distinctly female ways of experiencing the world so as to operate without unbearable stress within the received urban forms;
- they may actively resist such pressures and demand that their way of experiencing the world, which results in relationships of mutual dependence, must be allowed to contribute to the reimagining of the city. We should notice that Robert Moses' outburst provoked by the resistance of 'a bunch of mothers' is revealing in that it clearly demonstrates how the experiences of women, of mothers, brings to light the limitations of the rationally planned city;
- their reaction may be a pathological one in the form of agoraphobia. As Milun says in a memorable phrase, 'Agoraphobics are the miner's canaries in the public space of our cities' (Milun 2007: 48).

In the cities of the South

In chapter 2 we briefly noted some of the patterns of contemporary urbaniza-tion in the Global South, especially in Africa and China. Across the southern continents there were urban settlements that long pre-dated the modern world. China, for example, has an urban history stretching back 3,000 years and it is still possible to see 'the remains of a rich urban culture of the past as it was adapted to different geographies and climates' across this vast country (Atkinson & Thielen 2008: 155). On the continent of Africa, cities such as Alexandria played a crucial role in the history of the ancient world, while our earlier reference to the urban theology developed by Augustine of Hippo is a reminder of the importance of the cities which once dotted the coast of North Africa in Roman times. But elsewhere on this continent, as Aylward Shorter points out, towns and cities have existed for centuries, whether sacred enclosures governed by divine kings, or settlements created as the result of the spread of early forms of Christianity or Islam:

> Under the influence of the Coptic Church, indigenous Christian towns developed in medieval Sudan and Ethiopia. . . . Along the southern fringes of the Sahara Desert, and down the coast of eastern Africa, towns like Djenne and Timbuktu, Mombasa

and Kilwa grew up as inland or coastal emporia. Islamic culture in Africa was, and is, essentially urban (Shorter 1991: 22).

When H. M. Stanley entered the capital of Kabaka Mutesa's African kingdom in 1875, he discovered a settlement with a population of 5,000 in which there were broad roadways and dwellings surrounded by well-kept courtyards. Stanley was amazed at the sophistication and splendour of this traditional town, out of which the modern city of Kampala would eventually grow.

The mention of Stanley serves to remind us that the key factor in the modern growth of many cities in Africa, Asia and Latin America was the economic and political expansion of Europe. Beginning in the sixteenth century, European colonialism brought peoples throughout these continents into direct and often painful contact with the revolutionary forces of the modernizing process. As Bryan Roberts observes, from 1492 onwards the European powers 'influenced the urbanization of developing countries through imperialism, and through investments in transport and infrastructure designed to facilitate the extraction of primary products' (Roberts 1995: 23). The Spanish and Portuguese conquests in the 'new world' resulted in Latin America becoming embedded within the European economy on terms set by the colonists and in ways that radically altered the socio-economic structures of the entire continent. History thus appeared to repeat itself in that the ancient Roman policy of establishing imperial control through the building of compliant cities was now employed by the European colonial powers. The Spanish and Portuguese invaders destroyed the indigenous cities which they discovered in South America, replacing them with urban centres built on the basis of their own models and designed to facilitate their social and economic objectives across the continent. Havana, Mexico City, Cuzco and Arequipa, provide examples of city-building as the instrument of colonial policy. Such cities became part of an imposed urban system intended to ensure 'the control and administration of the new domains'. Roberts describes the development of the town of Potosi in Bolivia, which by 1545 was producing half the world's output of silver and quickly became the largest city in South America. Such urban developments suggest that from the beginning of the colonial era, 'integration into the European economy favoured commodity circulation and undermined the self-sufficiency of local agrarian structures in Latin America' (ibid.: 30).

Similar patterns of urban development occurred on the continent of Africa, where cities like Lagos, Nairobi and Kampala were shaped by the colonial enterprise, the built environment consisting of state houses, army barracks, government offices, cricket grounds and, let it be noted, cathedral churches.

There was an underlying assumption that these cities existed for the benefit of Europeans and that the appropriate place for native Africans was the countryside, or, as it was somewhat contemptuously called, 'the bush'. African access to these cities was restricted by laws that often amounted to a form of *apartheid* – requiring passes issued to meet specific labour demands. Thus, urban housing for Africans in the Copperbelt and in Kenya was constructed on the 'bed space' principle to accommodate single male labourers (King 2002: 528). In India as late as the 1940s New Delhi was still being constructed as a city built to meet the needs of the colonial power 'with virtually no attempt made to plan for industrial development' (ibid.: 527).

Clearly, we cannot attempt to offer a detailed account of the history of the cities of the South during the colonial era. However, there are certain consequences of the establishment of the kind of urban systems described above which we need to highlight since they offer us a way of understanding some of the key features of the urban world which we now inhabit.

First, the narrative of modernization, which includes urbanization as a key instrument for the achievement of its goals, has resulted in the marginalization and denigration of the native peoples of the southern continents. Where such peoples have survived, their voices have gone unheard amid the trumpeting of 'progress' through development and modernization. Tragically, this narrative has all too often become internalized by traditional peoples, with the result that they have experienced terrible crises of identity and have frequently ended up demoralized and living on the margins of post-colonial cities.

Second, in many countries previously under colonial rule, the cities built as the command centres of the colonial enterprise have expanded to become megacities, sucking in huge numbers of people and dominating the political and economic life of entire nations. Sociologists speak of *primate* cities in contexts where a single urban centre expands to become much larger than any other city within the nation. This phenomenon can be found in Africa and Asia and was the dominant trend in Latin America in the nineteenth century. By 1920 most nations across this continent had primate urban systems. Mexico City, for example, grew to become three times the size of any other Mexican city, while Buenos Aires, which was developed to provide administrative structures for trade with Britain, had a population of one-and-a-half million by 1914, or 20% of the population of Argentina.

The phenomenon of megacities across the southern hemisphere demands that we give attention to the issues of poverty and injustice that shape the lives of millions of city-dwellers around the world. Bryan Roberts describes the situation of the urban poor as 'appalling' and comments that in Latin America 20% of the entire population 'have incomes that are insufficient for adequate

levels of food or shelter'. He concludes that the free-market economic policies imposed on developing nations in recent decades have 'excluded most of
Latin America's population from the benefits of growth' and that for millions
of city dwellers, 'solutions to the problems of urban poverty are as distant now
as they were when masses of rural migrants struggled to find whatever work
and shelter they could within the city' (ibid.: 209). In a sobering account of
slum conditions throughout the cities of the Global South, Mike Davis writes
that,

> . . . the cities of the future, rather than being made of glass and steel as envisioned by
> earlier generations of urbanists, are instead largely constructed of crude brick, straw,
> recycled plastic, cement blocks, and scrap wood. Instead of cities of light soaring
> toward heaven, much of the twenty-first century urban world squats in squalor,
> surrounded by pollution, excrement, and decay (Davis 2006: 19).

Actually, the situation is even worse than Davis's comment suggests, since
the cities of 'glass and steel . . . soaring toward heaven' *do* exist, but they stand
right beside the *favellas* which he so well describes. Take, for example, Nigeria's
capital city of Abuja which, as we noticed earlier, reflects the Le Corbusier-
inspired 'International Style', with broad, tree-lined boulevards and a forest of
shining skyscrapers. The Federal Government minister responsible for this
city has been quoted as saying that Abuja is 'not a city for the poor', ignoring
the expanding slums around the edges of the shining capital, housing (among
others) the civil servants who staff the gleaming offices during the daylight
hours. One of them, Dayyabu Haruna, describes his frustration at living a
schizophrenic existence in which he appears in a spotless, air-conditioned
office by day, only to return to his family amid the garbage, blocked drains and
lack of sanitation by night (Murray 2008).

While conditions in urban slums are indeed appalling and rightly provoke
a sense of moral outrage, we should not imagine that life within the privileged
and protected enclaves built of glass and steel and sealed by armed guards,
is ultimately satisfying. The Sante Fe district in Mexico City is one of Latin
America's most prestigious and high-profile urban development projects.
Like Abuja, it reflects a modernist vision and is promoted by developers as
providing high-quality educational facilities, corporate offices, 'and the most
renowned malls and recreation centers in Mexico City'. Sante Fe has been
lauded as showcasing Mexico City's 'transition from urban catastrophe to
global city'. But the phobias and anxieties that have surfaced in modernist
cities from Los Angeles to Brasilia are also evident within the 'glass cage' that
is Sante Fe:

Driving around the streets of Sante Fe, one is immediately struck by its sterility and anonymous, rather unhuman character. Compared to the hustle and bustle one finds all over Mexico City, Sante Fe's streets are devoid of life; pedestrians are few and far between. . . . In aspiring to exclusivity and modernity, it seems, Sante Fe has lost the very element that gives Mexico City its character: public space (Furniss 2008: 48–49).

This loss of 'public space' and the virtual demise of street life, while conforming (at least in this respect) to Le Corbusier's vision for the cities of the future, results in what is perhaps the most radical social and economic polarization in the whole of human history. Sante Fe has been designed on an American model 'that is being adopted in globalising cities all over the world, from Johannesburg to Mumbai and Buenos Aires to Shanghai', providing space for a 'globalised class to withdraw from public life' (ibid.). We thus witness the creation of dualist cities in which parallel communities are divided by gross disparities of wealth and opportunity, the one suffering from material poverty, while the other knows a dehumanizing poverty of spirit which is corroding the very qualities that have historically been regarded as necessary for defining the human person.

Storm clouds over the city

The prospects for the urban world in the twenty-first century are in many respects discouraging and threatening. It is not difficult to discover careful and respected scholars who view the future of cities with an almost apocalyptic foreboding. Nan Ellin, in a comprehensive review of postmodern urbanism, notes that many commentators analyse the contemporary situation in language that is unmistakably eschatological, even apocalyptic. She warns of the dangers that lie ahead if an 'extreme relativism and disengagement' resulting from the repudiation of meta-narratives were to 'eliminate any possibility for communication, ethics and democratic practice'. In that case we would be likely to witness a deepening of the 'alienating sense that there is no "real"', leaving people vulnerable to forms of 'artifice which allows for easy manipulation by the deft imagery of advertising and other forms of persuasion' (Ellin 1999: 292).

A striking example of the apocalypticism to which Ellin refers is provided by James Howard Kunstler's prediction of a series of 'converging catastrophes' which will bring the expansion of cities to a juddering halt and compel a return to earlier, sustainable urban models. Kunstler's alarming study focuses on the imminent end of cheap sources of energy and a looming ecological crisis which will, he argues, expose the unsustainable nature of the entire modern way of life, resulting in the social and physical collapse of the kind of cities built in the course of the twentieth century. In particular, American suburban sprawl has a 'tragic destiny' since it depends upon 'liberal and reliable supplies of cheap oil and natural gas' which are even now disappearing (Kunstler 2005: 248). Downtown skyscrapers will also be at risk and Kunstler envisages a nightmarish scenario in which powercuts cause the lights to go out and the loss of gas supplies results in ruptured water pipes in the cold of winter:

> What will happen in a city full of skyscrapers when the electric grid goes out unpredictably for hours at a time? What will happen to people stuck in the elevators? What will happen to people down at street level who need to get upstairs to their twenty-ninth floor office or apartment? What will happen to the elderly? (Kunstler 2005: 253).

If we are tempted to dismiss Kunstler's predictions as simply too pessimistic, it is sobering to discover that the last book published by Jane Jacobs, one of America's most respected urbanists, bore the ominous title, *Dark Age Ahead*. Jacobs, who had earlier explored the factors which result in the *death* of cities, believed that there were worrying indications that the developed, urban culture of the Western world might be 'rushing headlong into a Dark Age'. Perhaps the most chilling aspect of her analysis is to be found in a discussion of the collapse of the ancient cities of the Fertile Crescent, which we described in the previous chapter. How and why did those once great cities end up as ruins surrounded by utterly barren landscapes? The following passage provides food for thought and may suggest that this historical precedent indicates that Kunstler's warnings are not as fantastic as we might assume:

> In ancient times, much of the Fertile Crescent and eastern Mediterranean was covered with forests. But to obtain more farmland and more timber, and to satisfy the plaster industry's relentless demands for wood fuel, the forests were cut faster than they could regenerate. Denuded valleys silted up, and intensified irrigation led to salt accumulations in the soil. Overgrazing by goats, allowing new growth no start in life, sealed the destruction (Jacobs 2005: 15).

The final act in this tragic drama, which results in the designation the 'Fertile Crescent' becoming a complete misnomer, was played out under Saddam Hussein when the Marsh Arabs, who had occupied the wetlands of southern

Iraq for thousands of years, were expelled to make way for a drainage scheme which created 'another barren, salt-encrusted desert'.

Jane Jacobs viewed the loss of the Fertile Crescent and the collapse of its once great urban cultures as a warning to the modern world, and especially to the urban culture of North America. She suggested that peoples elsewhere in the world, including Europe, who are inclined to view the United States as an 'exemplary model', must discriminate between 'much that is constructive and vigorous' and much that is 'destructive and deadening' (ibid.: 26). The language here may be more measured and moderate than that of Kunstler, but the message is essentially the same. Thus, when Kunstler points out that urban development on America's arid Great Plains has been possible only as the result of massive irrigation schemes that have depleted underground supplies of water which accumulated 'over the geologic ages', it is to warn that a tragic urban history may be about to repeat itself. Like Jacobs, Kunstler regards most American cities as unsustainable in their present form and proposes that *downscaling* 'is the single most important task facing the American people' (Kunstler 2005: 239).

Given that urbanization is now taking place on a global scale, and that it invariably involves an uncritical use of Western, modernist models of development, the warnings sounded by scholars like Jacobs and Kunstler have a relevance and urgency far beyond the USA. For example, with the fading of the Communist ideal in China and its replacement by a capitalist economy, urban development has taken place using models of planning and architecture that are essentially foreign in nature and fail to address 'the escalating problems that China faces as its cities grow and transform on a scale never before witnessed by humankind'. China's 'rigorously marketed computer generated utopias' suppress the lessons of history and create 'a virtual world of inaccessible mega-structures' (Denison 2008: 215). Yet these very cities are threatened by inundation because if sea levels rise as predicted, the entire Pearl River Delta will be overwhelmed. As Atkinson and Theilen put it,

> ... focusing on what is actually happening and likely to happen within the wider policy framework and as a result of many millions of isolated actions, we see a very threatening future of the Chinese development process as a whole and especially for the coastal cities that are the power house of this process (Atkinson & Theilen 2008: 158)

The mushrooming of modernist cities around the world, designed on the basis of ideas that can be traced back to the European Enlightenment with its trust in secular rationality, is thus creating massive ecological problems and results in untold human suffering as the result of the socio-cultural impact of such structures. We have seen how the rise of the modern city in Europe and North America disrupted traditional patterns of human society and resulted in the appearance of acute forms of psychological distress for large numbers of people who had been driven by economic necessity into these settlements. The crucial question demanding attention in the light of this history is, *how will similar types of experience impact the lives of millions of people across the Global South who have made – and continue to make – their own migration from traditional societies into the megacities?*

The tragedy that could unfold in our urban world can be envisaged when we recall the plight of the native peoples driven from the Great Plains of North America and forced to relocate 'out of their collective forms of social organization' in the vain hope that they would assimilate within modern society, becoming 'proper farmers and raising nuclear families' (Milun 2007: 22). Without in any way minimizing the scandal of the slums, the fact is that millions of poor people in cities like Mumbai, Cape Town, Nairobi and Rio de Janeiro survive appalling conditions with extraordinary dignity because traditional patterns of kinship and social organization have been transferred to, and adapted to, life in the city. What would happen if governments across the Global South, pressured by international organizations to 'develop' and 'modernize', were to respond to this situation by flattening the informal settlements and erecting in their place forests of tower blocks? It would surely be a tragic irony were such forms of housing to mushroom in the cities of the South at the very time when the last of them, having proved destructive of social cohesion, were being dynamited in Europe and North America.

Back to the future?

The pessimistic urban scenario sketched above need not result in despair over the future of the city in a postmodern world. Leonie Sandercock notes the appearance of apocalyptic thinking in urban studies at the turn of the millennium, but argues that this context offers an opportunity for fresh and creative approaches to planning theory. What is needed, she insists, is a vision for the future of the city which embraces 'concerns for social and environmental justice, for human community, for cultural diversity, and for the spirit'. The hubris of the modernist approach to the city resulted in much human suffering because planners 'killed communities and destroyed individual lives by not understanding the loss and grieving that goes along with losing one's home and neighbourhood and friends and memory' (Sandercock 1998: 208).

Perhaps the most remarkable aspect of Sandercock's vision for the future relates to the *return of the sacred*, which she regards as essential if a way is to be found to prevent total environmental degradation. Not only so, but cities need to be built in such a manner that they do not frustrate 'our unrequited thirst for the spirit, for the sacred'. Noting (as we have seen in the previous chapter) that the cities of medieval Europe were built around the sacred sites of monasteries and cathedrals, Sandercock recognizes the vital role that churches, synagogues and mosques continue to play in the social life of many communities and insists that the city of the future must provide space for 'the nourishing of the spirit, or soul' (ibid.: 213). Sandercock's work continues and expands the feminist critique of modernist urban planning to which we have made previous reference, and it constitutes 'an eloquent, impassioned and challenging manifesto for a radically different post-modern approach to cities' (While 2005: 6).

We will complete this survey of the history and development of the city by identifying a number of specific 'signs of hope' that, without minimizing the enormous challenges confronting the urban world of the twenty-first century, offer some grounds for optimism.

First, in the United States of America the reaction against modernist planning and architecture has created space within which fresh thinking concerning the design of urban settlements is taking place. Andreas Duany and Elizabeth Plater-Zyberk have developed, with other leading American urbanists, an intellectual movement known as *New Urbanism*. In 1998 this subversive group drafted the 'Charter of New Urbanism' in which they committed themselves to work for 'the restoration of existing urban centers and towns within coherent metropolitan regions' and the reshaping of 'sprawling suburbs into communities of real neighborhoods'. The charter set New Urbanism the bold task of seeking to reverse the patterns of urban development that had shaped American cities for half a century and more, insisting that the built environment must be designed 'for the pedestrian and transit as well as the car', and that urban places must 'be framed by architecture and landscape design that celebrate local history, climate, ecology and practice' (Jacobsen 2003: 180).

The radical nature of the movement's rejection of modernist presuppositions and its willingness to utilize and adapt historic urban models can be seen from the extended quotation below from a contribution Duany and Plater-Zyberk made to a volume with the significant sub-title, *Toward an Architecture of Community*:

> The suburbs and cities of today continue to separate the naturally integrated human activities of dwelling, working, shopping, schooling, worshipping and recreating.

The hardship caused by this separation has been mitigated by widespread automobile ownership and use, which in turn has increased the demand for vehicular mobility. The priority given to road building at the expense of other civic programs during the last four decades has brought our country to the multiple crises of environmental degradation, economic bankruptcy and social disintegration.

The New Urbanism offers an alternative future for the building and rebuilding of regions. Neighborhoods that are compact, mixed-use and pedestrian friendly; districts of appropriate location and character; and corridors that are functional and beautiful can integrate natural environments and man-made communities into a sustainable whole (Duany & Plater-Zyberk 2007: 196).[4]

These New Urbanist principles have been applied in the design and construction of numerous developments both in the USA and in Europe, including Prince Charles' controversial building of Poundbury, an 'urban village' designed by the architect Leon Krier according to the New Urbanist ideas which he helped to shape (Miles 2006). Mention of this development is sufficient to indicate that New Urbanism (perhaps more accurately described as *neo-traditional* urbanism) is a controversial movement that is not without its critics. However, what makes the movement particularly significant for this study is the fact that, despite the overwhelmingly suburban character of North American Christianity, New Urbanism has attracted the enthusiastic endorsement of Christian professionals from across the denominational spectrum. Thus, Philip Bess, a Catholic teacher of architecture, having made the trenchant observation that empirical evidence suggests 'that modernist social fantasies underestimated the pervasiveness of what theologians call sin, while overestimating the redemptive power of steel, glass and electricity', endorses the New Urbanist movement as a significant attempt to employ 'the best practices of city-making from the past, toward the end of making better cities for the future' (Bess 2006: 123). Meantime, Eric Jacobsen, a Protestant pastor concerned to relate Christian theology and mission to the urban issues discussed in this book, has urged fellow-believers to identify with the Congress for New Urbanism 'on the basis of their Christian convictions'. Aware that the heartlands of Protestant-Evangelical religion in the USA are located firmly within the suburban sprawl which this movement seeks to challenge and transform,

---

4. Mike Davis comments that the 'young environmentally conscious architects' who lead the New Urbanist movement have 'sketched, with admirable clarity, a regional planning model that cogently links issues of social equity . . . with high priority environmental concerns' (Davis 2002: 102).

Jacobsen acknowledges that North American Evangelicals were not compelled to live in the suburbs, but chose to do so 'because *we have been worshipping false gods in the name of American values*' (Jacobsen 2003: 21, emphasis added).

The *second* sign of hope relates to developments in the cities of the Global South where the uncritical acceptance of Western urban models based on Enlightenment assumptions is increasingly challenged by intellectuals and professionals eager to reclaim neglected cultural and religious values and to apply the wisdom within these traditions to the task of city-building and development today. Earlier in this book we noticed the possible significance of African concepts derived from primal religious and cultural traditions to the task of urban development on that continent. At the same time, we have seen the problems created by the manner in which China's headlong rush toward modernization and urbanization has bypassed and marginalized that nation's traditional wisdom. Adrian Atkinson and Korinna Thielen have observed that Western faith in 'progress', translating into the 'creative destruction' of the modernizing process, is 'fundamentally at odds with the traditional, Confucian culture that gave structure to Chinese civilization for over 2000 years' (Atkinson & Thielen 2008: 155). Yet China's capitulation 'to an Occidental idea of what life should be all about' is likely to be increasingly questioned as experience within modernized cities creates a profound sense of need for 'a new formula for the organization of its society, productive processes and settlements that will put these back onto a sustainable path and provide the population with an enjoyable life' (ibid.: 159). It seems highly likely that the traditional wisdom repressed in the pursuit of 'progress' will return to provide both a critical perspective on recent developments and to offer a positive contribution to the Chinese urban future.

Perhaps the most striking examples of urban regeneration from the so-called developing world are to be found in Latin America in the transformation of cities like Curitiba in Brazil and Bogota in Columbia. The UN-HABITAT report, *State of the World's Cities, 2008/09*, concentrated on the challenges posed by rising inequalities in the world's cities, noting that 'Africa and Latin America have the world's highest levels of inequality, with many countries and cities experiencing widening disparities between the rich and the poor' (UN-HABITAT 2008: 50). The report contained alarming evidence of the dire social consequences of the widening gulf between the wealthy and the deprived, warning that when disadvantaged people realize that 'they will never attain their desired living standard', society becomes 'primed for political instability and high risks of generalized civil conflict' (ibid.: 57).

However, the cities of Curitiba and Bogota provide examples of the kind of transformation that is possible when visionary political leaders win the support of an urban populace eager to contribute to, as well as benefit from, radical social and structural change. Curitiba witnessed very rapid population increase in the second half of the twentieth century, yet as the result of three decades of 'thoughtful city planning' it achieved significant improvements in the quality of life of its citizens. The city is noted for its innovative public transport system, but other developments have included 'the preservation of the city's cultural heritage, the large expansion in the number of parks and green areas, the integration of social programmes and environmental educa- tion . . . and the "garbage exchange" programme' (Rabinovitch 1992: 62). In the case of Bogota, the transformation is yet more remarkable since here urban renewal has involved a megacity of 7 million people, with a high popu- lation density and a history of four decades of serious civil conflict. However, a succession of courageous mayors were able to imagine an alternative future for Bogota, culminating in the proposals of Enrique Peñalosa who 'presented his fellow citizens with a vision of urban harmony focused on equity – the cornerstone of a great city' (UN-HABITAT 2008: 190).

The renewal of Bogota resulted from the simultaneous pursuit of multi- ple aims, including the reclamation of public space through the recovery of pedestrian pavements and the creation of parks and plazas, the provision of a high-class public transport system, offering affordable fares and managed by a non-profit public company, and the promotion of non-vehicular transport through restrictions on motorized travel within the city and the creation of 'the world's longest pedestrian corridor', the 17 kilometre *Alameda Porvenir*. In addition, Mayor Peñalosa's administration 'built schools, nurseries and libraries where most needed: the poorest quarters of Bogota', and initiated a programme to reform urban land use and develop micro-credit schemes and public-private partnerships for small businesses and local communities (ibid.: 190). Research on the outcomes of this programme of urban transformation provides clear empirical evidence of significant economic, environmental, and social benefits for the citizens of Bogota (Wright 2004). For example, air quality has drastically improved, traffic accidents have been reduced, with road deaths falling from 1,387 in 1996 to 697 in 2002, and crime levels (including the murder rate) showed marked reductions. The success of this programme has attracted worldwide attention, with urban officials from more than fifty countries visiting the city to learn from its experience.

The description given above may leave the impression that Bogota's regeneration has resulted from a series of policy enactments, bringing about structural changes in a mechanistic manner designed to make the urban system function more efficiently. Nothing could be further from the truth; at the very core of this transformation is a *vision* of a different kind of city, one in which justice and equality are fundamental, underpinning values, and urban policy and planning are therefore intended to operate to the benefit and well-being of all citizens. In other words, there is a return here to something like the ancient vision of a community united in the pursuit of virtue, with a consequent repudiation of the dogma according to which market forces must be allowed free rein without reference to their social consequences. Enrique Peñalosa is very clear about this: 'Defining what makes a good city is more a matter of heart and soul than of engineering. It is more akin to an art than a science' (Peñalosa 2008: 307). He insists that government intervention is essential to the well-being of the city and that, since there are alternative urban models, urbanism 'is one of the few remaining realms of ideology'. The leading architect of the remarkable transformation of this Latin American megacity could hardly be more open and honest about the ethical values providing the foundation for his policies:

> A government has many roles, but to try and construct equality is a fundamental one under democratic rule. For legitimacy to exist within a society, citizens must perceive that a fundamental objective of their state is to generate inclusion and some form of equality. With the collapse of communism, many thought that equality as an issue was a thing of the past. But it has too long a history to disappear so easily. Western civilization's roots in Greece, Rome, and Judaeo-Christianity cannot disengage from equality (ibid.: 310).

The *third* and final sign of hope I wish to identify may cause surprise and even alarm. We have seen that earlier urban settlements were 'sacred' cities in which religious beliefs shaped the form and practice of the city. The loss of such religious visions, whether those of the ancient world, or the medieval Christian model of the holy city, has led to a situation in which it is widely assumed that a secular urban model is the only one available to us. Quite apart from the alternative approaches emerging from the Global South discussed above, this assumption ignores the existence of cities that are profoundly shaped by an *Islamic* vision. Cities like Cairo and Karachi, with populations exceeding ten million people, or Tehran, which has a smaller population yet possesses enormous symbolic significance on account of Iran's Islamic Revolution, form part of what has been described as the 'Qur'anic Belt' stretching from Morocco to Indonesia, and from Kazakhstan down the east coast of Africa to Tanzania, an area that is home to the great majority of the world's estimated 1.2 billion Muslim people. As Paul Lubeck and Bryana Britts observe, today's Muslim city,

> ... remains the epicenter of a burgeoning public sphere in which informed publics debate highly contested discourses regarding social justice, urban public space,

legitimate government, political action, and gender relations (Lubeck & Britts 2002: 306–307).

Within the cities mentioned above, and elsewhere throughout the Islamic world, the failure of nominally Muslim governments to deliver social justice in accord with the explicit promises which form part and parcel of this most political of all religions, has resulted in the emergence of radical movements, generally classified as 'Islamist'. This term distinguishes such movements from more apolitical Islamic traditions, such as the Sufi orders, in which the stress on subjective spirituality often results in withdrawal from the world and a consequent passivity in contexts where Westernized Muslim intellectuals and rulers have reached an uneasy accommodation with liberal socioeconomic ideas stemming from the Enlightenment. The failure of such regimes to apply Islamic law to the spheres of government and economic management, together with the obvious corruption of elite groups within these nations, created a powder-keg situation in urban settings similar to those described earlier in this chapter as existing across the Global South. For example, it has been estimated that six million people live in areas of extreme social deprivation in Cairo, with at least 500,000 of these existing on the rooftops of slum dwellings. The levels of pollution in these areas are such as to result in brain damage and mental disorders in small children. And yet, within a single decade toward the end of the twentieth century, the income of the top 10% of Egypt's urban dwellers grew from 26% of GNP in 1981 to 32.6% in 1991.

The sparks which ignited the explosion of Islamist reaction and radicalization within this context included, first, the implementation of Structural Adjustment Programmes devised by neo-liberal economists from outside the Islamic world, which had the effect of destroying 'the social contract between state elites and urban dwellers'. These programmes increased the hardship experienced by millions of people already suffering from injustice in the cities, but they also violated Islamic prohibitions on usury, 'as well as the obligation for Muslim states to distribute alms or subsidies to the poor'. Thus, Structural Adjustment Programmes were perceived to be alien impositions and their enforcement by non-Muslims living in prosperity on the other side of the globe 'rapidly evaporated any residual fig-leaf of legitimacy possessed by secular political elites' (ibid.: 310).

The second spark to ignite the explosion of Islamist movements was the Iranian Revolution in 1978–9. This involved an urban insurrection which overthrew 'a corrupt, secular authoritarian regime' and, in doing so, offered excluded and oppressed young Muslims living on the margins of cities across the Islamic world demonstrable evidence that their religion could provide 'a rational, feasible, alternative political project' (ibid.: 311). The result has been that for more than twenty-five years radical Islamist movements have expanded within the cities of the Islamic world, 'fuelled by a vast reservoir of young, impoverished, and disillusioned recruits' (ibid.: 325). Ironically, the withdrawal of the state from the provision of social services as these were handed over to private companies in line with the requirements of Structural Adjustment Programmes, created the space within which socially active Islamic groups could develop a host of projects providing economic, medical and social support to millions of poor urban dwellers. In Egypt, for example, Yahya Sadowski noted that Islamist primary schools offered 'not only religious indoctrination but a rigorous education superior to that available from badly-overcrowded public schools', and medical clinics providing high quality care for the poor, in contrast 'with state-run hospitals with their low sanitation standards and long delays' (Sadowski 1987: 45). Observers have noticed that Islamist groups have repeatedly out-performed national governments in their responses to emergencies created by floods and earthquakes, a fact which highlights the substantial support provided to such movements by Muslim intellectuals and business people who pay their obligatory tithes to provide the funding of such charitable activities.

The inevitable question that arises at this point is how such Islamist movements can be described as a 'sign of hope' in the urban world? Have these very movements not spawned the wave of terror and violence that resulted in the destruction of parts of the urban fabric of New York, London, Nairobi and Madrid, inflicting great suffering on thousands of ordinary citizens across the world? Tragically, the actions of the Islamist extremists responsible for such acts of terror have obscured the fact that the movements briefly described above have indeed been the agents of hope and social transformation in urban settings characterized by grinding poverty and injustice. But in addition, they offer an alternative vision of our shared urban future, one which needs to be understood and taken seriously beyond the Islamic world. In the words of Lubeck and Britts, urban theorists and policy makers (and, I would add, urban theologians),

> ... must become far more realistic about the complex, contradictory tendencies contained within Muslim discourses. In practice, this means distinguishing the violent insurrectionists like bin Laden's al-Qaida from the moderate and then entering into a dialogue with modern, civil society-based Islamist movements ... For, like it or not, Islamism will constitute a powerful social force shaping Muslim-majority cities in the twenty-first century (Lubeck & Britts 2002: 332).

The really big issue

In the foregoing discussion words like 'equality', 'justice' and 'hope' have surfaced fairly frequently. We have described an urban world in which millions of
people live in great poverty, often within sight of others whose wealth enables
them to exist in the kind of luxury which makes them appear to the poor as
inhabitants of a different planet. We have seen the disturbing predictions of
a growing number of social and urban analysts that the pattern of life which
has developed within this deeply divided urban world is unsustainable and is
leading inexorably toward catastrophe. At the same time, we have noted the
existence of some 'signs of hope', both in the shape of a radical rethinking
concerning the city in the postmodern West, and in the emergence of alternative models for the urban future from the Global South and in the Islamic
world. Such fresh visions, seeded in the soil of the post-colonial experience,
are welcome and encouraging, but they cannot disguise the simple truth that
the rich and prosperous urban dwellers of our world must confront: *we cannot
go on as we are.* Unfortunately, both Western political rhetoric and the ideology of consumerism suppress this truth, employing forms of double-speak in
which economic growth is presented as the solution to the ills of the world,
when in fact, in the form it currently takes, *it is the source of those ills.*

In an earlier chapter I cited the work of the geographer, David M. Smith.
In the conclusion to a study of the deeply divided, post-apartheid city of
Johannesburg, Smith identifies the fundamentally *ethical* challenges which now
confront the entire human family:

> [S]ocial justice as equalization cannot be envisaged as bringing up the mass of the
> poor to the living standards of the well-to-do minority, for this is both economically
> unattainable and environmentally unsustainable. The satisfaction of everyone's
> basic needs, everywhere, entails more equal sharing of the means of a more modest
> conception of the good life. . . . The challenge ahead is thus not so much social
> scientific as ethical: to help devise a new theory of the good, incorporating inclusive
> material living standards combined with an ethic of responsibility to the weak and
> vulnerable, persuasive enough to be a source of moral motivation as well as of social
> understanding. This would be progress in 'urban studies' (Smith 2002: 78).

This present book is written with the conviction that the Bible and Christian
theology have something important to contribute toward such 'progress'.
What that contribution consists of will be explored in later chapters.

5. CITY SKYLINES, CITY MEANINGS

> Monuments have lost their power to persuade, and enshrine permanent memories, but society has hardly lost its appetite for grand structures. Quite the opposite: the self-important building characterizes our time. . . . So a strange mood has developed, something of a double-bind, where the architect and society both have misgivings about the iconic building but cannot help producing it, in ever greater numbers and ever weirder form (Jencks 2006: 3).

In the survey of urban history outlined in the previous chapters we have noticed the significance of particular types of constructions as providing us with clues to the *meaning* of the city at different stages in its development. For example, we have seen how the appearance of walled cities, and the dominating presence of the palace and the temple within them, indicates the belief of the earliest urban dwellers that this was *sacred space*, sealed off from the chaos and danger of the surrounding world. We may thus read the meaning of the cities of the ancient world from their skylines, and a similar exercise is possible with regard to the Greek *polis* and the imperial city of Rome. At a later stage in urban history, the Christianization of Europe changed the urban skyline as, for example, Gothic cathedrals and church spires, and the earliest universities, were erected in medieval cities. A sense of sacredness remained within these cities, but some of the new shapes appearing on their skylines suggest that significant changes were taking place and hint at even greater transformations to come.

Of course, in the contemporary world urban skylines have become far more crowded and complex than they ever were in ancient times, so that the horizon of a postmodern city presents us with a veritable 'forest of symbols' which need to be decoded. This chapter attempts to offer an analysis of one particular contemporary city through a reading of its skyline and, in so doing, provides a model that may be applied to the study of urban contexts elsewhere.

The complexity of the city today reflects the loss of the once-unified understanding of its meaning. A city built in obedience to the command of the gods and united by a shared mythical worldview had a limited number of significant buildings and a simple, uncluttered skyline. By contrast, the erosion of belief in the sacred and the growth of secularization bring major transformations within the city, in which once-dominant religious institutions become *monuments* to a past glory, and new buildings – the factory, the town hall, the corporate headquarters – become the icons of power on the urban skyline.

David Martin has suggested that we can illustrate the varied patterns of secularization in different urban contexts by visualizing the layout of cities and noting the relationship between certain iconic buildings. For example, he describes Washington DC as 'a sacred field, surrounded by Greek and Roman temples, with an Egyptian (or Masonic) obelisk in the centre'. Churches, somewhat incongruously called 'national cathedrals', lie 'at a discreet distance', symbolizing the separation of church and state. Yet within the Lincoln Memorial is an American summary of the biblical narrative, suggesting that this is 'New Rome and New Israel combined'.[1]

By contrast, Paris has a classical temple, the Pantheon, which was previously the church of St Genevieve, patroness of the city, now 'the mausoleum of the Republic, militant and triumphant'. Martin comments:

> The Arc de Triomphe, higher and bigger than any Roman arch, proclaims that Paris
> is yet another New Rome. This New Rome is in conflict with Roman Catholicism,
> represented in the old centre of the Ile de la Cite by Notre Dame, and on Montmartre
> by the Sacre Coeur, built expressly to rebuke the faithless city below. Looking at
> this ensemble of rival locations of the sacred you see how an older France, once the

---

1. Richard Horsley discusses 'the image of the United States as the new Rome' and comments that this is nowhere more clearly seen than 'in the architecture of the great public buildings in the nation's capital, which are all patterned after the great buildings of ancient Rome' (Horsley 2008: 2).

powerhouse of Christendom in the early days of the University of Paris, became the powerhouse of global secularity (Martin 2005: 48).

What Martin is doing here is reading urban skylines to gain an understanding of the meaning of particular cities, and then using this information to note the contrasts in the historical, cultural and physical development of a variety of modern cities. He goes on to undertake similar analyses of London, Budapest, Prague, Vilnius, Helsinki and Amsterdam, drawing fascinating conclusions regarding the ever-changing and ambiguous nature of the relationship between the sacred and the secular.

Even more interesting for our purposes here is the 'genealogy of urban shrines' developed by Maria Kaika and Korinna Thielen in which they trace the historical development of iconic urban buildings across the centuries, identifying the key points at which particular 'shrines' lose their power and become monuments to a past glory (Kaika & Thielen 2006). Such transitions occur as power moves from those who have held and used it for centuries (popes, priests, kings and the aristocracy), to a new elite, or, hopefully, to 'the people' themselves. Such revolutionary changes are reflected on the urban skyline as new 'secular shrines' are built to celebrate the movement of liberation and to house those who manage power in the new arrangement. The genealogy provided by Kaika and Thielen offers a valuable tool of analysis which we will employ in exploring the skyline of a particular city: Glasgow, in the west of Scotland.

From sacred centre to preserved monument

Since the birth of cities, it has always been monuments dedicated to state or religious power that have dominated the urban skyline. . . . In medieval times, cathedrals and town halls were the most important landscape landmarks, and hosted an array of public activities, from coronations to weddings, and from political intrigues to religious festivals. The sheer volume and height of these constructions made them prominently visible, while their visual domination was further pronounced by the choice for their location – on a hill, in the centre of the town, or in front of a public square that was often purpose built to host functions related to the building. . . . The buildings were committed to be standing proudly for as long as the authority that they represented remained in power (Kaika & Thielen 2006: 59).

The city of Glasgow is closely associated with the industrial revolution, and with the manufacture of ships, railway engines and a host of other heavy industries developed in the nineteenth century. It would be easy to overlook the fact that this city, which came to be known as the 'Second City of Empire', retains on its northern outskirts distinct traces of the presence here of an army sent to defend the extreme limits of the Roman *imperium* two thousand years ago. There is obvious irony in the fact that a city which grew with astonishing speed as the direct consequence of the global expansion of British power in the Victorian era, actually exists within the line of the Antonine Wall which marked the furthest boundary of that earlier urban empire.

That 'monument' to the once-dominant power of Rome is itself part of the Glasgow skyline that needs to be considered when we ask concerning the 'meaning' of this city. However, when Rome collapsed, and then discovered in the Christian faith a religion capable of providing a new social cohesion, power shifted from deified emperors to a church that confessed a crucified Messiah as its Lord. That transfer of power is reflected on Glasgow's skyline in the shape of the city's cathedral, symbolizing the centuries-long dominance of ecclesiastical power and the persistence of belief in a sacred city.

There are many reminders in and around this cathedral of the Christian past. Links to Celtic Christianity are found in the tradition that Ninian dedicated a burial ground on the site in the fifth century, while a hundred years later Mungo arrived, founded a monastic community and built a church which, it is said, was visited by Columba. The tomb of Saint Mungo (or Kentigern, to give him his official name) is to be found in the lower church of the cathedral, part of which dates from 1136. In the Middle Ages its reputation was such that pilgrimage to Glasgow Cathedral was declared to be equal in merit to that made to Rome and at the start of the fourteenth century King Edward I made no less than three pilgrimages to the site in a single year.

The cathedral thus became the locus of power and prosperity in early Glasgow, reaching the peak of its influence in 1492 when Glasgow was made into an archbishopric. Throughout this period the population of the city remained small, but now other centres of power had begun to appear: the university had been founded in 1451 and within a decade had moved to a new site on the growing High Street, lower down the hill which leads to the River Clyde. Ecclesiastical power remained strong, but gradually an alternative centre took shape at the bottom of the hill as the city's 'bi-focal urban structure comprising the ecclesiastical upper town . . . and the more temporally oriented commercial settlement of the lower town' began to grow apart (Pacione 1995: 11).

As we have seen, the revolutionary changes introduced by the Protestant Reformation resulted in significant social and economic developments as the work of bankers, merchants and tradesmen was invested with new significance. Professional activities came to be recognized as divine callings with a dignity no less than that of the priest or bishop. Rising up behind Glasgow Cathedral is an extraordinary burial ground known as the Necropolis, and at the highest point on this hill is a dominating statue of John Knox. The Reformer holds the Bible out towards the city below, a powerful symbol of the Reformed vision of a 'Holy Commonwealth' and a reminder of the Calvinist conviction that urban prosperity would only come about through 'the preaching of God's word and the praising of His name'. The Knox statue (erected in 1825) stands above hundreds of impressive monuments to departed merchants, theologians and ministers, and the story of the Glasgow they represent in the centuries after the Reformation perfectly illustrates the struggle to preserve Knox's vision for the city against the growing power of money.

Moving down the hill

[W]ith the shift to a modern, industrialized, secular society, state and church power, along with the power of the landed aristocracy, gave way to the power of the emerging bourgeoisie. The belief in god was complemented or even replaced by belief in money power and the power of technology. . . . As part of its new role the bourgeois state quickly became the key manager of the rationalization of urban space (Kaika & Thielen 2006: 59–60).

Michael Pacione observes that the Reformation effectively undermined 'the old clerico-social order on the hill', replacing it with a 'new mercantilism nearer the river', so relocating the centre of gravity in the emerging town at the bottom of the High Street (Pacione 1995: 14). The city's Tollbooth, of which only the tower now remains, was erected in 1626 and as the growing merchant class prospered, Glasgow began expanding toward the west. The arrival in the city of the first cargo of tobacco from Virginia in 1674 signalled the beginning of an era of great prosperity and in the following century the old cathedral town was increasingly eclipsed by the growth of a sophisticated, commercial urban culture. More than 50% of Britain's tobacco trade was under the control of the Glasgow merchants and the conspicuous wealth of these traders resulted in growing social and spatial divisions. Pacione describes the emergence of distinct classes as follows:

The most extravagant display of the wealth and power of the tobacco lords was their promenade on the plainstanes of the Trongate arrayed in satin suits, scarlet cloaks,

powdered wigs and three-cornered hats and carrying gold-headed canes, which they
wielded against any who dared trespass on their exclusive right to walk on the only
piece of pavement in Glasgow (ibid.: 42).

The area of the city developed in this period has recently been dubbed
the 'Merchant City' by a local government anxious to preserve this part of
historic Glasgow and to provide it with a brand name capable of attracting
tourists. However, the existence of roads bearing names such as Virginia
Street and Jamaica Street serves as a reminder of the dark side of this history,
that associated with the Atlantic slave trade. Many Glasgow merchants made
great fortunes through the ownership of estates in the West Indies as, from
the middle of the eighteenth century, they developed trade in sugar, cotton
and rum imported from the Caribbean and produced by slave labour (Whyte
2006: 44).

This initial expansion of Glasgow corresponds to the transition described
by Kaika and Thielen above in which religious belief 'was complemented
or even replaced by the belief in money power'. In Glasgow religious belief
remained strong and, as we shall see, actually increased during the nineteenth
century, a growth that was accompanied by a massive programme of church
building which transformed the urban skyline. However, the move 'down the
hill' and the growth in the power of the merchant class signalled the emergence of a new form of privatized religion which was allowed little influence
in the spheres of commercial and economic activity. R. H. Tawney quotes the
Scottish theologian Robert Woodrow who in 1709, with Glasgow poised 'on
the eve of a triumphant outburst of commercial enterprise', lamented the 'sin
of our too great fondness for trade' and warned of the divine judgment that
would result from placing such activity 'in the room of religion'. But it was too
late for such warnings; the early Calvinist demand that economic activity be
subject to biblical ethics had already given way to the assumption that 'business affairs should be left to be settled by business men, unhampered by the
intrusions of an antiquated morality or by misconceived arguments of public
policy' (Tawney 1936: 238–239). The stage was thus set for the appearance
of quite new 'sacred shrines' on Glasgow's skyline as the cathedral on the hill
increasingly became a monument to past glories.

The forest of symbols

From the second half of the nineteenth century, cathedrals were built not to house
god, but to house money, technology and innovation. From banks to factories, from

pumping stations and water towers, to gas works and train stations, a whole new array of secular shrines were created and dedicated to money flows, technological innovation and industrial production (Kaika & Thielen 2006: 60).

In the nineteenth century Glasgow became an industrial city and experienced explosive growth. The city possessed the fastest-growing population in Europe, expanding from just over 100,000 in 1811, to 762,000 in 1901. The initial phase of this expansion was based on cotton as textile production came to dominate the city. Around the middle of the century the banks of the River Clyde filled up with the emerging ship building and repair yards and the city became home to an enormous range of heavy industries, earning it the title 'the workshop of the world'. Sean Damer points out that, in addition to ship building (represented by the phrase 'Clyde-built'), Glasgow produced the carpets in the British, Australian, New Zealand and South African Houses of Parliament, and manufactured 80% of the world's sugar-crushing and refining machinery. In addition, almost three-quarters of the world's steam locomotives came from engine-building works in Glasgow and were shipped around the globe, including to Russia, India, China, Kenya, Argentina and Paraguay. At the peak of its industrial development contemporary photographs reveal 'a jam-packed, filthy-dirty metropolis bristling with chimneys belching out smoke into an already over-polluted atmosphere, the streets black with people' (Damer 1990: 40).

Where did those people come from? The workforce required for an industrial take-off on the scale we have described came from three main sources: Highlanders driven south by rural poverty, and with the history of the Clearances creating an abiding suspicion of landlords;[2] Lowlanders from Ayrshire and the Borders, where both the memories of the Covenanters and the radical tradition expressed by Robert Burns were strong; and Irish immigrants who fled a land devastated by famine as the potato harvests failed year after year. The narratives which each of these groups brought with them into the city fed into the streams which created a remarkable and distinctive working class culture in Glasgow.

---

2. The Clearances involved the removal of the traditional communities which had inhabited the Highlands of Scotland for centuries in order to create huge sheep farms providing meat for the burgeoning cities of the south and profits for the new, aristocratic, landowners. The Scottish Highlands have come to be viewed as a vast natural wilderness but, as the descendents of the people expelled from the area might point out, they are also one of Europe's tragic human wastelands.

The mention of class divisions serves to highlight the fact that the physical growth of the city took place in a manner that further segregated the rich and the poor. As far as the latter were concerned, they were initially concentrated in the overcrowded alleyways, or wynds, in the area around the High Street. An official report from 1839 (later to be cited by Friedrich Engels in his *Condition of the Working Class in England*) describes conditions as follows:

> I have seen human degradation in some of its worst phases . . . but I can advisedly say that I did not believe, until I visited the wynds of Glasgow, that so large amount of filth, crime, misery and disease existed in any one spot in any civilised country . . . It is my firm belief that penury, dirt, misery, drunkenness, disease and crime culminate in Glasgow to a pitch unparalleled in Great Britain (quoted in Pacione 1995: 86).

Meantime, owners of the industrial enterprises were making vast fortunes and an emerging middle class sought new accommodation out of sight and sound of the squalor in which the workers existed. In 1841 the Great Western Road was built and new suburbs designed by distinguished architects appeared on either side of it, creating easy access into the city without the need for exposure to the conditions in which the poor lived their lives. New iconic buildings appeared in the West End; the Botanic Gardens was opened in 1842, and the university moved from its old site beside the squalor of the High Street to its present location in 1870. And there were churches – dozens of them from all denominations, with the significant exception of the Roman Catholic Church. Most of these magnificent buildings remain today, largely converted for secular use and so monuments to the success, wealth and social standing of those who thronged them in the nineteenth century. When Lansdowne United Presbyterian Church was opened on Great Western Road in 1863, the well-heeled congregation was shocked to discover the following lines chalked on the main door:

> This church is not built for the poor and needy,
> But for the rich and Dr. Eadie;
> The rich may come in and take their seat
> But the poor must go to Cambridge Street.

The words of the anonymous poet expressed the widespread belief among the underprivileged that 'the flight to the suburbs had created a church divided between rich and poor' (Hillis 2007: 49). Describing the nature of the relationship between religion and the growth of the industrial city of Glasgow, social historian Callum Brown concludes that the middle class developed 'a penchant for evangelicalism' and found this faith to be consistent with their desire to create beautiful churches 'suitably isolated from the industrial working classes . . . in the context of a rapidly expanding city' (Brown 1981: 336).

So, among the new 'shrines' to appear on the Glasgow skyline in the nineteenth century were the huge cranes beside the river and the elegant spires of the middle-class churches in the West End. Examples of both types of iconic constructions remain today, but all of them have now become, like the cathedral before them, monuments to past power and influence.

However, before we leave nineteenth-century Glasgow it is important to notice that the transition to the 'secular shrines' which Kaika and Thielen describe was *not* as clearcut and decisive as their language might suggest. To be sure, the 'shrines' they list – banks, factories, pumping stations, railway stations – were all built in nineteenth-century Glasgow, and many remain to this day, gracing the urban skyline and earning this most industrial of cities a justified reputation for the quality of its architectural heritage. But while this transition reflected a major *transformation* in the character of religion, it did not indicate the 'replacement' of belief in God by a secular worldview. Callum Brown points out that explaining 'how religion adapted to urban society in Glasgow is long and complex' (Brown 1988: 10).

The point we are making here can be illustrated by noticing the significance of a very cathedral-like building that stands at the heart of the city: Glasgow's massive City Chambers (or 'Town Hall'), built in 1883, and the open expanse of George Square which it overlooks. As in other British cities in this period, this building symbolized the emergent power of the middle classes and is a striking expression of civic pride. Its vast frontage is decorated with impressive statues and is topped by a dome which appears distinctly ecclesiastical, confirming the claim that the new shrines 'borrowed the architectural language of the past to invoke *grandeur* and to assert the power of the new authorities that produced them' (Kaika & Thielen 2006: 60). However, the social policies and political decisions conceived and enacted within this building during the second half of the nineteenth century were shaped to a considerable degree by Christians who had come to realize that 'the single-minded grasping for wealth in a free market economy was detrimental to the moral, physical and spiritual condition of the working classes' (Brown 1981: 433). Scotland witnessed a succession of remarkable Presbyterian ministers who engaged with the challenges which urban culture presented to their faith and warned their prosperous, middle-class congregations of the perils of neglecting the biblical imperative for social justice.[3]

The result of such ministries was that in Glasgow 'outwardly secularized bodies like the Corporation' were dominated by socially-aware Christians who advocated progressive policies such as 'municipalizing the gas works and the trams, laying main sewers, bringing fresh water to the city, and doing something about insanitary and overcrowded housing'. Evangelical religion in Scotland thus retained, perhaps recovered, its links to the Calvinist heritage which we have described earlier in this book and so attempted to relate the vision of a 'Holy Commonwealth' to the unprecedented social problems experienced in an industrializing city. The extent of this influence is described by Callum Brown as follows:

> Evangelical councillors voted across party lines . . . trying to use municipal collectivism to create the 'Godly Commonwealth'. Religious visions of 'democratic cities of God' were important to the advance of social welfare at local level in the nineteenth century, and churchmen organized religious campaigns for social reform (Brown 1988: 11).

In the opening chapter of this book we mentioned the scheme to pump clean drinking water into Glasgow through a pipeline from the distant Loch Katrine. This was a major feat of civil engineering and was a costly project, funded by taxation. There were periodic revolts by rate payers who objected to the demand that they should finance a scheme designed to alleviate the suffering of the poor and weak in the slums. However, middle-class opposition was overcome largely because Evangelical ministers preached passionate sermons in defence of the project and provided pastoral and theological support to the members of their congregations who were politically active within the City Chambers.

Mention was made above not only of the new 'shrine' of the City Chambers, but of George Square onto which it faces. Typical of the open public spaces which were a feature of urban design in this period, the square replaced

---

3. For example, Thomas Guthrie (whose statue stands on Edinburgh's famous Princes Street) published *The City: Its Sins and Its Sorrows* in 1851. He welcomed the emergence of cities as 'the cradles of human liberty' yet warned of the catastrophe that faced society if it ignored the plight of the poor. 'We first condemn them to crime and then condemn them to punishment. And where is the justice of that?' (Guthrie 1857: 98).

Glasgow Green as a focal point for the expression of social and political protest. In January 1919 it became the site for the largest working-class demonstration ever seen in the city when a huge crowd of protesters crammed into every corner to demand a forty-hour working week. The authorities, fearful of revolution, attempted to break up the assembly and the following day tanks were ordered into the square and machine gun posts put in place on the roofs of surrounding buildings. This event created the image of the 'Red Clyde', establishing Glasgow's reputation as a centre of radical politics. It is worth noting, however, that when three years later the Independent Labour Party won ten seats in the 1922 General Election, the crowd which gathered at the Central Station to send their representatives to Westminster sang *both* 'The Red Flag' and the 124th Psalm ('If it had not been the Lord who was on our side . . . when men rose up against us'). The new MPs issued a public manifesto which reflected the influence of the Christian faith in the shaping of an emergent socialist agenda:

> The Labour Members of Parliament for the City of Glasgow . . . inspired by zeal
> for the welfare of humanity and the prosperity of all peoples . . . have resolved to
> dedicate themselves to the reconciliation and unity of the nations of the world and
> the development and happiness of the people of these islands (quoted in Damer
> 1990: 134).

Thus, while new secular shrines did appear on the Glasgow skyline in this period, the influence of a socially-engaged faith remained significant among the middle classes and (perhaps more surprisingly) within the working class. The first Labour MPs from Glasgow publicly committed themselves to 'abjure vanity and self-aggrandizement' and to pursue the 'righteous purpose' of promoting 'the welfare of their fellow-citizens and the well-being of mankind'.

Visions of utopia

> After the Second World War, the need to house millions of homeless people and the
> commitment of western states to social welfare projects led to the mass production
> of housing projects. . . . These historical circumstances gave Le Corbusier the chance
> to realise his dream of building 'machines to live in' . . . massive apartment blocks for
> functional and efficient living (Kaika & Thielen 2006: 64).

The urban visions of modern planners and architects discussed in the previous chapter were reflected in the development of the city of Glasgow in the course of the twentieth century. Large swathes of the city were identified as 'Comprehensive Development Areas' (CDAs) requiring the wholesale clearance of slum housing and the erection of multi-storey tower blocks and council housing schemes. In the Gorbals, on the south side of the River Clyde, the old tenements were replaced with high-rise buildings designed by the distinguished architect Basil Spence and opened by the Queen in 1972. Very quickly it became clear that these buildings would be 'a social and architectural disaster' and within thirty years they were demolished. Michael Pacione's conclusion concerning Glasgow's slum clearances has a sobering relevance in a world in which the growth of slum housing in the megacities of Global South presents such a huge ethical challenge:

> While the physical removal of slum housing was to be welcomed, the social costs of the CDA strategy are incalculable and it is reasonable to suggest, albeit with hindsight, that a more sensitive approach would have brought greater social benefits to the affected communities. Overall, the comprehensive development strategy proved to be expensive, disruptive of traditional communities . . . and unpopular with many of those moved out to bleak peripheral housing estates (Pacione 1995: 165).

By 1982 the city skyline was dotted with no less than 321 tower blocks, including the Red Row flats, designed to house 4,000 people in each thirty-one-story skyscraper. If this sounds reminiscent of Le Corbusier's 'machines to live in', his influence was even more evident and long-lasting in the shape of the M8 motorway, driven through the city as part of a planned network of urban expressways. In his vision of the 'contemporary city' Le Corbusier had specified the necessity of 'great arterial roads for *fast, one-way traffic*, built on immense reinforced concrete bridges', so that the city could be 'traversed and the suburbs reached without having to negotiate any cross-roads' (Le Corbusier 2007: 326).

Urban planners in Glasgow caught sight of this heady vision and in the 1960s they proposed building three concentric ring roads connected by arterial motorways like the spokes of a wheel. Had this plan been realized the devastation of Glasgow's urban fabric would have rivalled that resulting from Robert Moses' road building in New York. As it was, only the M8 was built, its ghost-like exits to nowhere and partially constructed bridges now serving as reminders of the original plans and the havoc they would have wreaked on familiar areas of the city such as the ancient High Street, Sauchiehall Street and the Great Western Road. Motorists who now discover the motorway invariably clogged by some of the 15,000 plus heavy lorries which trundle down it every day might find it difficult to believe that this iconic structure was inspired by Le Corbusier's belief that a 'city made for speed is made for success'.

A city without meaning?

> The 19th- and 20th-century preoccupation with large-scale landscaping and planning gave way to a practice of urban design that aimed at producing 'postcard views' of the city, that could be photographed and used to promote the contemporary metropolis to the tourist industry and to international capital. . . . From museums and stadiums to shopping malls, the recent public-private projects that act as symbols of prosperity for a location bear remarkable similarities in style and function, and use almost identical architectural language (Kaika & Thielen 2006: 66).

Where do we look for new 'sacred' buildings in a secular age? If the cathedral, the Tollbooth, the City Chambers, the steeples and spires, have all become *monuments* to a past glory, which buildings are now the locus of power and the icons of a postmodern culture? With the fading of the religious vision for Glasgow, a vision which had been encapsulated in the prayer-like motto that the city might flourish through the preaching of the Bible and the worship of God, the social and political objectives of planners and politicians inevitably became restricted to material ends. Like other post-industrial cities, Glasgow set about overcoming negative perceptions of decline and decay in order to attract both investment and tourism. This involved programmes of urban regeneration and the creation of fresh images of the city through what is now known as rebranding. In 1983 a marketing campaign was launched using the banal slogan, 'Glasgow's Miles Better'.[4] A subsequent campaign reflected the shift toward economic globalization and the culture of consumerism as Glasgow was promoted as 'Scotland With Style'. The creation of such images was accompanied by major developments at the heart of the city and along the banks of the Clyde, involving both the conservation of what has been described as 'the finest surviving example of a great Victorian city', and new buildings providing housing, shopping, conference and recreational facilities. However, as Kaika and Thielen note, massive economic and socio-political transformations at the global level

---

4. The slogan prompts the question, better than what? At one level the answer was simply – better than is generally realized. But locals recognized the implied sideswipe at Edinburgh – a fact illustrated by that city's response with a counter slogan, 'Edinburgh's Slightly Superior'.

resulted in 'inevitable changes in the production of urban space' as the state retreated from its previous role to become 'a networking institution and a hands-off manager of projects that would be fully developed by private entrepreneurs' (Kaika & Thielen 2006: 65). Thus, the iconic buildings of the early twenty-first century can be viewed in the shopping malls that now encircle Glasgow, retaining in their design reminders of previous sacred buildings, and shamelessly plundering sacred language in promotional campaigns – especially in the run-up to Christmas. The new iconic buildings that now stand beside derelict cranes along the banks of the Clyde exhibit radically new architecture and eye-catching shapes in the attempt to attract attention to a post-industrial city attempting to gain rank in an urban world.

What then becomes of the *meaning* of the city? What is the *reality* behind the image? Michael Pacione points out that the benefits of Glasgow's 'cultural renaissance and image repackaging have not trickled down to the disadvantaged residents in the deprived estates' and that, while the city centre 'is being physically remade the problems affecting large parts of the working-class areas of the city have not gone away' (Pacione 1995: 250–251). When I pointed out to a class of postmodern theological students the completely disproportionate amount of investment poured into the fashionable areas of the centre of Glasgow compared to that available in districts characterized by multiple deprivation, some reacted by asking why I should be surprised by this, since 'this is how the market operates'.

We are back once again to fundamental ethical questions. However, just as we have earlier noticed urban theorists, planners and geographers raising moral concerns about urban trends, we will now discover similar questions being asked in relation to the role of urban planners and architects. In the quotation at the head of this chapter Charles Jencks notes that 'the self-important building characterizes our time'. His explanation for this is, first, that in late-capitalism huge amounts of money are paid for innovative designs capable of satisfying the desires of wealthy patrons to be associated with iconic buildings. Second, Jencks points out that such secular 'shrines' are the inevitable result of a global culture driven by the ideology of consumerism and 'without common religious beliefs or shared culture'. The use made of urban space inevitably reflects underlying cultural values, so that when 'scanty-clad celebrities are emulated almost like saints, and money is the only universal in which a global culture believes', we cannot be surprised that this 'confusion of values finds its counterpart in the architectural free for all' (Jencks 2006: 5–10, and see McNeill 2006).

There may be a further explanation for the appearance of spectacular buildings which refer to nothing beyond themselves. Deyan Sudjic suggests that building is about more than the simple provision of shelter; it reveals human values and psychology and can be a means 'for inflating the individual ego to the scale of a landscape, a city, or even a nation' (Sudjic 2005: 324). The shapes of our buildings reveal 'the ambitions and insecurities' of the builders and are 'a faithful reflection of the nature of power, its strategies, its consolations, and its impact on those who wield it' (ibid.: 325). Sudjic argues that in a world devoted to the pursuit of money power, it is the rich and powerful who shape urban spaces, but he concludes:

> An understanding of what it is that motivates us to build, and the nature of the elusive relationship between architecture and power, is a key insight into our existence and can allow us to free ourselves from its most pernicious aspects (ibid.: 327).

Readers of the Bible will be struck by the parallel between this statement and the ancient narrative of the tower of Babel, built (so the author of Genesis tells us) by people who desired 'to make a name' for themselves and so be assured of a kind of immortality. But this is to anticipate the contribution that the Bible may make to our debates concerning the city today, a subject which will occupy us in the remainder of this book.

Figure 5.1: Glasgow: old and new. Photograph © Gordon Nicol, used with permission

PART TWO: BIBLICAL AND THEOLOGICAL PERSPECTIVES

Glasgow: three tower blocks. Photograph © Gordon Nicol, used with permission

6. THE BIBLE AND THE CITY: FROM PATRIARCHS TO PROPHETS

Contrary to popular opinion, the Bible has more to say about cities than it does about the countryside. The romantic view that the Bible paints a bucolic setting, one of 'green pastures' and 'still waters', for faith and practice is woefully one-sided. Even the so-called Shepherd Psalm ends with reference to the 'House of the Lord', that is, the sanctuary in the city. According to scripture, the city constitutes a central context for faith and practice (Brown & Carroll 2000: 4).

At the conclusion of chapter 2 we suggested that the challenge which the urban world presents to Christian theology and practice demands, among other things, a willingness to listen afresh to the Bible, attuned to the responses of poets, prophets and of Jesus and his apostles, to the cities which formed a crucial component of the contexts within which their ministries were conducted. We suggested that too often studies claiming to provide a biblical foundation for urban ministry and mission use a proof-texting approach to Scripture in which favoured passages are isolated from the flow of the biblical narrative, creating distorting lenses in the quest to understand the theme of the city in the Bible.

It may help to illustrate what is meant by citing two examples in which the texts selected result in radically different conclusions regarding the Bible's teaching concerning the city. Jacques Ellul's 1970 book, *The Meaning of the City* is both stimulating and controversial. It is, as John Wilkinson points out in his introduction, a 'theological counterpoint' to Ellul's earlier work, *The Technological Society*, providing a critical analysis of that society and the urban form it has taken, in the light of the teaching of the Bible. It must be stressed that Ellul is certainly not a superficial exegete, treating the biblical narrative at a surface level. On the contrary, all his work offers profound and deeply challenging insights, and it has attracted great interest, especially among thoughtful young Christians in the United States. Nonetheless, the fact remains that Ellul's theological interpretation of the meaning of the city is founded upon his reading of the Genesis narrative of Cain and Abel, and the conclusion he draws from that text that the city 'is the direct consequence of Cain's murderous act and of his refusal to accept God's protection' (Ellul 1970: 5). The very first city-builder mentioned in the Bible is thus a man in flight from God who, refusing the offer of divine grace and protection, endeavours to create his own paradise, east of Eden. According to Ellul, Cain the murderer, living under a divine curse, attempts to make his tragic situation bearable by two actions: 'he knows his wife sexually, who then gives him a son; and he builds a city.' Cain determines to live without grace and sets about remaking the world, reducing God 'to a hypothesis, to the domain of the superfluous and the unreal' (ibid.: 6). In this story, Ellul says, we discover the seed of all man's searching for a place in which 'his need for security might be satisfied'.

Ellul is aware that by granting this narrative a foundational role in his analysis of the city he risks being accused of anti-urbanism and of constructing 'an entire theory on the basis of a word, a sentence from the Bible'. His response is to argue that, in fact, the judgment of the city found in the Cain story turns out to be the consistent and unvarying position taken by the whole Bible, and this fact absolves him of the charge of bias. He writes:

> If we discover a doctrine of the city, complete, coherent, with an undeniable bearing on man's life, his destiny, his relations with God, and at last his salvation, if we discover a history of the city, incorporated into the Lordship of Jesus Christ, we will then be obliged to admit that it is a question of something other than the invention of a professor bent on a new theology (ibid.: 8).

Ellul's reading of the Bible results in a profoundly negative verdict on the city, unfolded with a consistent and unrelenting pessimism. Within two pages we find the city described as 'a parasite', as preying on the living creation 'like a vampire', as 'made of dead things for dead people', as being 'an enormous man-eater', and as receiving and consuming things from outside its boundaries while contributing nothing of value to those who are not its denizens (ibid.: 150–151). We are certainly justified in asking whether this is indeed the view of the city to be found in the whole of the Bible, or whether Ellul's starting point has in fact skewed his reading of Scripture, so validating the theological presuppositions with which he began?

Harvie Conn is in no doubt concerning the answer to this question. He regards *The Meaning of the City* as a deeply anti-urban book in which the city is treated as a symbol of the technological society so dreaded by Ellul. This then becomes a 'controlling perspective', reinforced by a Barthian dialectic and resulting in a position which treats the city as simply 'a citadel of sin' (Conn 1992: 13). However, Conn then introduces his own 'favoured text' from the early chapters of Genesis and proceeds to build a different interpretation of the Bible on this foundation. He describes Genesis 1:26–28 as the 'cultural mandate' in which the first human beings are made 'regents' and are called 'to rule over a world whose imagery appears uniformly agricultural' (ibid.: 14). This divine mandate to 'fill, rule, and subdue the earth' is said to be 'nothing more than a mandate to build the city', while the summons to procreate amounts to a way of 'providing the citizens of the city'. What are described as 'sheltering structures' in Eden anticipate 'the physical architecture of the city', while the life of the primal family contains the seeds of 'centralized government'. Conn concludes this remarkable feat of interpretation with the following claim: 'Urban culture, *built in perfect obedience to God,* would typify our hope in Jehovah' (ibid.: 15, emphasis added).

The problems with both these approaches are surely obvious. They result in extreme positions, not dissimilar to the 'two opposing imaginaries of the city' which, as we noticed in chapter 2, are embedded within pro- and anti-urbanist movements within the social sciences. It is difficult to avoid the conclusion that in both the examples cited above, theological presuppositions have been brought to the text of Scripture and, consciously or not, have shaped its interpretation. As a result, the variety and tension found within the biblical narrative as a whole is lost; the different – sometimes even contradictory – perspectives regarding cities within the purposes of Israel's God are flattened out. The 'favoured texts' which form the foundation of these approaches are used as tools in a process of harmonization designed to ensure that the biblical authors speak with one voice on the subject of the city. *But the truth is, they do nothing of the kind, and it is only by a careful listening to what they actually say that we can discover the range of theological perspectives on urban cultures that are to be found within Scripture – a range that, in contrast to the monochrome pictures of the anti- and pro-urban readings, actually does justice to the complex reality of empirical cities.* Our task in the remainder of this chapter will be to attempt such a process of listening.

In the beginning

Clearly, within the limits of this volume we cannot survey every biblical text relating to cities, so a decision must be made as to how we might identify those passages which are indispensable to the discussion of an urban theology. Where are the critically important narratives in which the challenge of the urban context for faith and obedience is obvious and unavoidable?

We begin at the beginning with the opening chapters of the Bible, which have sometimes been described as containing 'primeval history'. In the survey of the earliest cities of the ancient world in chapter 3 of this book, we noted the rise of urban empires with sophisticated political structures and ground-breaking innovations in what we would call the arts and observed that this was the context within which the biblical tradition took shape. In fact, Genesis 1 – 11 contains a highly compressed account of developments which actually occurred over a vast stretch of time. As K. A. Kitchen put it, the opening chapters of the Bible provide a 'vista of early antiquity, drawn in broad outline' (Kitchen 1977: 19). This 'outline' has a clear purpose in that it offers a sharply critical view of the directions taken by the dominant cultures of the ancient world, whether in Egypt, Babylon or Palestine. Of course, there are many points of contact between the biblical authors and the beliefs and assumptions of those who laid the religious foundations of the ancient city states and the urban empires which grew from them. However, as Gordon Wenham points out, while Genesis 1 – 11 is part of the inheritance we receive from the ancient world, and must *not* therefore be read with modernist assumptions about its meaning, 'most of the stories found in these chapters are best read as presenting an alternative world-view to those generally accepted in the ancient Near East' (Wenham 1987: xlv).

The key question here concerns the response these chapters make to the city. However, before we attempt to consider this it is very important to remember that 98% of the population of the ancient world remained outside city walls and that, despite their growing influence, most of these cities remained very small in comparison with the urban developments seen during and after the industrial revolution. The use of the term 'city' must not mislead us into reading back into the Bible modern assumptions about urban life and the attitudes which have come to accompany it since this would inevitably distort our understanding of the biblical texts. For example, Richard Bauckham has pointed out that urban dwellers in ancient times were *not* alienated from the natural world in the way that modern city people frequently are and he insists that we recognize that 'the Bible's world is pre-industrial and that this made both living in towns and living off the land very different from both urban (increasingly post-industrial) and rural life today'. He continues:

Ancient literature of all kinds simply takes it for granted that human life is embedded in the rest of nature and inextricable from it. . . . To read the texts ecologically we have to make the effort to think in a creation-embedded way which will catch the resonances of texts for which constant and immediate relationship with non-human nature is as everyday and unremarkable as relationship with the built environment is for modern urban people (Bauckham 1999: 1).

This embeddedness within the natural world was characteristic of all ancient societies and is reflected, for example, in the fertility religions of the city states of Canaan which, as we shall see, came to play such a crucial role in the history of Israel. At the same time, the biblical writers refused to accept the claims of pagan rulers and priests at face value and engaged in a process which involved the deconstruction of the myths which underpinned the dominant worldviews. While there is much that is noble and beautiful in the literature of the ancient world, and while it contains evidence that serious doubts and questions arose *within* these cultures, the fact remains that the myths and rituals which dominated the lives of people and gave physical shape to the ancient cities, formed the basis of the authority of urban elites whose wealth depended on the labours of an army of 'peasants and herders, craftsmen and traders' (Gottwald 2008: 9–10). In other words, from its very first pages the Bible is engaged in a confrontation with certain aspects of the prevailing religious ideas and this conflict had profound social and ethical implications.

This confrontation can certainly be seen in the texts with which Jacques Ellul begins his exposition of the theme of the city in the Bible. It appears to be the case that the first city-builder mentioned in Genesis is a man who has 'gone out from the Lord's presence' to live 'east of Eden', so that from its beginnings the city becomes a symbol of human independence and arrogance (Gen. 4:16–17). And by the time we reach chapter 11 with its famous story of the building of the Tower of Babel, the biblical critique of both the philosophy underlying the city and its architectural expression, has become more explicit than ever. As Wenham says, while the whole of Genesis 1 – 11 contains 'a strong polemic against the mythic theology of the ancient world', in the Babel narrative discretion is thrown to the winds and 'the assault on Babylonian pretensions becomes open and undisguised' (Wenham 1987: 244).[1]

---

1. It is worth noting the element of irony and humour in this passage. The tower was 'only a human building, and who would chose brick in preference to good Palestinian stone? And as for its vaunted height, so far short of heaven did this

Why should the Tower of Babel be subjected to such withering criticism? After all, this was one of the great wonders of the ancient world, a construction surpassed in size and magnificence only by the two largest pyramids of Giza. The answer is that, like those pyramids, the ziggurat carried enormous symbolic significance and was the site at which the central rituals of the Babylonian religion were annually enacted. As Arend van Leeuwen explains, this building was the focal point of the New Year Festival rituals in which the mythical victory of Marduk over Tiamat was re-enacted and the *Enuma Elish* was solemnly recited.

> Careful study of each verse of the biblical saga of the tower shows that it is concerned to refute the whole ziggurat mythology. The cosmic significance of the ziggurat is fully recognized, but at the same time is exposed as a fully human attempt at self-realization on a superhuman level, a reaching for the stars, a manifest example of the inordinate ambition to take heaven by storm (van Leeuwen 1964: 78).

As we shall see, the consequences of the human attempt to rule the world without reference to its Creator becomes a central and constant theme of the Bible and is at the heart of its critique of the cities of the ancient world. Indeed, Donald Gowan suggests that in Genesis 11:1–9, the primary focus of the narrative is on *the city* since, while both city and tower are mentioned in verses 4–5, 'at the end the tower is forgotten; *only the abandonment of city building is cited*' (Gowan 1975: 28, emphasis added). The human grasp for ultimate power is thus expressed in the attempt to build 'a city with a sky-high tower', which suggests that this seminal passage is essentially a negative judgment on a particular type of urban culture. In so clearly identifying this aspect of the biblical witness and stressing its importance with regard to our understanding of the 'meaning of the city', Jacques Ellul has done us a great service. However, when he then concludes that the 'very fact of living in the city directs a man down an inhuman road' taking him into 'the service and worship of a somber goddess' (Ellul 1970: 22), we feel bound to part company with him.

From the perspective of the early chapters of the Bible then, the fundamental problem with the cities of the ancient world relates to the mythical beliefs of those who built and shaped them. The root of the urban evils denounced by Israel's prophets are not to be found in the urban form itself (as

---

Footnote 1 *(cont.)*

so-called skyscraper fall that God could hardly see it: he had to come down to look at it!' (Wenham 1987: 244–245).

Ellul appears to think), but rather in the megalomania that results in delusions of grandeur and the denial of death. The existential question posed by God to alienated human beings in the garden – 'Where are you?' (Gen. 3:9) – needs, therefore, to be asked with even more urgency amid the forest of skyscrapers in the city where the danger increases that the reality of the human condition may be concealed and forgotten.

The relevance of this biblical perspective to the urban world we have described in the first part of this book is illustrated by the work of Mike Davis, Daniel Bertrand Monk and their fellow authors, charting the rise of what they describe as *Evil Paradises*, contemporary cities that 'arise from the toil of migrant workers' for the benefit of an elite who withdraw into 'gilded dreamworlds', sealed off from 'the tragedies overtaking the planet' (Davis & Monk 2007: xvi). Although these scholars make no reference to the Bible, the parallels between their disturbing analyses of contemporary cities and the critical insights of the author of Genesis are striking.

As we shall see, the Bible offers alternative visions for life in the city and a central aspect of Israel's calling was to model in the sight of the nations a form of community which had the potential to revolutionize urban life. Even within the primal chapters we have discussed here, there is evidence of a certain ambivalence concerning the city and signs of hope for its future. The builders of cities are not only people in flight from God, they are also men and women who bear the *imago Dei* (Gen. 1:27). That 'image' may be broken, but it is not entirely lost, so that the creative gifts, the faculty of the imagination and a sense of morality, which all form part of the 'likeness to God' which defines the human being, means that the city reflects something of the *glory* of humankind, as well as its wretchedness. John Goldingay has noticed that while Genesis 4:17–24 describes the human search for security apart from God and charts a rapid descent into terrible violence and blasphemy, it also recognizes developments in art and technology, such as the invention of musical instruments and the mastering of craft skills. It is in the city that writing is first invented, so that 'had there been no city, it seems there would have been no history, no theology, no science, no Bible' (Goldingay 1989: 6).

Before we leave the early chapters of Genesis we should note the significance for our topic of the frequently overlooked Table of Nations in chapter 10. This remarkable text, which is without parallel in the ancient world, describes how humankind fulfilled the divine mandate to 'fill the earth and subdue it'. It charts the spread of peoples, 'each with its own language', and identifies some of the key urban locations which will later be subjected to prophetic critique. Babylon, Erech (known to us as Uruk), Akkad, Nineveh, Sodom and Gomorrah, all of them are there. When, two chapters later, we are told about the call of Abram and hear God promising that 'all peoples on earth' will eventually be blessed by his obedience and faith, the extent of that blessing has already been mapped out for us in this survey. The entire known world, with its diversity of peoples *and its cities* is the object of God's love; these peoples, these cities, despite being presently in the grip of ideologies that result in bondage, injustice and despair, will see the glory of God and will experience his *shalom*. This neglected text thus has considerable significance for a biblical theology of the city. As Claus Westermann says,

> It is the most forceful and heavily underscored statement of the Bible about the effect of God's blessing, which extends over the whole earth and the whole of human history, whereas his saving action is of necessity bound to a people that has been chosen. . . . It means that all people existing in the present, all of them, belong to the human race that God created. . . . One thing only is said of them – all of them with all their differences go back to one common origin . . . God's history with his people went on through the centuries so that his action on Israel's behalf was of positive significance for other peoples, for humanity (Westermann 1984: 528–530).[2]

Let my people go

Within the ancestral narratives of Genesis 12 – 50 there are 'urban texts' of considerable significance. For example, the story of Sodom and Gomorrah contains important lessons regarding prayer for the city (18:16–33) and provides the classic example of the terrible fate to which cities become liable when all the foundations of ethics and morality, both personal and social, are destroyed (19:1–29; and see Ezek. 16:49–50; Isa. 1:9–10; Jer. 23:13–14). The dismal description of Abraham looking toward the location of the twin cities of the plain and seeing only 'dense smoke rising from the land' (19:28) is a stark reminder that once vibrant cities can reach a point of no return and be reduced to rubble. What is more, the use later made of this example in both the prophetic literature and in the ministry of Jesus (Matt. 10:15; 11:23–24), suggests that the death of these cities is not to be treated as an abnormal,

---

2. In an important study of this text, James Scott describes the Table of Nations as 'part of a tradition that pervades the OT'. He goes on to demonstrate its importance in the letters of Paul in the NT, arguing that the geographical vision in this ancient literature formed the basis for Paul's missionary strategy, a strategy which, as we shall see, centred on cities (Scott 1995: 14).

extreme case, but rather offers a sobering warning of the potential fate of all urban communities. Yet again, the work of Mike Davis, this time in his disturbing book *Dead Cities*, suggests parallels between the biblical story and contemporary urban realities (Davis 2002).

From the point of view of this study, the major development in the ancestral narratives concerns the movements of Abraham and Joseph which shift the focus from Mesopotamia to the imperial cities of ancient Egypt. The Patriarchs are depicted as experiencing close encounters with the pharaohs, with Joseph (like Moses after him) becoming thoroughly assimilated within Egyptian culture and politics (Gen. 41:41–45). Mircea Eliade comments that Egypt 'had no great cities of the Mesopotamian type' but was a country 'constituted by a rural mass ruled by representatives of an incarnate god, the pharaoh' (Eliade 1971: 85). The role of the pharaohs in Egypt suggests that, notwithstanding the significant contrasts between the civilizations which developed beside the Euphrates and the Nile, both societies operated with similar conceptions of sacred kingship. A court official in Egypt described the pharaoh as 'a god who makes us live by his acts', a statement which illustrates the manner in which the security and prosperity of peoples in states ruled by sacred kings across the ancient world depended absolutely upon the actions of their divine rulers. It is of enormous significance that, having depicted Abram as abandoning one ancient civilization in his search for 'the city with foundations', the Bible then relates how his descendants found themselves in close contact with another in which similar beliefs gave shape to state and society. The scene is thus set for what van Leeuwen describes as the Old Testament's unique account of Israel's 'struggle to preserve their peculiar genius by breaking away from the pattern of a primary civilization' (van Leeuwen 1964: 158).

The reference above to the 'rural mass' of Egypt and its relationship to the sacred power located at the urban centre and embodied in the pharaohs is strikingly illustrated in the Joseph story. The theological purpose of this narrative concerns the mystery of the outworking of the will of God, but it also highlights the dangers that accompany close association with imperial power. The dark side of Joseph's rise to influence within this system is seen when, during one of the periodic famines which drove multitudes of starving peasants into Egypt in search of food, he provides relief for the refugees at the price of their reduction to abject servitude (47:20–24). The appropriation by the state of 'all the land in Egypt' and the virtual enslaving of the population, anticipates the later plight of Joseph's own descendants who, as slave labourers, were to 'build store cities for Pharaoh' (Exod. 1:11). In a strange irony it is the patriarch's own policy in the service of the god-king which creates the precedent for the oppression of his descendants when a new pharaoh 'who did not know about Joseph' took the royal throne in Egypt. However, whereas the veneration of the divine king in the time of Joseph led the Egyptian masses to express *gratitude* for their bondage to Pharaoh (47:25), the cries of the oppressed peoples at the start of the book of Exodus results in a theophany of revolutionary significance which creates the promise of a different future with new social possibilities (Exod. 3:1–10). At this critical moment the power of sacred kings is decisively challenged and an alternative vision of human life under the rule of God is introduced into the world.

The historical setting for the emergence of early Israel was one in which existing power structures were disintegrating across the ancient world. During the mid-thirteenth century before Christ there is evidence of widespread destruction and great loss of life resulting in 'an economic and political dark age'. This was the context within which Israel 'developed its distinctive patterns of thought' which involved the rejection of the authority of divine kings, including that of the pharaohs (Mendenhall 1973: 64). In place of the myths which underpinned the power of sacred kings, Israel celebrated the direct acts of God, experienced in actual history through the events of the exodus from Egypt. The veneration of kings was replaced with the worship of Yahweh and obedience to his ethical demands. As Mendenhall puts it:

> If the center of old paganism was concern for perpetuating the king's control over all his enemies, the new proclaimed that no one but God was, or could be, in control. His authority was exercised in the first place by the community's obedience to His commands, and secondly, by His control over all those powers of nature and history that man individually and corporately could neither control nor predict, but the functioning of which was also subjected to ethical interpretation in the covenant formula of curses and blessings (ibid.: 25).

The biblical account of the exodus has the pharaoh, the god-king who is the object of unquestioning veneration and obedience, saying to Moses: 'Go, worship the LORD as you have requested' (Exod. 12:31). This is the precise point at which the power of sacred kingship is broken, replaced by devotion to a saving and liberating God who provides those who love him with the gifts of Torah and covenant, and with the promise of his blessing on condition of the spiritual and ethical faithfulness of a freed people. However, Israel's encounter with divine kingship, and with the temptations it presented, was far from over. Ahead of this liberated people lay the land of Canaan and its fortified cities, ruled by an urban elite operating on the basis of the similar patterns of divine kingship that had been left behind, first in Mesopotamia, then in Egypt. Palestine at this time was divided into a multitude of city-states ruled by kings who regarded all productive land as their personal property, and sustained in power by a 'military aristocracy'. Meantime, as in Egypt, the mass of people existed in virtual slavery, their labours supporting the urban elite, which used the surplus resources accumulated on the backs of the poor 'to support an ambitious building program – of temples, palaces, fortifications, a sumptuous and expensive art in ivory, gold and silver' (ibid.: 222).

At this point it is important to underline the significance of the theophany in which Israel's distinctive understanding of the nature of God is rooted (Exod. 3:1–15), and the gifts of covenant and Torah which were to shape the ethical and social life of this liberated people (Exod. 19:3–6; and see Deut. 4:5–8; 6:4–9). The vision of God was the basis upon which the authority of sacred kings was repudiated, so that the peoples freed from tyranny might become a nation under Yahweh's rule. As Mendenhall says, ancient Israel refused to delegate power to a centralized political system:

> The deification of productivity and power were rejected in favor of an ethic, and economic prosperity and security were presented as by-products of ethical obedience rather than as evidences of divine authority and proof of divine favor (ibid.: 224).

The rejection of this covenantal ethic would result in the loss of *shalom* which, tragically, is 'precisely what happened with the reestablishment of monarchy under Kings David and Solomon'. Israel's history thus contains the warning that a state, or a city, 'which sacrifices ethical obedience for temporary gain must be destroyed by God Himself' – a warning that becomes the central theme of classical prophecy and is later reaffirmed by Jesus.

The question that arises at this point concerns the *content* of this kingdom ethic. What kind of society would liberated Israel become? What social vision would replace the unjust urban systems defended with seemingly impregnable power within the city-states of Canaan? The answer is to be found in the frequently overlooked fact that the Torah displays distinctively urban characteristics, so that 'much of Deuteronomy is comparable to a city charter' (Brown & Carroll 2000: 7). The negative experience of urban life in Egypt, and the awareness of similar patterns of domination and injustice within the city-states of Palestine, forms the context for the laws and statutes which gave concrete shape to Israel's hope for the future. This context is made explicit in passages like the following:

> When the LORD your God brings you into the land he swore to your fathers, to Abraham, Isaac and Jacob, to give you – *a land with large, flourishing cities you did not build*, houses filled with all kinds of good things you did not provide, wells you did

not dig, and vineyards and olive groves you did not plant – then when you eat and are satisfied, *be careful that you do not forget the* LORD, *who brought you out of Egypt, out of the land of slavery* (Deut. 6:10–12, emphases added).

John Goldingay describes Deuteronomy as 'the most urban of the Old Testament's law codes' and he traces the ways in which its regulations provided Israel with a covenantal, urban ethic. Read within its canonical and literary setting, Deuteronomy is given to Israel 'on the edge of the promised land, and thus on the edge of life in an urban setting which Israel will share as it takes over Canaanite cities' (Goldingay 1989: 6). From the perspective of the critical study of the Old Testament, the book belongs in its final form to the context of 'urban Jerusalem' and is designed to preserve the practice of Torah at a point at which this was being set aside in the interests of what would today be called economic modernization. Either way, the urban character of the work is clear, and is reflected, for example, in the demand that the cities previously governed in the interests of powerful elites, be transformed to reflect the sovereignty of Israel's liberating God:

> Appoint judges and officials for each of your tribes *in every town* the LORD your God is giving you, and they shall judge the people fairly. Do not pervert justice or show partiality. Do not accept a bribe, for a bribe blinds the eyes of the wise and twists the words of the righteous. *Follow justice and justice alone, so that you may live and possess the land the* LORD *your God is giving you* (Deut. 16:18–20).

This fundamental principle of the practice of justice 'and justice alone', is not an abstract ideal but is given concrete and structural form, particularly in the institution of the jubilee, designed to prevent the accumulation of wealth on the part of the powerful at the expense of the poor and disadvantaged (Deut. 15:1–11). If, as Walter Brueggemann has noted, cities are characterized by money economies because urbanization creates surplus wealth and 'the capacity to live off the produce of others' (Brueggemann 2007: 10), then this vision of a society in which debts are regularly cancelled to ensure that 'there should be no poor among you' is truly revolutionary. The jubilee institution clearly recognized that Israel's hope for social and economic equality under the rule of Yahweh was likely to be constantly *vulnerable* and liable to erosion and loss. For this reason, the survival of the new nation is made conditional on the implementation of the law, together with the practice of social solidarity at the local level. The ethos of this society would be one characterized by an open-handed generosity and love toward those who, despite their misfortune, remain both neighbours and brothers (Deut. 15:7–8; 24:19). However, what makes this covenant ethic remarkable is the fact that it is gifted to Israel as an *urban* society, so that Deuteronomy reflects 'an urban tradition that endorses city life as one setting in which early Israel encountered and served Yahweh'. Thus, from the foundational period of its history Israel demonstrated the possibility of being 'both thoroughly urban and authentically Yahwist' (Benjamin 1983: 304–305).

The challenge of the cities of Canaan

Before we move on from the story of early Israel we need to consider elements in these texts that may be considered difficult, or even offensive. Not everything in the Mosaic law codes is congenial to the modern mind and much in the story of early Israel as told in the book of Joshua is profoundly troubling. As John Hamlin observes, colonialists from Christianized nations have frequently justified both their violence toward native peoples and their seizure of land and resources by appeal to the book of Joshua, and in a postcolonial era the Bible's apparent justification of mass killings is deeply repulsive to many people (Hamlin 1983: xi). It will no longer do either to ignore these problems, or to sidestep them by a spiritualizing interpretation which dehistoricizes the Old Testament and fails to respond to serious questions concerning these texts.

According to the canonical scriptures, the Hebrew slaves liberated from bondage in Egypt found the promise of their entrance into Canaan frustrated by the discovery of cities which were 'fortified and very large'. Moreover, these cities were occupied by people whose military strength and prowess struck terror into the hearts of those who had witnessed it (Num. 13:26–33; Deut. 1:26–28). The account within the book of Joshua of what has usually been described as the 'conquest' of the land, presents many difficult problems, both at the level of ethics and with regard to the interpretation of the texts and the relationship between what they appear to claim and the findings of modern archaeology. Clearly, the resolution of such problems must be left to scholars with the knowledge and expertise which enables them to address such issues, but our concern with cities, together with the use that has been made of these texts in the history of interpretation, justifies us in asking questions concerning the nature of the urban settlements in Canaan and the circumstances in which the slaves liberated from Egypt came to form the nation of Israel.

We have already traced the manner in which both the migration of Abraham and his descendants from Mesopotamia and the liberation of the slaves from Egypt involved the repudiation of systems of sacred kingship which had resulted in the domination and oppression of peasant populations. The absolute authority previously ascribed to divine kings was transferred to Yahweh, whose rule over those who came to love and worship him resulted in a social revolution which promised justice 'and justice alone'. The question then becomes whether the entrance of the freed slaves into Canaan was in fact an extension of the saving acts of Yahweh, overthrowing the absolute monarchs who governed those cities in ways that destroyed the poor and denied the claims of justice.

From the 1970s onward a series of studies suggested that the situation within Palestine at the time that the liberated slaves made their entrance was already like a powder keg, needing only a spark to ignite an explosion. For example, George Mendenhall suggested that archaeological and historical evidence indicated that villagers whose labour sustained the urban elite within Canaan had no rights or entitlements to the land they tilled and were simply 'given enough of their own produce to keep them alive'. Meantime, surplus wealth was creamed off by the rulers whose power and glory was justified by myth and by the central role which they played in religious rituals enacted in elaborate and costly temples. This intertwining of religion and politics meant that any opposition to the kings was not simply a political act, but constituted 'an offense against the gods' and placed the entire system of production and the maintenance of peace and security in jeopardy (Mendenhall 1973: 223). In other words, the prevailing ideology was surrounded with such an aura of sanctity as to be presented as unalterable and without any possible alternative.

The arrival within Palestine of a band of former slaves confessing allegiance to Yahweh and committed to a vision of social life which clearly had revolutionary implications, provided the spark capable of igniting rebellion against tyranny *within* the walled cities of Canaan. The Joshua narrative itself indicates that the progress of the liberated slaves had been observed with mounting concern, creating panic among the urban elite who feared the impact that their entrance into the land might have on an oppressed and increasingly restless peasantry (Josh. 2:8–11, 24). Given this scenario and the realization that, as John Bright expressed it, the overthrow of the sacred kings was to some degree 'an inside job', some Old Testament scholars began to question the appropriateness of the language of 'conquest'. Bright himself described the early history of Israel as follows:

> Large numbers of Hebrews were already long settled in Palestine, and these joined
> with the Hebrews coming from the desert. Their joining struck the spark that ignited

Palestine; and it was from the fusion of the two that the Israelite tribal league in its normative form emerged (Bright 1981: 138).[3]

The conclusion to which the studies mentioned above appeared to point was that, when read carefully within their context, the narratives recording the formation of biblical Israel described a clash between two absolutely opposed and contrasting worldviews, with the Canaanite kings representing not merely the people who happened to occupy the land, but 'practitioners of an urban system that defeats and diminishes the peasant population with whom YHWH is allied, indeed has been allied since the slave emancipation from Egypt' (Brueggemann 2007: 13). There is then continuity between the exodus from Egypt and the entrance into Canaan, in the sense that *both* events bring release from oppression and bondage, *both* involve unavoidable violence, because those who benefit from the existing power arrangements refuse to accept the demands of Israel's God, and *both* are related to the hope of a new social reality shaped by the Torah. It is significant that the book of Joshua opens with a ringing re-affirmation of the Torah (1:6–9), presented as the primary 'weapon' with which Israel enters the land. It is this vision rather than the military prowess of the liberated peoples which terrifies the Canaanite kings, leading them to recognize the social alternative represented by Israel as a dire threat that had to be eliminated (Josh. 11:1–5). Archaeologist William Dever has said that the evidence pointing to a revolutionary movement within Canaan, driven by the dynamic faith in Yahweh brought into the land by the slaves freed from bondage and oppression in Egypt, is clear and convincing. He concludes:

> The [archaeological] evidence surveyed here of social upheaval, mass migration to the hill country, and the relatively sudden emergence of a distinctive rural lifestyle, is all best explained by positing a social revolution of some kind (Dever 2003: 187–188).

Seen in this light, the Joshua story begins to resonate in unexpected and surprising ways with the realities of the urban world we have described earlier in this book. While the violence that is part of the struggle to establish the reign of Israel's God in a context of oppressive power and deeply entrenched privilege may offend the sensibilities of rich Christians who have never known the experience of hunger, or the humiliation of poverty and homelessness, it

---

3. Note the statement of Pekka Pitkänen: 'Thus, Israel is born in Egypt and grows in and *from* Canaan' (Pitkänen 2004: 175, emphasis added).

may be more readily understood in the shanties and *favellas* which continue to mushroom within and around megacities across the Global South. Norman Gottwald sees disturbing parallels between the 'abusive and degrading features' of the tributary system by means of which the urban elite in Canaan 'siphoned off the produce of distant peasant villages', and the manner in which a globalized economy now drains resources from small cultivators 'to bolster the profits of agribusiness, energy and finance corporations' (Gottwald 2008: 11). His subsequent observation that these parallels explain why Bible readers across the Global South are able to recognize 'the stark realities of biblical economics' is strikingly illustrated by the work of the African theologian, Jean-Marc Ela. He describes the context within which millions of Christians read the book of Joshua today as one which provides them with an understanding of the strength of resistance to social transformation which is too often hidden from their fellow believers in Europe or North America:

> At a time when millions of black peasants are working – not to feed themselves but to sell for a wholly inadequate price export crops that will bring in foreign exchange and profit only for an urban minority – African theologians must listen to their people and ask themselves, 'How long will this go on my God?' . . . The question of 'God' is being asked today from the bottom of society, there where racism and segregation develop and where famine results from a policy of domination rather than from natural disasters due to climate (Ela 2001: 175).

Clearly, the approach to the history of early Israel which we have briefly described is capable of connecting this narrative to social realities within our contemporary urban world in a manner that suggests the transformative potential of the biblical story. However, there are still significant hermeneutical problems to be addressed, not least those related to the violence with which, according to the Joshua account, the land and its walled cities were taken. How is it possible that people who had been delivered from tyranny and gifted the knowledge of a God who demanded the practice of justice and mercy, a demand enshrined in a legal code which made their own deliverance from slavery a motivation to care for *aliens* living among them (Deut. 16:11–12), could apparently show such a lack of mercy to the inhabitants of the cities of Canaan?

It is important to notice that critical Old Testament scholarship locates the production of the book of Joshua in its final shape during the reform movement in the time of King Josiah, some six centuries *after* the events it describes. If this conclusion were to be accepted, the time gap involved between the reported events and the context in which the book came to be written – a period that would take the readers of this present book back to the middle ages – is clearly significant and prompts questions concerning the manner in which the narrative has been shaped by the theological agenda of Josiah's reformation. John Hamlin's commentary interprets the book of Joshua against the background of this royal programme of moral and spiritual renewal, and demonstrates how, when read in this way, it continues to act as a word of revelation capable of speaking powerfully to our divided, urban world today (Hamlin 1983).

However, if we grant that the redactional history of the book, together with the archaeological evidence, and (most significantly of all) a careful reading of the text itself, combine to compel a revision of the received understanding of the history of early Israel, the problem of the violence involved in the taking of the Canaanite cities still remains to be addressed. As we have noticed, the extent to which this is felt to be an issue is to some degree determined by the social and cultural contexts of contemporary readers and for many poor Christians in the southern hemisphere suffering the profoundly negative consequences of a globalized, capitalist economic system, the occurrence of violence on the route to social transformation is unsurprising. Increasing numbers of Christians in such contexts are likely to read the Scriptures as being deeply subversive of the dominant ideologies and as an inspiration to work for radical social and economic change (see Vaage 1997).

In addition, we may notice the response of William Foxwell Albright – known as the 'father of biblical archaeology' – who suggested in the early 1940s, at the start of the Second World War, that the use of violence against urban populations based on military policies designed to create 'shock and awe', is not exclusive to ancient peoples whom we want to designate as 'primitive'. Albright proposed that 'the reciprocal massacres of Protestants and Catholics' in seventeenth-century Europe, the deliberate targeting of non-combatants in the Spanish civil war, or the German bombing of Rotterdam in 1940, all suggested that modern people are in no position to condemn the ancients for the practice of 'total warfare' (Albright 1957: 279–280).

The essential correctness of this claim can be demonstrated simply by a roll-call of modern cities that have fallen victim to 'man's inhumanity to man' – Guernica, Coventry, Leningrad, Dresden, Hiroshima, Nagasaki, Srebenica, Falluja – and the list goes on! The RAF's saturation bombing of German cities in the Second World War was designed to produce 900,000 civilian deaths and a million serious casualties, while 'Operation Gomorrah' in 1943 created firestorms at the heart of the city of Hamburg in which seven thousand children were among the carbonized victims (Davis 2002: 70–71). After the Germans launched their V1 and V2 bombs on London, Winston Churchill proposed a response involving poison gas attacks on Berlin, describing the discussion of morality in such a situation as 'absurd' and demanding that the plan be 'studied in cold blood by sensible people, and not by psalm-singing uninformed defeatists' (ibid.: 75–76).

The systematic targeting of urban populations in modern warfare, or what has been called the policy of *urbicide*, has actually influenced the design and construction of contemporary cities, as is demonstrated by Stephen Graham's observation that Le Corbusier's 'obsession with loosely spaced modern towers set in parkland' was not just the result of his vision of cities characterized by light and space, but was a 'reaction to a widespread obsession in 1930s Europe with the need to completely re-plan cities *so that they presented the smallest possible targets to the massed ranks of heavy bombers*'. Le Corbusier's response to the 'sinister apotheosis' of death heralded by aerial bombardment was the total destruction of the old city and its replacement by a modern utopia 'capable of emerging victorious from the air war' (Graham 2004: 175, emphasis added). The studies of urban sociologists like Graham and, more recently, Saskia Sassen, suggest that the policy of deliberately attacking urban targets, bringing terror and death to their populations, has become a characteristic feature of modern war, resulting in an ever-increasing sense of insecurity as warfare becomes asymmetric and creates a new 'urban map of terror' (Sassen 2009: 32).

Finally, it is vitally important to notice that, whatever the actual level of violence may have been in the establishment of ancient Israel, it must be seen within the broader setting of the biblical revelation of God's promise of *shalom*. As we have seen, that promise originates in the revelation granted to Abram and, from the beginning, embraces *all* the peoples listed in Genesis 10. The extent of the promise, and the depth and richness of the universal *shalom* that is the goal of God's redemptive work in the world, will gradually be unfolded as the story progresses, but the ultimate end is that war and violence should cease and all peoples come to live in a world of peace and justice:

> He makes wars to cease to the ends of the earth;
> he breaks the bow and shatters the spear,
> he burns the shields with fire.
> 'Be still, and know that I am God;
> I will be exalted among the nations
> I will be exalted in the earth.' (Ps. 46:9–10)

The mention of the destruction of the weapons of war in this seminal text alerts us to a significant aspect of the Joshua narrative. Joshua 11 describes an alliance of Canaanite kings which brought together 'a large number of horses and chariots' and a 'huge army' with the intention of crushing the Israelite incursion (vv. 4–5). Walter Brueggemann notes that the horse and chariot is the symbol of the military power of sacred kings and he tracks the repeated rejection of an idolatrous trust in such weaponry through the Old Testament. The motif is found in the Psalms in statements such as,

Some trust in chariots, and some in horses,
but we trust in the name of the LORD our God (Ps. 20:7).

Similar statements are scattered elsewhere (Pss 33:16–19; 76:6–7; 147:10–11; Prov. 21:30–31), and occur repeatedly in the prophetic literature where, for example, Hosea records God as saying, 'I will show love to the house of Judah; and I will save them – not by bow, sword or battle, or by horses and horsemen, but by the LORD their God' (Hos. 1:7).

Throughout the prophetic writings a trust in 'horses and chariots' is seen as inconsistent with faith in Yahweh and is set over against it in terms of radical contrast (see Isa. 31:1; 30:15–16; 43:16–17; Mic. 5:10). However, Brueggemann suggests that all these statements 'are rooted in and derived from the much more primitive statement' in which, confronted by the massive military might assembled by the kings of northern Canaan, God is heard instructing Joshua to 'hamstring their horses and burn their chariots' (Josh. 11:6). This is the only place in this chapter where God is recorded as speaking directly, which means that his mandate to Joshua is restricted to violence against horses and chariots, in other words, against *weapons*. The revelation in this text, says Brueggemann,

. . . is the gift of authorization by which Joshua and Israel are legitimated for their own acts of liberation, which from the side of the king of Hazor are perceived as acts of violence. What is 'disclosed' is that the world of the city-kings is not closed. It is the purpose of 'horses and chariots' to close that world and so to render the peasants hopeless and helpless. But the world ostensibly controlled by oppressive city-kings is now dis-closed, shown to be false, and broken open to the joy of Israel. The revelatory decree of Yahweh breaks the fixed world of the city-kings. What we label as violence on Yahweh's part is a theological permit that sanctions a new social possibility (Brueggemann 2009: 30).

That 'new social possibility' becomes evident within the book of Joshua as the land gifted to a liberated people becomes the scene for the application of the Torah in the actual life of the nation. For example, the establishment of 'cities of refuge', intended to provide shelter and protection to people involved in the accidental shedding of blood, prevented the urge for revenge from descending into endless cycles of violence, while also providing displaced persons with acceptance, security, and the means for rehabilitation (Josh. 20:1–9). These cities were thus intended to contribute to the social health and *shalom* of the covenant nation and were locations within which 'justice reigned, superseding in some cases the more provincial customs of family and clan, "so that the blood of an innocent person may not be shed..." (Deut 19:10)' (Brown & Carroll 2000: 7).

Clearly, the accomplishment of Yahweh's *shalom* in a disordered world too often characterized by the hubris of the powerful and the insatiable greed of the wealthy, where deeply entrenched evils are defended at almost any cost by powers both human and demonic, must necessarily involve conflict. There is no magic wand that can be waved to bring about the reign of God; rather, the divine purpose is worked out amid the complexities and ambiguities of human history. This means that the ways of God are often hidden or difficult to discern in contexts where evil appears to triumph and the might and power of privileged elites often seems impregnable. But the narratives of the exodus and the gift of the promised land reveal a God who, as John Hamlin puts it, enters into battle 'against the powers of death', liberating the oppressed and granting them a new, truly revolutionary vision of life in the world, including life in the city. As Hamlin says,

> This does not mean that the cruelty, terror and destruction of war are either
> God's doing or God's will. God's 'warfare' is his concerned, costly effort to create
> righteousness and peace. In some mysterious way, God's will may be accomplished
> even in the midst of the brutalities of war. The human agents probably do not realize
> or intend what God wills (Is. 10:7). In fact, it is God's will that wars come to an end
> (Ps.46:9), and that nations should not make war with each other (Is. 2:4) (Hamlin
> 1983: 96–97).

Holy Zion: the promise and the failure

With the founding of the monarchy in Israel social and political developments were set in motion which resulted in the appearance of new urban forms. The establishment of a royal house and the creation of a formal state led inevitably to new building programmes, including the fortification of Jerusalem. The institutions of statehood – requiring the creation of a bureaucracy in the form of court and administrative officials – resulted in extensive building works to provide accommodation for these officials. Volkmar Fritz observes that urbanization had a new beginning in Israel around 1,000 BC:

Leaving aside the fact that the city has a long history in Palestine, the urbanization during the period of the monarchy represents a new beginning, in which older elements are incorporated but have a completely new concept and new building forms as their vehicle (Fritz 1995: 14).

The reigns of David and Solomon witnessed 'a wave of new city foundations', many of which were built on the ruins of long abandoned urban sites, such as Dan, Hazor and Lachish. In the case of Jerusalem, the ancient Jebusite city appears to have survived the earlier collapse of the Canaanite city states and was captured by David and transformed into Zion, the 'Holy City'. The historian describes these events, which in fact marked an absolutely crucial turning point in the story of biblical Israel, with few words:

> David then took up residence in the fortress and called it the City of David.
> He built up the area around it, from the supporting terraces inward. And
> he became more powerful, because the LORD God Almighty was with him
> (2 Sam. 5:9–10).

The evolution of the urban form within Israel at this point becomes evident when we are told that Hiram, king of Tyre, offered to supply 'cedar logs and carpenters and stonemasons' in order to assist the building of 'a palace for David' (2 Sam. 5:11). It will be remembered that royal palaces and temples were the iconic structures which dotted the skylines of the cities of the ancient Near East and this fact alone is sufficient to flag up the dangers inherent in this development. Indeed, when the historian tells us a few verses later that 'David took more concubines and wives in Jerusalem' (5:13), we witness the appearance of a model of kingship that was bound to exist in tension with the ethical demands of the Torah gifted to liberated Israel in wilderness. It was precisely this which so troubled Samuel when the desire for a king 'such as all the other nations have' first surfaced in Israel. The warning of the aged prophet is worth quoting at some length:

> This is what the king who will rule over you will do: *He will take* your sons and make
> them serve with his chariots and horses, and they will run in front of his chariots. . . .
> *He will take* your daughters to be perfumers and cooks and bakers. *He will take* the
> best of your fields and vineyards and olive groves and give them to his attendants.
> *He will take* a tenth of your grain and of your vintage and give it to his officials and
> attendants. . . . *He will take* a tenth of your flocks, and you yourselves will become his
> slaves (1 Sam. 8:11–17, emphasis added).

While Samuel's central objection to the institution of the monarchy concerned the implicit rejection of the rule of Yahweh, his language also reflects
the memory of the harsh and unjust urban regimes from which the tribes had
been delivered. The old man knows that it is in the nature of kings to *take* what
they will, and while the traditions of Torah and covenant might restrain royal
power in its initial stages, the centralizing tendencies of monarchy might too
easily overwhelm the ethics of the kingdom of God and result in tyranny and
slavery. Samuel warned a generation for whom the old story of exodus and
liberation was a fading memory that the kingship they demanded would come
at a tremendous social and economic cost.

However, it is worth pausing here to notice that the contrasting attitudes
found within Israel towards Jerusalem provide us with an example of the tensions within the Bible concerning the city to which reference was made earlier
in this chapter. On the one hand, the growth of this royal city was understood
by many as an inevitable development given the particular historical context
within which Israel found herself at this time, and one that was not necessarily inconsistent with the fundamental vision gifted to the tribes in the shape
of the Torah. Indeed, it could be asked whether the establishment of this
city provided a stage on which it became possible to show to the world an
alternative form of *urban existence*. Were the ethics of the kingdom bound to
be compromised when removed from the context of the tribal confederacy
which had given shape to Israel's social and political life until this point, or
might they be adapted and re-interpreted in a way that made possible the
creation of an *urban* culture within the royal city of David reflecting Yahweh's
will for human society? After all, the book of Deuteronomy itself anticipated
that when the nation obtained 'rest' and 'lived in safety', God would choose
one place 'from among all your tribes' where his glory would be displayed
and all the people would come to 'rejoice before the LORD your God' (Deut.
12:4–14). As Brown and Carroll comment, 'The city is an integral feature of
the theological topography of the promised land, no less than God's gift to
Israel', and Jerusalem is understood to be the place in which God's name
'lodges' in a particular, *urban* sanctuary (Brown & Carroll 2000: 7).

The psalmists depict Jerusalem as a place of gladness and security within
which the reign of God is indeed a sign to 'all nations' of the transforming
power of Yahweh's salvation (Pss 46:4–7; 47:5–9). The city is 'beautiful in its
loftiness', but its greatest glory is in the fact that it is 'the city of the LORD
Almighty' (Ps. 48:8). The conviction that the God of the exodus and Sinai
was *present* in the worship of Israel finds expression again and again in the
psalms and prompts joyful celebration: 'Great is the Lord and most worthy
of praise, in the city of our God' (Ps. 48:1). As Brueggemann points out,

there was great joy in the knowledge that Yahweh had 'established govern-
ing control' and 'enunciated policies of justice and well-being (*shalom*)', and
Israel's liturgical worship 'had the effect of imposing a life-giving order on
every aspect of Israel's life and on the life of the world' (Brueggemann 1997a:
655–656).

The blessings of this urban centre extended outward to 'the villages of
Judah' (Ps. 48:11) and had significance for all nations because the justice and
mercy of Israel's liberating God offered hope to 'all the earth' (Ps. 47:7). And
it is not only Jerusalem which is celebrated as the locus of human well-being
and security; the wider process of urbanization which we have noted above is
viewed in positive terms since the expanding cities offer relief from the hunger
and thirst which characterized life in the harsh environments of the wilderness. Psalm 107 strikingly illustrates this perspective when it contrasts the
experiences of those who, having faced starvation as they 'wandered in desert
wastelands', cried out to God in their distress and were 'led by a straight way
to a city where they could settle' (107:4–9, emphasis added). Here is the basis for an
urban spirituality in which God's goodness is recognized in the gift of the city
within which hungry people are filled 'with good things'. Later the psalmist
returns to this same theme, contrasting the desperate struggle for existence in
harsh locations with the security of life in the city:

> He turned the desert into pools of water
>   and the parched ground into flowing springs;
> there he brought the hungry to live,
>   *and they founded a city* where they could settle (Ps. 107:35–36, emphasis added).

During the period of Israel's classical prophets, when Samuel's fears about
the long-term consequences of the changes he witnessed taking place at the
end of his life proved to be more than justified, the prophet Isaiah recalled a
time when life within the city of Jerusalem had made it a holy place providing
'light to the nations':

> See how *the faithful city*
>   has become a harlot!
> She *once was full of justice;*
>   *righteousness used to dwell in her* –
> but now murderers! (Isa. 1:21, emphasis added).

We might well ask at precisely which period in its history the city had been
'full of justice'? Walter Brueggemann observes that although the reign of

David was to witness an increasing borrowing of social, political and ethical practices from surrounding nations, its earliest phase is presented by the biblical narrators as being 'rooted in Yahwistic covenantal traditions', so that any move toward pagan practices of monarchy on the assumption that the king might *take* whatever he desired, was met by fierce prophetic opposition (see 2 Sam. 12:9–10). The subsequent decline into moral chaos should not obscure the fact that Jerusalem was developed as the capital city at a time when the memory of Israel's calling to present the world with an alternative model of social life within an urban context remained alive.

However, we must also take account of a far more negative and pessimistic view of life in the city which also surfaces within the Old Testament writings. The same city that can be celebrated as the sphere of security, joy and well-being, can become a context for violence, division and fear. The psalms reflect on this dark side of urban life, reversing the comparison between the desert and the city which we have mentioned above, so that the former becomes a place of 'shelter' from the turmoil and threat which leads to 'fear and trembling' within the city. The psalmist now wishes for the 'wings of a dove' to fly away from the city and his prayer in this situation has a note of desperation:

> Confuse the wicked, O Lord, confound their speech,
>   for I see violence and strife *in the city*.
> Day and night they prowl about on its walls;
>   malice and abuse are *within it*.
> Destructive forces are at work *within the city*;
>   threats and lies *never leave its streets* (Ps. 55:9–11, emphasis added).

This negative perception of the city may be connected to the increasing loss of memory concerning Israel's origins which, as we shall see, resulted in a dangerous syncretism which eroded, and eventually all but eliminated, the covenant ethic. However, as Volkmar Fritz points out, the institution of the monarchy itself brought about far-reaching social changes which, almost from the start, had a negative impact on the lives of many people within the city:

> The kingship brings the Israelite various obligations that were hitherto unknown and affect not only his independence but also his income. Detailed mention is made of military service, duties, collection of property and taxation. All these rights of the king mean an economic restriction for the Israelite, for he is now no longer master where his own productivity is concerned or sole beneficiary of the fruits of his labour (Fritz 1995: 166).

The potentially oppressive character of the forms of bureaucracy which accompany the emergence of the state and profoundly alter the urban form are nowhere more clearly described than in the book of Ecclesiastes. Here it is not simply a matter of the loss of security or peace in the city, but of a profound sense of alienation that results in a loss of *meaning*. The author is a quintessentially urban person, undertaking great building projects (2:4), amassing enormous personal wealth (2:8), and pursuing pleasure in familiar forms of escapism (2:10). Yet the meaning of life, and the meaning of the city, has been lost, with the result that he sees through the pretensions of urban civilization to uncover a pervading 'meaninglessness'. The city is structured in ways that are oppressive because all human labour and achievement is ultimately driven by 'man's envy of his neighbour' (4:1–4). We might wonder whether any modern analysis of bureaucracy can match this author's acute insight into the structural evils which result in the oppression of the urban poor:

> If you see the poor oppressed in a district, and justice and rights denied, do not be
> surprised by such things; for one official is eyed by another one, and over them both
> are others higher still. The increase from the land is taken by all; the king himself
> profits from the fields (Eccl. 5:8–9).

The traditional view of the authorship of this book associated it with Solomon and, although that connection now seems unlikely, the book serves to highlight the part played by the royal household in the erosion of the ethic of the covenant and the growing sense of crisis within the city. Martin Buber analyzed Solomon's prayer at the dedication of the magnificent temple in Jerusalem (1 Kgs 8:12–61) and concluded that, while this acknowledged God as 'the Lord of the heavens' and 'Lord of the cult', it left no place for God 'as leader of the people':

> The functions of YHVH are to be reduced so that they *do not bind* the king: the
> cosmic spheres are left in His control, as is the Holy of Holies, whereas for the
> government of Israel full power has been given to His anointed one, and with this
> YHVH, so to speak, surrendered His influence in this domain (Buber 1949: 83).

Certainly, all the aspects of questionable behaviour which we identified above as being confessed by the author of Ecclesiastes are to be found in the life of Solomon (and some more), and they result in an alien practice of kingship which creates dangerous religious and social tensions within Israel and brings him into direct conflict with Yahweh. The charge against Solomon could not be more serious: 'Since this is your attitude and you have not kept my covenant and my decrees, which I commanded you, I will most certainly tear the kingdom away from you and give it to one of your subordinates' (1 Kgs 11:11). The promise of Holy Zion, the vision of God's *shalom*, was fatally undermined by Solomon's compromises which Brueggemann discusses in detail before summing up as follows:

> The common theme of all these theological-*cum*-socioeconomic commitments is that they commonly assume that enough power and wealth will permit self-securing for the state and the economy, without the costliness of an inconvenient social ethic. Thus, that Solomon's heart should be turned away from YHWH also means that his heart has turned away from the neighbor, which in turn led to social policies that disregarded the neighbor. Disregard for the neighbor in the formation of urban policy becomes, predictably, a hallmark of urban economy, characteristically intoxicated as it is with the love of opulent grandeur and the autonomy of self-serving acquisitiveness that is never curbed by social reality (Brueggemann 2007: 23).

However, if the promise of a different kind of city was lost from view among those who had much to gain from the adoption of pagan ideas concerning urban life, it was kept alive by faithful people who boldly and persistently questioned God concerning the apparent miscarriage of his purpose within history. There is, in other words, a tradition of prayer for the city that, far from being weakened and destroyed by disappointment and frustration, actually becomes more urgent and honest in situations that seem utterly desperate. This is the tradition of the lament psalms in which the poor and oppressed ask, 'Why have you rejected us forever, O God?' (Ps. 74:1). In a context marked by terrible destruction and deep despair, Yahweh is reminded that he once 'purchased' this people and that he had dwelt on Mount Zion, but now the voice of prophecy is silent and 'none of us knows how long this will be' (Ps. 74:9). If, as we suggested above, an urban spirituality will recognize God's goodness in the gift of the city, it must also include a commitment to prayer for the city when the basis of hope becomes reduced almost to vanishing point. As Goldingay says, 'The pain, suffering and oppression of the Psalms of lament are often those of the city. . . . The city is supposed to be a place of refuge, of safety, but it is not; so the Psalms challenge God to do something about that' (Goldingay 1989: 13).

The prophetic perspective

The great prophets whose writings make up such a substantial part of the Old Testament scriptures were, to a considerable degree, preachers and poets whose work was fundamentally concerned with the city. Our emphasis on the critical importance of an understanding of the contexts of the biblical narratives and a grasp of the flow of the history within which they appear is especially important in regard to these books. The prophetic books can be arranged and classified in relation to the position they occupy in relation to the terrible events of the Babylonian invasion, the utter destruction of the city of Jerusalem, the removal of the pathetic survivors to Babylon, and their exile there. These traumatic events constituted a radical turning point in the history of Israel, creating a huge crisis for faith and placing previously unheard of questions on the theological agenda. Where was Yahweh when Zion was over-run and heathen invaders 'poured out blood like water all around Jerusalem' (Ps. 79:3)? How was it possible to retain hope in the meaning of history, or of some purpose for one's own life, when the very foundations of faith seemed shaken and the silence of God appeared to be unending (Ps. 74:9)? And what of the glories of the city of Babylon itself, now encountered directly for the first time by Jewish exiles who were tempted to interpret the supremacy of the empire as evidence of its superiority and success? When one of the prophets, speaking precisely into the context of these exiles, warned of the terrible dangers of spending 'money on what is not bread' and working 'on what does not satisfy' (Isa. 55:2), it is clear that he was aware of the strength of the temptations which Babylonian civilization presented to people who had lost everything in the holocaust of 587 BC.

The message of the prophets in the context of this tragic history is centrally concerned with *cities*: the city of Jerusalem, broken, empty and apparently now a dead city; and the city of Babylon, proud, successful, wealthy, and celebrating its complete dominance and the seeming ability of its gods to actually deliver human well-being. *The nature of a prophet's message, whether the announcement of impending disaster, or the offer of fresh hope and a voice of comfort, was determined by the point at which they were called to deliver God's word on the timeline that ran from the early days of Israel's monarchy, through the decline and the destruction of the kingdom, to the exile and beyond.* Klaus Koch, who describes Israel's great prophets as 'towering far above all comparable intuitive diviners or soothsayers' in the ancient world, observes that in the earliest phase, the primary concern of the prophets was not with human suffering, but with the fact that 'far too many people are getting on far too well, and that in the near future this is going to lead to inescapable catastrophe'. This profoundly critical view of their own society, and especially of its anointed kings and religious leaders, was 'new and unique in the ancient world'. However, *after* the catastrophe, with Jerusalem a heap of smoking ruins and the survivors in chains, the prophetic message underwent a change as a new generation recognized that 'there was a surplus of suffering on the part of the innocent' and that the ending of the old regime in Jerusalem had created space for the emergence of Yahweh's surprising and wonderful newness (Koch 1983: 4).

The prophetic critique of the ruling and privileged elites in the city of Jerusalem and their courageous and relentless warnings of the inevitable disaster that loomed ahead in the absence of genuine repentance, provide models for urban ministry in a cultural context in which the official ideology of growth, success and happiness conceals the unpleasant and alarming realities known to those familiar with the underside of the city. Or again, the experience of deep loss, which brings an outpouring of almost inconsolable grief, and the exile from all that had been familiar and loved, is paralleled by the journey travelled by large numbers of Christians in the modern world who have found themselves in a new, unfamiliar and anxiety-inducing situation at the cultural margins of societies which, not long ago, knew and respected their faith. Thus, in identifying some of the prophetic themes which offer direction for an urban theology today, we can take heart, observing Walter Brueggemann's insight that one of the key revelations provided by biblical faith 'is the awareness that only anguish leads to life, only grieving leads to joy, and only embraced endings permit new beginnings' (Brueggemann 1978: 60).

The critique of urban religion

Following the reigns of David and Solomon, Jerusalem became the centre of Israel's political life and its great temple was at the heart of her religious worship and the focal point of pilgrimage. As we have seen, the psalmists repeatedly celebrate the beauty of Zion, 'the city of our God', where Yahweh displays his glory in an urban shrine and his worshippers experience both indescribable joy and the conviction that God makes this city 'secure forever' (Ps. 48:1–8). As long as this worship remained rooted in the covenant made with Moses and so resulted in obedience to the demands of the Torah, thus creating personal, family and social life which reflected the divine holiness, love and justice, the people's confidence in Yahweh's presence and protection was justified. However, the reign of Solomon marked a change, in which patterns of ruling authority, economic activity, and what might be called 'defence policy', were imported from other nations and led to the transformation of the city of Jerusalem and its temple. Brueggemann describes Solomon's reign as involving the 'uncritical embrace of anticovenantal urbanism', seen in his expansive building projects, the growth of international trade, the formation of a standing army, the imposition of forced labour and the erosion of Israel's sexual ethics (Brueggemann 2007: 23). The fears of the old prophet, Samuel, proved to be entirely justified as the changes initiated in the reign of Solomon bore bitter fruit in later years. Under the kings the *language* of devotion and worship remained in place and religious practice persisted, and even underwent significant revivals, but the power of the royal state increased, progressively eroding the vision of a community and a city that might offer the world an alternative social model. By the eighth century, as John Bright says, 'though Yahwism remained the national religion, with lip service given to Yahweh's covenant, covenant law had in practice come to mean little' (Bright 1981: 260).

In this context, the role of the earliest prophets at the start of the 'timeline' we have described above, was to *confront* king and people with a message of warning and judgment. Their courage in denouncing apostasy, challenging the privileged and powerful with vivid reminders of Yahweh's holiness and wrath, and exposing the hypocrisy and emptiness of urban forms of religion which had become mere ideology, led them into inevitable tension and conflict. The prophets refused to accept the official propaganda which concealed 'inconvenient truths' beneath inanely optimistic assessments of national life. They refused to deny or conceal the dysfunctional nature of the city and gave public voice to the pain and grief of the victims of the royal system. When the psalmists' celebration of Jerusalem as the 'city of God' turned into a religious ideology which screened out of consciousness the *conditional* demands of the covenant relationship and viewed the city as unassailable on account of God's protection, the prophets understood that their message would need to confront an urban religion which now sanctified a corrupt and evil society and would lead inexorably to *the death of the city*.

This critique of urban religion can be heard in the message of Amos, the first of Israel's classical prophets, who reports God as saying,

I hate, I despise your religious feasts;
   I cannot stand your assemblies.
Even though you bring me burnt offerings and grain offerings,
   I will not accept them.
Though you bring choice fellowship offerings,
   I will have no regard for them (Amos 5:21–22).

The context here seems to be one in which urban shrines are full of joyful worshippers who celebrate their faith with rousing songs and high quality music (5:23), but this empty triumphalism is dismissed because it fails to deliver a way of 'life together' that reveals a true knowledge of Israel's God. Thus Amos's great cry: 'But let justice roll on like a river, righteousness like a never-failing stream!' (5:24).

This prophetic critique of popular urban religion, including direct confrontation with those religious professionals who serviced it, is characteristic of all the classical prophets. Isaiah dares to address the powerful in Jerusalem as 'rulers of Sodom', and the population as 'people of Gomorrah', dismissing temple worship as a mere 'trampling of my courts' to meet in 'evil assemblies'. The sea of hands lifted up in corporate prayer is shockingly described as 'full of blood' and Yahweh is said to turn his face away from such worship, refusing even to listen to the intercessions endlessly offered by the crowds thronging the temple (Isa. 1:10–15). This is powerful and disturbing language, but the further we move down the timeline toward the catastrophe of the destruction of the city, the bolder and more strident the prophetic critique of urban religion becomes. The culmination of this strand of the tradition is reached with the extraordinary 'Temple Sermon' of Jeremiah in which, standing at the very heart what constituted 'sacred space' in Jerusalem, he declared the temple liturgy to involve 'deceptive words', dared to name this shrine as 'a robber's cave', and challenged the ideology that both it and the city were inviolable by announcing the imminent destruction of both.

> If you really change your ways and your actions and deal with each other justly, if you do not oppress the alien, the fatherless or the widow and do not shed innocent blood in this place, and if you do not follow other gods to your own harm, then I will let you live in this place, in the land I gave to your forefathers for ever and ever. But look, you are trusting in deceptive words that are worthless (Jer. 7:5–8).

At the conclusion of this most courageous of prophecies the preacher was faced by an angry lynch-mob demanding his immediate execution for having 'prophesied against this city' (26:7–11).

Here is a direct clash between the representative of the prophetic tradition, which reaches back into the foundational sources of Israel's existence in the shape of the revelation of Yahweh granted to Moses, and the guardians of a form of state power and religion which has turned into an ideology justifying the way things are. In a clash of this nature the preacher comes to be viewed not simply as a rather odd person whose views can easily be dismissed as cranky, but as a dangerous subversive whose language poses a dire threat to the status quo. He is, in fact, a *traitor*. Jeremiah is only too well aware of this and in some of the most pathos-filled texts in the Bible, laments the calling God has laid upon him:

> O Lord, you deceived me, and I was deceived;
>   you overpowered me and prevailed.
> I am ridiculed all day long;
>   everyone mocks me.
> Whenever I speak, I cry out
>   proclaiming violence and destruction.
> So the word of the Lord has brought me
>   insult and reproach all day long (Jer. 20:7–8).

We must pause to ask how these texts might relate to the nature of urban ministry in the world we have described in the first part of this book, in which, according to United Nations' estimates, 940 million people currently live in urban squalor, and one person in every three will be a slum dweller within thirty years. Does contemporary urban religion offer what Karl Marx described as 'false comfort' to the oppressed, while concealing from Christians their own involvement in a world system which results in such immense human suffering? We should be under no illusions about this; the potential cost of prophetic preaching is likely to be no less painful for us than for Israel's classical prophets because when religion ceases to be perceived as an innocuous, private concern and begins to probe the underlying myths, ideologies and structures of 'the world', it is likely to be seen as a subversive force and its advocates may attract the interest of state security forces. Walter Brueggemann contrasts the 'royal consciousness' associated with Solomon and his successors, with 'prophetic criticizing' and concludes:

> We also are children of the royal consciousness. All of us, in one way or another, have deep commitments to it. So the first question is: How can we have enough freedom to imagine and articulate a real historical newness in our situation? . . . We need to ask if our consciousness and imagination have been so assaulted and co-opted by the royal consciousness that we have been robbed of the courage and power to think an alternative thought. . . . It is the vocation of the prophet to keep alive the ministry of imagination, to keep on conjuring and proposing alternative futures to the single one the king wants to urge as the only thinkable one (Brueggemann 1978: 44–45).

Love in the city

One of the most obvious and striking contrasts between the contemporary debates concerning urban life which we have described in the earlier chapters of this book and the prophetic perspective found in the Bible is that the latter never separates social, political or economic issues from an even more fundamental concern – that of *love for God*. The calling of Israel to be a community characterized by the practice of justice and equality is indissolubly connected to her sense of being a redeemed people, delivered from oppression and bondage and liberated to love and serve Yahweh. As Deuteronomy so dramatically expresses it, an enslaved and landless people had been 'brought out of the iron-smelting furnace' of Egypt to be God's own inheritance among the nations (Deut. 4:20). However, the same book makes it clear that the continuing relationship between God and this freed people depended upon their knowledge of his great love for them, because without this the motivation for obedience to the requirements of the Torah would be replaced by a dead legalism, rendering Israel powerless to resist the temptations posed by the more normal 'way of the world'. It is emphasized again and again that God's mighty acts to bring about Israel's salvation, delivering them from death and opening up a path to life, were driven by his unconditional love, so that the bond between Yahweh and Israel is called a 'covenant of love' (Deut. 7:9). The continuing knowledge of God's love for them, the return of that love in heartfelt worship, devotion and obedience, and what might be called the 'overflow' of the love of God in their social life and family relationships, all of this is embedded within Israel's core confession of faith which summons the people to 'Love the LORD your God with all your heart and with all your soul and with all your strength' (Deut. 6:5). As Martin Buber wrote,

> Because they love Him with all their heart and with all their soul, they do what they do for Him with all their heart and with all their soul (Deuteronomy 26:16). Moreover the love between a man and his neighbor flows from the love of God (Buber 1949: 161).

Not surprisingly, the pre-exilic prophets have much to say about the erosion and loss of Israel's love for Yahweh and they regard this as the source of the urban pathologies which are the harbingers of the death of the city. The descent into lifeless legalism, anticipated in Deuteronomy, becomes a reality when God complains of urban worshippers who 'come near me with their mouth and honour me with their lips, but their hearts are far from me' and their religion is 'made up only of rules taught by men' (Isa. 29:13). Empty and

spiritless religion of this kind leaves the city exposed to a host of evils, and the
failure to love God from the heart leads to various forms of spiritual adultery
in which other gods – far less ethically demanding, and tolerant of practices
which run directly counter to Yahweh's concern with social justice and mercy
– become tolerated and followed within Jerusalem. In a remarkable text, Isaiah
has the inhabitants of the city confessing to Yahweh that 'other lords besides
you have ruled over us', and as a result, 'We have not brought salvation to the
earth; we have not given birth to the people of the world' (26:13–18).

The loss of the knowledge of the love of Yahweh results not only in forms
of spiritual adultery, but has profound consequences for the stability of marriage and family life and brings about a change in the understanding and practice of human sexuality. Jeremiah reflects these changes when he describes
Israel as behaving like 'a prostitute with many lovers' and repeatedly claims
that the citizens of Jerusalem had so far abandoned the ethics of the covenant that *nothing causes them to blush* (Jer. 3:3; 6:15; 8:12). Walter Brueggemann
trenchantly observes that when a society reaches a point at which it 'loses its
capacity to blush, it indicates that all norms outside of self-interest have collapsed' (Brueggemann 1987: 62).

If then the Hebrew prophets know all about 'sex in the city', nowhere is
the depth of social disorder and the personal tragedy that can result from it
described with greater clarity and pathos than in the book of Hosea. The syncretistic form of religion practiced in Jerusalem in his time involved a formal
confession of faith in Yahweh combined with rituals based on fertility cults
involving sacred prostitution. This separation of sex from love and its elevation into a form of the sacred resulted in the collapse of normative ethics,
as the loss of faithfulness led to the abolition of 'all bounds' (Hos. 4:1–3).
Prostitution and adultery came to be accepted as normal behaviour, but
Yahweh clearly distinguishes between those who are the victims of a sexual-
ized culture and those who promote it for their own evil ends:

> I will not punish your daughters
>   when they turn to prostitution
> nor your daughters-in-law
>   when they commit adultery,
> because the men themselves consort with harlots
>   and sacrifice with temple prostitutes –
>   a people without understanding will come to ruin! (Hos. 4:14).

What makes the prophecy of Hosea unique is, first, the degree to which the
sexual chaos in Jerusalem impacted upon his own married and family life, and

second, the manner in which his tragic biography is seen to reflect the pain and anguish within the very being of God himself. There are considerable problems of interpretation in relation to the precise nature of the prophet's experience, but it seems clear that his wife, the mother of his three children, was unfaithful and left him in order to take a lover (3:1). Hosea is then asked to redeem his wife, to 'love her as the LORD loves the Israelites', so imitating in his own tragic, real-life situation, the character of the God he served. Israel's compromise with Baalism was an act of spiritual adultery which grieved the heart of God, yet such is the nature of his love that he cannot give this people up and declares his intention to 'allure' Israel, to 'speak tenderly to her', so that she returns to him and finds a new joy which enables her to 'sing as in the days of her youth' (2:14–15).

Commenting on the relevance of this prophecy in our contemporary, urbanized world, Terence Fretheim observes that 'the place of God in the life of the world has become increasingly problematic' because a God-of-the-gaps is crowded out of the few spaces that remain available to him in a highly technological culture. Meantime, the language used by Christians to describe God appears 'to be divorced from common human experience' and irrelevant to the true concerns of modern life; our traditional images of God 'seem to float above the maelstrom of actual life or are narrowly associated with one or another segment of society' (Fretheim 1984: 15–16). By contrast, consider the language which Hosea employs to describe Yahweh's reaction to the unfaithfulness of his covenant people:

> What can I do with you Ephraim?
>   What can I do with you Judah?
> Your love is like the morning mist,
>   like the early dew that disappears (Hos. 6:4).

Later, in one of the most lyrical passages in the Bible, God describes himself as like a father who taught his infant child to walk, and now, having been rejected by his beloved son, confesses an anguish that lies almost too deep for words: 'My heart is changed within me; all my compassion is aroused' (11:1–11). As Fretheim says, statements like these (which are paralleled by similar texts elsewhere) give us a glimpse into the very being of God, revealing a deity who is 'deeply wounded' by the broken relationship:

> God's suffering is not such that he is overwhelmed by the experience; his emotions do not get out of control or lead to incapacitation. . . . God is able to absorb all the arrows of outrageous fortune that pierce him through and, instead of becoming

callous or removing himself from the line of fire, still seeks to bring about a future which is good for those who inflict the wounds. . . . God's steadfast love endures forever (Fretheim 1984: 124).

The tragic experience of Hosea demonstrates in the most deeply moving way what happens to life in the city when a community loses contact with the ultimate source of love, turns sex into a false sacred, and abandons moral and ethical norms beyond a concern for self-interest and self-fulfilment. The relevance of this to the urban world of the twenty-first century can be seen in Zygmunt Bauman's discussion of what he calls the 'liquid love' that characterizes a culture in which people 'yearn for the security of togetherness' while resisting all relationships involving faithfulness or permanence, since these 'would bring burdens and cause strains they neither feel able or willing to bear' (Bauman 2003: viii). As a sociologist Bauman traces the source of this dilemma to the shifts that have taken place under the impact of what he describes as 'negative globalization'; the Bible, while in no way ignoring the cultural and sociological forces so brilliantly analyzed in Bauman's work, insists on a more radical explanation, warning us that a city without love will be a city of grief and pain, and that the recovery of loving relationships between human persons will be the outcome of a rediscovery of the ultimate source of all true love in the One whom Hosea reports as saying: 'I will show my love to the one I called "Not my loved one" . . . and they will say "You are my God"' (2:23).

Lament for the city

The further we move down the timeline of Israel's pre-exilic history, the darker the prophetic messages become and the greater is their certainty that the catastrophe of the loss of Zion is imminent. Isaiah of Jerusalem announces the judgment of Yahweh on the rebellious city from the very beginning of his ministry in what scholars have called the 'Great Assize' in chapter 1. In the oracles that follow, the critique of city is, in Brueggemann's words, 'harsh and relentless because it exposes the systemic self-deception of the royal-temple establishment' (Brueggemann 1987: 33). Those who held power within the city are said to have 'entered into a covenant with death' as the result of which they are supremely confident that Jerusalem will be spared when 'an overwhelming scourge sweeps by'. They believe themselves to be untouchable by disaster or invasion because, having rejected the prophet's message of doom as ridiculously pessimistic, they are confident that their own

politics and military strategies can secure peace and safety. God's message
through Isaiah is that this covenant with death will offer no protection and
when the 'overwhelming scourge sweeps by' it will result in comprehensive
destruction and loss (Isa. 28:14–19).

However, despite the insistent warning of judgment and the evident loneliness of Isaiah (see 8:16–17), it is clear that his preaching was underpinned by a
deep love for the city of Jerusalem and a hope that his warnings might yet be
heeded and the city saved from destruction. If that proved not to be the case,
Isaiah still believed that, once purged of its evils through God's 'strange work'
of judgment (28:21), Jerusalem would become the source of light and healing
for all the nations. In John Bright's words, Isaiah saw 'the judgement that was
coming as a chastisement . . . not a total destruction', so that it would 'purify
and refine, and make Jerusalem once again the city God has intended it to be'
(Bright 1976: 105).

When, a century later, we arrive at the ministry of Jeremiah, no such hope
for the city of Jerusalem remains and, like his younger contemporary, Ezekiel,
it is his painful and costly task to announce, 'The end has come! The end has
come!' (Ezek. 7:1–9). Walter Brueggemann writes that Jeremiah 'knew long
before the others that the end was coming and that God had had enough of
indifferent affluence, cynical oppression, and presumptive religion'. He understood that God's own freedom 'had been so grossly violated . . . that death was
at the door and would not pass over' (Brueggemann 1978: 51). The pain and
deep anguish of the prophet was heightened by the fact that he had witnessed
what appeared to be a sincere and genuine attempt to bring about repentance within Jerusalem. As the Babylonian empire began to expand across
the ancient world, capturing the city of Nineveh in 612 BC and defeating the
Assyrians at Haran in 609 BC, Jerusalem had witnessed a movement of reform
designed to reshape the religious, political and social life of the city in line with
the Torah. In 621 BC, as work to refurbish the temple was already underway,
the 'Book of the Law', neglected, forgotten and eventually lost, was dramatically rediscovered and read in the hearing of King Josiah (2 Kgs 22:8–13). The
dissonance between what was read (which is believed to have been part of
the 'urban charter' we know as Deuteronomy) and both the royal ideology
that had come to dominate Jerusalem, and the actual practice of religious and
social life within the city, was immediately obvious. As John Bright puts it, the
ethical demands of the Torah and the conditional nature of the covenant convinced Josiah that the nation existed in a 'fool's paradise', so that the demands
of the Mosaic Law came to him as 'the veritable thunderclap of conscience,
like the trumpet announcing the Last Day' (Bright 1976: 141–142). The result
was a movement of reformation which Jeremiah, despite his recognition of

the inadequacy of the changes, was to praise when later confronting Josiah's son over his complete failure to follow his father's example:

> 'Does it make you a king
>   to have more and more cedar?
> Did not your father have food and drink?
>   He did what as right and just,
>   so all went well with him.
> He defended the cause of the poor and needy,
>   and so all went well.
> Is this not what it means to know me?'
>   declares the LORD (Jer. 22:15–16).

This conflict with the palace was paralleled, as we have already seen, by Jeremiah's confrontation with the religious leaders in the temple, as the result of which he trod a pathway of almost unbearable isolation, loneliness and danger. Unable to marry (16:1–4), rejected and betrayed by his own family circle (12:6), and the object of suspicion and hatred by practically the entire population (15:10), this weeping prophet expressed his deep anguish with a candour and boldness that is unique within the biblical narratives. In a series of agonizing prayers that scholars have sometimes described as 'Jeremiah's Confessions', he gave vent to the personal crisis that was the consequence of his divine commission and boldly questioned whether his belief in the justice of God could be squared with the apparent confusion, suffering and violence of the chaotic times through which he lived (12:1–2). Aware that people in his own home town were plotting to kill him and so silence the voice of prophecy which caused them so much embarrassment and shame, Jeremiah described himself as 'like a gentle lamb led to the slaughter' (11:19).

We can identify three sources of the urban laments of the prophet Jeremiah. First, his *personality* is such that he is unable to dissemble; he cannot disguise his inner conflict with audible expressions of faith or hope which might have reduced the hostility directed toward him, but would have rung hollow in his own ears as well as before God. In other words, when he cries out, 'Oh, my anguish, my anguish! . . . Oh, the agony of my heart!' (4:19), he is being true to himself and refreshingly honest before God. Second, Jeremiah's message concerning the judgment and destruction of Jerusalem and its people was not delivered with the mechanical efficiency of an automaton, but came through a person of flesh and blood who knew profound emotions and was *deeply disturbed by the content of his own message.* Here is no dogmatic preacher who declaims the death of the city in a detached manner that exposes a self-righteous satisfaction within his own soul; on the contrary, Jeremiah knows the true nature of the human suffering that lies ahead and cries out longingly:

> O my Comforter in sorrow,
>   my heart is faint within me.
> Listen to the cry of my people
>   from a land far away:
> 'Is the LORD not in Zion?
>   Is her king no longer there?' (Jer. 8:18).

And third, his grief was related to the *negative reception given to his message,* so that he is left almost totally isolated and outside the prevailing consensus, which remained absurdly optimistic concerning the prospects for Jerusalem. The prophet is thus left facing a dilemma: to declare what he *knows* to be true, and face inevitable rejection, hostility and derision, or to keep silent and avoid conflict and pain, but at the terrible price of the loss of his integrity and self-esteem. It is a mark of Jeremiah's authenticity as a prophet that, in fact, there is *no choice*:

> But if I say, 'I will not mention him
>   or speak any more in his name,'
> his word is in my heart like a fire,
>   a fire shut up in my bones.
> I am weary of holding it in;
>   indeed, I cannot (20:9).

We cannot here describe the details of this prophet's biography, except to say that he lived through the terrible events of the siege and destruction of the city and is last heard of as an exile in Egypt where, as an old man, he continued to faithfully deliver the prophetic word of God. However, Jeremiah's name is traditionally associated with the biblical book of Lamentations which, from its opening words, laments the death of the city: 'How deserted lies the city, once so full of people! How like a widow is she, who once was great among the nations!' (Lam. 1:1). Whether or not the prophet wrote any of these poems, they express the same sense of desolation and confusion in the form of the utterly honest cries to heaven that we have seen to be characteristic of Jeremiah himself. In five poems composed after the destruction of the city, deeply traumatized survivors express their pain and struggle to discover a way forward when all grounds for hope have been lost. There is no word of prophecy in this book; the heavens remain silent and it appears as though the cries of the desolate and broken people go unheard (notwithstanding the light which breaks in 3:21–26, a passage often grotesquely wrenched from its context in modern worship). In a beautifully written study of this book, Kathleen O'Connor describes it as peering into the wounds of the suffering world and raising 'fierce questions about God'. She continues,

> For survivors of civil wars, destroyed cities and genocides, for refugees, and for those who subsist in famine and destitute poverty, the poetry mirrors reality with frightening exactitude. When, like me, readers live in relative safety and prosperity, Lamentations calls forth loss and pain more narrowly, personally and indirectly. Yet even in the prosperous United States there are normal losses to lament, deaths, disappointments, and hidden depression with which to contend. . . . Behind the wealth and power of the United States hide despair and a violent culture of denial that drains our humanity. For our sake and for the sake of the world over which we try callously to preside, these things demand lamentation (O'Connor 2002: 4–5).

As I write this I have before me a leaflet which I took from a woman at a roadside stall in the city of Jos in Nigeria. It was issued by three womens' groups, 'Mothers in Nigeria Prayer Network', 'Widows Outreach, Jos' and the Plateau State chapter of a movement called 'Wailing Women', and it contains a call to a day of prayer in Jos. The invitation is accompanied by a verse from Jeremiah which summons the women of Jerusalem to 'teach your daughters how to wail; teach one another a lament' (Jer. 9:20–21). The context in which I picked up this piece of paper was one in which there had been a fresh eruption of inter-tribal and inter-religious violence in Jos, the latest in a tragic series of such urban conflicts resulting in the deaths of hundreds of people, including many women and children. The homes of thousands of poor people had been torched and pathetic groups of refugees had made their way to safety, seeking shelter among coreligionists as the lines of division between people of different faiths hardened and solidified across a city which once boasted that it was 'The Home of Peace and Tourism'. In the midst of all of this were women who recognized that mere talk would achieve little to bring about healing, and that what was needed were *tears* and *wailing,* so that the grief and despair of those who had suffered so much might find expression and be heard in public. These women had recognized a crucial aspect of the Bible's approach to their own broken urban society, but they also offered an example to Christians in the privileged places of the northern hemisphere, where urban worship is so often celebratory and no space is left for lamentation. As a result, the broken-hearted are left in a state of denial and numbness, needing to smile even though this involves deception concerning the reality of their condition. By contrast, tears 'can give watery birth to hope', washing out 'space once occupied by despair, fury, or sorrow, and in that space hope can emerge uninvited' (O'Connor 2002: 130). And, as the psalmist knew so well, God honours tears and is even said to collect and preserve them as something precious to him (Ps. 56:8).

Hope for an urban world

From the time that Amos burst on the scene around 750 BC down to the terrible events we have described above, to which the aged prophet Jeremiah was a witness, the dominant note heard from all Israel's prophets was one of criticism, exposing a reality denied and covered up by those holding power, and warning of inevitable disaster in the absence of deep and lasting transformation. This is not to suggest that the pre-exilic prophets were without hope, far from it, since, as we have already seen, Isaiah anticipated a time when Jerusalem would be restored and would fulfil its calling to be a light to the nations. The Great Assize of chapter 1, in which the nation is charged with apostasy and declared to be guilty, nonetheless contains a clear promise of recovery beyond the inevitable judgment: '*Afterwards* you will be called the City of Righteousness, the Faithful City' (Isa. 1:26). Thus, hope was never entirely absent even when the dominant theme involved critical exposure and warning. Brueggemann describes how the message of the prophets, notwithstanding the contrasting emphases of individuals according to their contexts, when taken as a whole, combines lament and doxology:

> Jeremiah alone leaves faith in death where God finally will not stay. And Second Isaiah alone leads us to imagine that there is comfort without tears and tearing. Clearly, only those who anguish will sing new songs. Without anguish the new song is likely to be strident and just more royal fakery (Brueggemann 1978: 79).

The mention of 'Second Isaiah' directs us to the great book of comfort which begins the second half of the canonical book of Isaiah (40 – 55). Here a new prophetic voice is heard, *one which moves us across and beyond the great abyss of the death of Jerusalem and the exile of its survivors, and in a daring and wonderful act of inspired imagination describes the utterly 'new thing' that Yahweh is about to do in the world*. The audience addressed by this prophecy was facing a desperate crisis of faith. The impact of the death of a city extends well beyond the experience of the immediate survivors, leaving their children and subsequent generations scarred by the collective memory of the terror, suffering and humiliation endured by their forefathers. The anguished question of the first exiles as they sat weeping beside the rivers of Babylon – 'How can we sing the songs of the LORD while in a foreign land?' (Ps. 137:4) – was repeated by their children, so that the Psalms of Lament and the desperately honest account of the holocaust contained in Lamentations, came to shape the piety and worship of the exiled community. With memories of the rape and destruction of their city seared into their collective memory and the problems of practicing their faith in a strange and alien land, these people were tempted to feel that the God who seemed to have gone missing in 587 BC had, in fact, never returned. The closing cry of Lamentations in which the poet asked Yahweh, 'Why do you always forget us? Why do you forsake us so long?' (Lam. 5:20), was *still* being asked in Babylon by a later generation who, Second Isaiah reports, continued to assert, 'The LORD has forsaken me, the LORD has forgotten me' (Isa. 49:14; 40:27).

This represented the most serious crisis ever to confront the faith of biblical Israel and it demanded a prophetic imagination capable of bringing real comfort to the mourners and of articulating a new and enlarged vision of what Yahweh was doing in the historical movements of the time. To express this differently, there was an urgent need for a theology which moved beyond the framework of old Jerusalem and demonstrated the ways in which Yahweh, the God of both Israel and the nations, was working through the upheavals of the times to establish 'justice on earth' and bring even the most distant islands to place their hope in him (Isa. 42:4). So far as the healing of the deep wounds of the exiles was concerned, the opening announcement, 'Comfort, comfort my people', and the command to 'speak tenderly' and declare that the judgment is over (Isa. 40:1–2), would seem to be a direct response to the endlessly repeated cry of Lamentations that there was 'none to comfort . . . no one to help . . . no one to restore my spirit' (Lam. 1:2, 7, 9, 16, 17, 21). Kathleen O'Connor observes that while this lament 'contains no words of comfort and seems to dismiss its very possibility', in Isaiah 40 'God is present, vocal and repentant', becoming 'the comforter of Zion and her exiled children' (O'Connor 2002: 140). It is worth noting the parallel between the *tone* of the word of God to the exiles and a statement which the aged Jeremiah reports the Lord as making to survivors of the Babylonian invasion amid the ruins of the Jerusalem: 'I am grieved over the disaster I have inflicted on you' (Jer. 42:10).

The power of these texts to bring comfort, healing and renewed hope to people who have endured the death of their cities in modern times, people who are victims of *urbicide*, is undiminished. Marshall Berman, who we heard in chapter 4 lamenting the destruction of his community to make way for the building of the Cross-Bronx Expressway in New York in 1953, has testified to the ability of the biblical narratives to penetrate 'deeply into reality' and bring fresh hope to people displaced and marginalized as their familiar urban fabric was torn apart. Berman records that during his childhood hundreds of thousands of people were displaced and made homeless in areas like the South Bronx, Harlem, and elsewhere in East New York, and were left with an aching hole in their lives and a feeling that they would need 'to create the world again'. Berman himself was deeply affected by this destruction and felt that as the streets of his childhood disappeared it was as though his own flesh was being 'ripped away' (Berman 2010: 124). However, the books of Jeremiah and Lamentations, together with passages from the Psalms and the prophets, spoke into this situation, treating the death of the city, not in Greek fashion, as part of cosmic fate, but as 'part of an ongoing historical process that will eventually lead to renewal and progress'. Noting Jeremiah's remarkable instruction to the exiles to pray for the city of Babylon, and to seek its welfare (29:7), Berman concludes,

> It is only through losing our own city that we can find the right way to live in the city. The prophets' searing indictment of the city's past is meant to empower the people to transform the city's future. If we can learn why we were overcome yesterday, we will overcome tomorrow (ibid.: 132).

The promise of *shalom*

Two central themes that run through the Old Testament sustained the hope of the prophets in times of apostasy and loss and provided the foundation for a new theology of hope after the abyss of the destruction of Zion. The first of these themes relates to *the promise of God's* shalom. Walter Brueggemann writes that this term signifies the 'central vision of world history in the Bible' in which 'all of creation is one, every creature in community with every other, living in harmony and security toward the joy and well-being of every other creature' (Brueggemann 1982b: 15). If this is the case then the loss of *shalom* must result not only in the fragmentation of human society, but in the alienation of people from the rest of creation, and in a way of life which places the natural world under threat of destruction. In the twenty-first century we have come to recognize what is called the 'ecological footprint' of the city, which indicates the physical area affected by the existence of a particular city. Clearly, in the urban world we have described in the first part of this book the impact of urbanization on a global scale is placing unbearable strains upon the earth's resources, with the result that the issue of sustainability has become a major concern in urban studies. However, the Hebrew prophets already knew that when the covenant with Yahweh was broken and the city came to be built on greed and heartless accumulation, this would result in environmental degradation as the earth became barren and exhausted, destroyed beneath the crushing weight of the insatiable appetites of its inhabitants. In Isaiah's words,

> The earth dries up and withers,
>> the world languishes and withers,
>> the exalted of the earth languish.
> The earth is defiled by its people;
>> they have disobeyed the laws,
> violated the statutes
>> and broken the everlasting covenant.
> *Therefore* a curse consumes the earth;
>> its people must bear their guilt (Isa. 24:4–5, emphasis added).

The striking thing about this text is that it anticipates a crisis that is universal; no longer is the focus restricted to Jerusalem, but the threat posed by a way of life which ignores the values fundamental to all human well-being now extends to the whole world and all of its peoples. Cities everywhere will be left in ruins as 'all gaiety is banished from the earth' because the social, economic and ecological collapse which the prophet envisages as the consequence of the violation of the 'everlasting covenant' will leave no part of the earth unaffected: 'So it will be on the earth and among the nations' (24:13).

This awareness of the interconnectedness of all created beings surfaces repeatedly in the prophetic writings. Jeremiah has an apocalyptic vision of the total collapse of the natural world, which becomes emptied of both its human and animal populations as cities lie in ruins and previously fertile land is turned into deserts (Jer. 4:23–26). Hosea makes a direct connection between the loss of faithfulness and love and the failure to acknowledge God within the city, and the descent into social chaos and ecological devastation:

> Because of this the land mourns,
>> and all who live in it waste away;
> the beasts of the field and the birds of the air
>> and the fish of the sea are dying (Hos. 4:3).

Clearly, we need to bear in mind Richard Bauckham's warning concerning the mistake of making a direct application of these texts to our very different world today, but we may ask whether, as the planet warms, sea levels rise, and scientists report that 1 in 4 of all flowering plants, 1 in 5 of all mammals, and 1 in 8 of all birds face an 'immediate threat' of extinction, are we now rediscovering the terrifying forces of nature and the threat they pose to our urban civilization (Jowit 2010: 5)? There is a growing realization today that the dangers confronting us have their roots in a failure to allow normative ethics to underpin and control economic development, or in the language of Isaiah, that we have broken the 'everlasting covenant' with the Creator. During the Copenhagen conference on global warming in 2009, journalist Madeleine Bunting traced a connection between the failure to curb 'the rapacious corporate drive to exploit natural resources, driven by the west's insatiable appetite for economic growth', and a world in which on every continent 'an environmental catastrophe is brewing that makes you want to weep'. The ultimate source of the unfolding tragedy, she suggested, was the 'decade of hubris' within a civilization 'which has been destroying the life systems on which human well being depends' (Bunting 2009: 25). In a not dissimilar situation, Isaiah predicted that previously strong, ruthless and arrogant nations would come to their senses, that 'the shroud that enfolds all peoples' would be destroyed as a prelude to a new world of *shalom* in which Yahweh would 'wipe away the tears from all faces' and 'remove the disgrace of his people from all the earth' (Isa. 25:6–8).

It is this great vision of a world transformed, of an age of God's *shalom*, which fills the pages of Second Isaiah, offering the exiles new hope both with regard to what Yahweh is doing through the tangled web of history, and in respect of their own place within this unfolding story as aliens who, not having forgotten their unique faith and testimony, can now bear witness to the liberating God in a strange land. This hope of a new age of universal blessing can be glimpsed scattered throughout the earlier prophecies of Isaiah, so that the dominant theme of judgment on the city is interspersed in chapters 1 – 39 with promises of a different future. Indeed, even in the Great Assize in the opening chapter, Isaiah anticipates that *afterwards*, beyond the coming judgment, the city will be transformed so as to merit the titles, 'the City of Righteousness, the Faithful City' (1:26). Furthermore, between this chapter and a description of empirical Jerusalem in which the city is said to be 'full of superstitions . . . full of silver and gold . . . full of horses [and] chariots . . . full of idols' (2:6–8), we discover one of the great visions of the Bible in which it is said that Yahweh will 'judge between the nations', bringing healing and reconciliation on a scale that will make war, or even preparation for it, redundant (2:1–4). It is this radiant vision of God's *shalom* which defines reality for the prophet, so that when the dream fades and he returns to the existing, mundane situation, he urges his disciples to 'walk in the light of the LORD' (2:5). That light, streaming back from God's promised future, illumines the darkness of the present, energizes the prophet and his circle to live by the values of the kingdom of God, and enables them to resist the destructive way of life which has come to be regarded as normal within Jerusalem.

Two generations later, when Zion had been devastated, the hope of the coming of the age of *shalom* reappeared and was elaborated in a wonderful outpouring of inspired poetry. The canonical book of Isaiah has been described as the great urban document of the Bible, and this poetry, including the later vision of a new heavens and new earth in 65:17–25, seems to have a direct and intended connection to Isaiah's hopes in the earliest chapters of the book. *Exiled Israel now exists in the 'afterwards' of which Isaiah had spoken all those years ago in Jerusalem and, with the old supports of faith stripped away, is in a position to discover Yahweh's wonderful newness.* The critique of Jerusalem, which had been the burden of Isaiah's preaching, was needed no longer; that message had been tragically vindicated by history, so that the priority now was the assurance that Yahweh's ultimate purpose lay *through and beyond judgment*. A people humbled, healed and renewed might now become Yahweh's witnesses among the nations, discovering new energies with which to begin 'rebuilding the ancient ruins' and renewing the 'ruined cities' (61:4). So great would be the transformation in the eschatological city that the sound of weeping would never be heard in it again, no infant would die prematurely, and an old person who lives to a hundred 'will be thought a mere youth' (65:20). The prophet thus highlights the peace and security of human persons who, in the present, are most vulnerable in an urban context: the baby and the child, so dependent and open to abuse, and the elderly, frail and weak, often forgotten and alone; these persons are singled out with the promise that they will be safe and cherished in the city of God. Nor is this blessed state limited to biblical Israel: people from all nations will become brothers (66:20) and 'all mankind' will join in the worship of God and rejoice in his glory (66:18, 23). The natural world, 'red in tooth and claw', will be transformed so that species no longer prey on each other but eat together and have their share in God's great *shalom* (65:25).

The cities of the world

The second foundational theme which underpins the prophetic hope concerns *the divine purpose for the nations of the world* – a topic which we discussed at the start of this chapter with regard to the Table of Nations in Genesis 10. That unique record of all known peoples on earth functions as a kind of ancient atlas for the biblical writers and its influence can be detected at many points throughout the Old Testament. James Scott has tracked this tradition through the Bible and finds explicit use of the Table of Nations in 1 Chronicles 1 – 2, Ezekiel 38 – 39, Daniel, with its repeated mention of 'peoples, nations and men of every language' (3:4, 7, 29; 4:1; 6:25; 7:14), and Isaiah, where the final vision of the glory of God displayed 'among the nations' and 'to the distant islands' (Isa. 66:19) 'clearly reflects the Table-of-Nations tradition' (Scott 1995: 10–13). Israel's worship is suffused with an awareness of the nations listed in Genesis 10, resulting in both a sense of her own calling in relation to them, and in the insistence that they are themselves directly answerable to 'the God of the whole earth'. The divine covenant with Israel in no sense contradicts or limits Yahweh's sovereignty, either in grace or in judgment, so that the psalmists often confess that 'the earth is the LORD's . . . the world, and all who live in it' (Ps. 24:1; see 8:1; 9:8, 19; 19:4; 22:27–28; 46:10, etc.). God's eyes are said to 'watch the nations' (Ps. 66:7) and the prayers of Israel are offered not merely for themselves, but for all the peoples, that they too may 'be glad and sing for joy', knowing that God rules all peoples justly and guides 'the nations of the earth' (Ps. 67:4–5). In Psalm 87 the influence of the Table-of-Nations tradition is especially clear in the sensational announcement that Egypt, Babylon, Philistia, Tyre and Ethiopia will be recorded among the peoples that know Yahweh and that these converted nations will be written 'in the register of the peoples' (87:4–6).

The significance of this in relation to urban theology is that, as we have seen, the Table of Nations makes explicit mention not only of the peoples, *but of their cities.* If, as Brueggemann expresses it, Genesis 10 offers 'an unparalleled ecumenical vision of human reality' which affirms that 'all nations derive their historical existence from the life-giving power of God and are called to be responsive to him' (Brueggemann 1982a: 93), then this revelation must also give shape to the prophetic response to the great cities of the Fertile Crescent and beyond. We cannot therefore be surprised to discover the prophets devoting chapter after chapter to those cities, especially Nineveh, Babylon, Damascus and Tyre.

Given that Israel's history unfolded against the background of the rise and fall of the great urban empires, and that she suffered continually as the result of their expansionism and violence, the oracles of the prophets are frequently *against* these cities. The judgment of God which the prophets announce as coming upon Nineveh or Babylon is related to particular features characteristic of all of them. First, they are denounced for their excessive use of violence against the peoples of the world and the oppressive nature of their rule. Isaiah anticipates Jewish exiles taking up a taunt song against the empire that has enslaved and abused them in which they celebrate the end of the oppressive nation which 'in anger struck down peoples with unceasing blows' and was guilty of 'relentless aggression' (Isa. 14:3–6). Elsewhere, Nahum anticipates the destruction of the city of Nineveh, which he calls 'the city of blood, full of lies, full of plunder, never without victims!' (Nah. 3:1). The prophet predicts that the collapse of this city will result in worldwide jubilation:

> Everyone who hears the news about you
>   claps his hands at your fall,
> for who has not felt
>   your endless cruelty? (Nah. 3:19)

Second, the prophets trace a connection between this use of violence and the systems of trade which operated within the empires, resulting in great wealth and luxury for the powerful urban elite, but in economic devastation for many, especially the weak and marginalized. Perhaps the most remarkable of all the biblical prophecies directed toward the cities of the world is Ezekiel's lament for the port of Tyre and the prediction that it will 'come to a horrible end' (Ezek. 28:19). It will be recalled that the king of Tyre supplied David with materials for the construction of the royal city of Jerusalem and the historian informs us that Solomon gifted Tyre twenty towns in Galilee 'because Hiram had supplied him with all the cedar and pine and gold he wanted' in order to complete his lavish building projects (1 Kgs 9:11). Ezekiel describes in great detail the international reach of Tyre's trade which made it 'the merchant of peoples on many coasts', bringing 'wealth and wares' which 'enriched the kings of the earth' (Ezek. 27:33). However, while the prophet recognizes Tyre's 'great skill' in trading, he traces the city's moral and ethical collapse as ever-increasing prosperity eroded honest practice and human kindness within its walls. The love of profit resulted in sharp practices and the obsession with trading created an urban culture in which violence became endemic (28:16). This ethical decline was accompanied by a growing arrogance as the enormous revenues generated by international trade led to a terrible pride, expressed in the saying: 'I am a god; I sit on the throne of a god in the heart of the seas' (Ezek. 28:2).

This hubris is another characteristic of all the cities addressed by the prophets; defended by overwhelming force and with their ideologies embedded within culture by means of myths, rituals and festivals, they presented themselves as the outworking of the purpose of the gods and as offering to the world civilizations to which there were no possible alternatives. Thus,

Babylonian propaganda declared that the city would 'continue forever' making the clearly blasphemous claim, 'I am, there is none beside me' (Isa. 47:7–8).

However, while announcements of Yahweh's judgment on these cities are frequent and uncompromising, the prophets also display remarkable insight into the specific factors which led to the decline of particular cities and an unshakeable conviction that divine grace and mercy extends to the urban populations of the empires. For example, at the conclusion of a long series of oracles in which he predicts that Babylon's oppression of the nations will end, causing 'all lands to be at rest and at peace' and to 'break into singing' (Isa. 14:5–8), Isaiah astonishes his hearers with a dramatic shift of emphasis as he anticipates the liberation of the Egyptians and the conversion of the Assyrians. In an extraordinary act of prophetic imagination, he anticipates the building of a highway between these two nations at opposite ends of the Fertile Crescent which will facilitate two-way traffic as former enemies travel in the company of Israel to worship Yahweh together, and hear him utter the astonishing words: 'Blessed be Egypt my people, Assyria my handiwork, and Israel my inheritance' (19:18–25). Here is an anticipation of the *shalom* of God which, according the closing visions of this book will include 'your brothers from all the nations' as 'all mankind' are liberated to find joy in worshipping Yahweh (Isa. 66:20, 23).

There are similar promises to the nations elsewhere, but we should note that these are not simply predictions of events that remain far off in the 'last days', but they indicate present responsibility for the people of Israel, especially after the destruction of Jerusalem and the exile in Babylon. Jeremiah's letter addressed to the first group of exiles, with its clear instruction to 'build houses, settle down; plant gardens and eat what they produce', and the startling advice to seek 'the peace and prosperity' of Babylon and 'pray to the LORD for it' (Jer. 29:4–7), rests on the prophet's conviction that Israel's unique testimony can now be offered at the urban heart of the empire. Indeed, when the Babylonians later return to Jerusalem to make a complete end of the city, we discover Nebuchadnezzar instructing his commanders to find Jeremiah and offer him protection and freedom (39:11–12), and we may wonder whether the letter to the exiles had been intercepted and had begun the work of testimony at the very heart of Babylon? If this seems far-fetched, remember that the Old Testament records how Jewish exiles did precisely as Jeremiah had instructed; settling in Babylon, rising to positions of considerable influence in the royal court, and becoming the agents of the conversion of Nebuchadnezzar, whose arrogant pride was replaced with the personal confession of the 'King of heaven' whose 'ways are just', who is able to humble all who 'walk in pride' (Dan. 4:37). Here is urban regeneration indeed!

Before we leave the Old Testament, I want to return to the remarkable prophecy of Ezekiel concerning the city of Tyre. The prophet is explicitly asked to utter a *lament* for this city, which indicates that precisely the language of loss, despair and regret that we have examined in relation to the destruction of Jerusalem is also to be used in connection with the decline and fall of this city. In fact, Ezekiel's extraordinary language suggests that, like Jerusalem, this great trading city has *fallen* from a previous state in which its religious, social and economic life reflected something of God's intention for urban societies:

> You were the model of perfection,
>> full of wisdom and perfect in beauty.
> You were in Eden,
>> the garden of God . . .
> You were blameless in your ways
>> from the day you were created
>> till wickedness was found in you (Ezek. 28:12–15).

The wickedness which corrupted this city is related explicitly to 'widespread trade'; Tyre prospered to such a degree that its wealth corroded human and ethical values until, 'By your many sins and dishonest trade you desecrated your sanctuaries' (28:18). This is not an easy text to interpret, but the implication of the prophet's lament would seem to be that urban cultures can result in genuine human flourishing when guided by a sense of the sacred, even when that sacredness originates beyond the tradition of Jerusalem. This should not surprise us since both the grace of God at work in the wider world and the high value which the Bible places upon human beings, on their skills, creativity, and sense of justice, can result in the building of cities characterized by wisdom and justice. Yet the text is equally clear that such progress is extremely vulnerable, that sacredness can easily become corrupted, and that the cities of the world can quickly be overwhelmed by forces that result in decline, despair and death. As Donald Gowan puts it:

> The Hebrew view of man is thus profoundly humanistic; tremendously enthusiastic about the man God made and the gifts God gave him. But it is also profoundly theistic, for the Israelite was convinced there is one thing that man cannot do, and that is replace the God who made him. Further, he was convinced that all the ills of human life are to be traced to the effort to do just that, and he saw in the successes and failures of the great governments of his time the evidence for man's near divinity, man's instinct to make himself a god over his fellows, and the brutalizing effects of man-made 'kingdoms of god' (Gowan 1975: 91).

We may conclude then that cities reflect the true greatness of human beings, but they also display the disastrous consequences of human greed, selfishness and propensity to violence. Which is why, according to the Jonah story, God looks upon the most corrupt of urban societies and asks his worshippers: 'Should I not be concerned about that great city?' (Jon. 4:11).

7. THE BIBLE AND THE CITY: FROM JESUS TO JOHN OF PATMOS

Probably starting in the thirties [of the first century] Christ confessing communities emerged in the Mediterranean societies of the Roman Empire. And it is noteworthy that we basically find them only in urban regions (Stegemann & Stegemann 1999: 266).

In the previous chapter we have attempted to engage in a process of listening to the witness of the Old Testament on the subject of the city, paying careful attention to the varied historical, cultural and social contexts within which the story of Israel and the nations unfolded. One of the dominant features of that narrative concerns the manner in which biblical Israel's history took place 'always in the shadow of empire'. The phrase comes from Walter Brueggemann who describes the 'endless conflict' which Israel experienced as the outcome of the tension between her covenant faith and the shifting socio-cultural and religious environments of a world dominated by successive imperial powers. As we have seen, the relevance of this to the present study arises from the fact that those empires – Egypt, Assyria, Babylon and Persia – operated from impressive *urban* centres which were presented to the world as the pinnacles of human achievement and glory. The conflict reached its most intense phase when, with Jerusalem a heap of ruins, the Jewish exiles came face to face with the glory of Babylon and found themselves the recipients of economic resources which seemed to provide concrete evidence of the superiority of the Babylonian system. The covenant faith of the Hebrews, 'displaced from their homeland and from all its sustaining institutional markers', now came under unprecedented pressure due to the ability of Babylonian culture to assimilate those it had taken captive and the capacity of its economy 'to substitute satiation for a faith identity' (Brueggemann 2000a: 82).

As we move into the New Testament we will continue to listen afresh to familiar biblical texts, taking particular note of the broad social and historical contexts within which the story progresses. In doing so, we are at once struck by the fact that the shadow of empire is no less present here than was the case with Old Testament Israel; indeed, that shadow now deepens and becomes more pervasive than ever, forming an inescapable feature of the world within which Jesus and his apostles lived and preached the message of the kingdom of God.

Jesus and the city

It has often been argued that while the early Christian movement clearly had a distinctly urban character, this characteristic cannot be traced back to Jesus of Nazareth since his life and ministry bore all the marks of a traditional, rural background. His Galilean origins, the connection to the village culture of Palestine, and the imagery and illustrations employed in his teaching, especially in the parables, reflect a prophet whose life was shaped by the countryside rather than the metropolitan centre. Dieter Georgi, who wrote one of the few serious studies to offer biblical foundations for an urban theology, argued that Jesus' teaching was 'oriented toward the small town and the surrounding countryside' and that Jerusalem was of no importance to his ministry (Georgi 2005: 54). Commenting on the return of the disciples to the city of Jerusalem after the resurrection, Georgi says,

> The concentration on Jerusalem after Easter did not rest on the authority of the earthly Jesus, at least on the basis of our limited knowledge about him. Those disciples, women and men, who chose the murderous city did so *despite their Galilean origin and their experience with Jesus in that region*. They did not depend on the historical Jesus for that (ibid.: 56, emphasis added).

We will return to the relationship of Jesus to the city of Jerusalem and the post-resurrection mission of the disciples below, but first we need to reflect on the assumption that the ministry of Jesus in Galilee showed little awareness of urban life and did not provide his followers with guidance and direction for their subsequent witness within cities. There is, of course, no question that the scene of the ministry presented to us in the Gospels is largely rural; the synoptic Gospels describe Jesus as moving 'throughout Galilee', entering village and small town communities and preaching to 'the lost sheep of Israel'. He uses vivid illustrations repeatedly drawn from nature, referring to birds, foxes and flowers as providing lessons to be imitated or dangers to be avoided. His followers are, for the most part, rural peasants, including fishermen whose lives have been spent beside the Lake of Galilee. All of this might seem to justify the image of Jesus communicated through Victorian religious art as a simple country rabbi, as far removed from the power and politics of the great urban centres as could be imagined.

However, this image completely ignores the reality of the wider *context* in Galilee during a time of massive social dislocation, increasing economic distress, and a rising tide of resentment, anger and resistance to the forces creating this situation. In other words, while the geographical context of Galilee is rightly described as rural, the social, political and religious situation in this area when Jesus began his ministry was marked by disturbance and upheaval as the result of the impact of the colonial rule of the Roman Empire. To express this in a different way, the peasant population of Galilee, including Jesus of Nazareth and his followers, lived in a social and historical context marked by a profound clash of cultures in which traditions and values which could be traced back to the period of Israel's earliest history were being overwhelmed by powerful forces representing a quite different worldview. Thus, while Jesus' teaching was indeed oriented toward 'the small town and the surrounding countryside', as Georgi claims, the population of those towns and villages consisted of people facing great tensions and distress on account of political and economic decisions taken by rulers far away at the centre of imperial power and implemented by their agents within Palestine. Consequently, as John Vincent observes, 'the peaceful, idyllic Galilean countryside was penetrated by many aspects of urban life, and was subject to them in many ways' (Rogerson & Vincent 2009: 52).

The Roman Empire had extended its control into Palestine in 63 BC and from that point it became the major power shaping the political and economic conditions of life both in Jerusalem and in Galilee. Richard Horsley summarizes the situation as follows:

> Roman legions conquered and reconquered Galilee and Judea. To terrorize the
> people into submission they destroyed villages, slaughtered or enslaved some of the
> people, and crucified leaders of resistance. Rome warlords laid the countryside under
> tribute. The Romans appointed client rulers, Herodian kings and Jerusalem high

priests, to control the country and collect the tribute. Roman governors crucified
bandits, prophets and other troublemakers. And to suppress wider insurrections led
by popular messiahs, they sent in the legions once again to devastate the countryside
and crucify the leaders of the insurgency (Horsley 2008b: 77).

The reference here to the payment of tribute demanded by the imperial
power and the creation of what was effectively two tiers of government within
Israel in the shape of the Herodian dynasty and the priestly elite in Jerusalem,
highlights how the populace found themselves subjected to demands for the
payment of taxes from no less than three sources: Rome itself, the Herodian
kings, and the tithes and offerings demanded by the priesthood (note the clear
reference to these three authorities in Luke 3:1–2).

Once the Romans had established control of the region, they set about the
task of bringing 'civilization' to the area. As we saw in chapter 3, Rome was
an urban empire not just in the sense that the greatest city in human history
lay at its heart, but also because of its policy of extending political control
and spreading its civilization through a programme of urban development
which left the ancient world 'dotted with cities, all patterned after Rome and
all submissive to Rome' (Gonzalez 1999: 106). In Palestine Herod the Great
and his successors undertook massive building projects, establishing the
Jerusalem temple in Graeco-Roman style, making it one of the marvels of the
imperial world, and building new cities in honour of the Caesars, including
Sepphoris and Tiberius in Galilee. In fact, archaeological excavations at the
site of Sepphoris, within an hour's walk from Nazareth and clearly visible
from there, reveal evidence of a sophisticated urban culture which must have
impinged upon the life of Christ. Almost two decades ago Richard Batey
observed that the Galilean culture within which Jesus lived and preached was
'much more urban than previously believed' and he concluded,

> The popular picture of Jesus as a rustic growing up in the relative isolation of a small
> village of four hundred people in the remote hills of Galilee, must be integrated
> with the newly revealed setting of a burgeoning Greco-Roman metropolis boasting
> upwards of thirty thousand inhabitants – Jews, Arabs, Greeks, and Romans (Batey
> 1991: 14).

The reference here to the ethnic diversity of the population of this Roman
city serves to highlight the major changes occurring within Galilee at the time
that Jesus was born and grew into manhood. He lived through a period during
which Herod Antipas, ruling as the agent of imperial power, not only rebuilt
the city of Sepphoris in Roman style, but also created a new capital within his

domain in the shape of Tiberias on the western shore of the Lake of Galilee. According to Marianne Sawicki, this new city formed the centrepiece of Antipas's policy which was designed to transform the lake 'as a tourist attraction, in furtherance of his geopolitical agenda' (Sawicki 2000: 134). Aware that streams of pilgrims from across the empire made their way toward the magnificent city of Jerusalem, either by entering Palestine at the newly built Mediterranean port of Caesarea, or, if coming from the east, through the area known as the Decapolis, from where they travelled down the east bank of the Jordon, Antipas sought to divert this international traffic by providing travellers with a reason to cross the lake and enter the region of Galilee. In other words, the building of Tiberias was part of a clear strategy of development intended to place this region on the international map and to promote business contacts 'not just for the Herodians, but for any local agricultural or food-producing interests astute enough to get a piece of the action' (ibid.: 146). Sawicki describes this policy as involving the attempt to 'mediterraneanize' the Sea of Galilee, turning it into 'Little Italy'.

The huge building projects undertaken by the Herodian dynasty involved vast expenditure and, while obviously creating employment for considerable numbers of skilled craftsmen and labourers, this had a significant economic impact on the population through the increased taxation required to fund such projects. Horsley describes how the 'extraordinary revenues' needed for the construction of these new cities in Galilee 'exacerbated the economic burden on peasant producers' and he concludes that these Roman cities, built 'by a king who had been educated in Rome, must have seemed like *an alien urban culture*' within 'the previously Israelite rural landscape remote from the dominant high culture' (Horsley 2008a: 46, emphasis added).

What made this imposed culture 'alien' however, was not simply its urban character, but the threat which the underlying worldview presented to a way of life shaped by the traditions, values and beliefs of Israel's ancient faith. That faith, rooted in the narratives we have explored in the previous chapter, involved the confession of Yahweh's supreme authority and the use of his gifts of land and resources in ways that reflected patterns of social life governed by 'justice and justice alone'. The Romans and their agents within Israel, in the shape of the royal and priestly elites, and an army of lesser people able to make comfortable livings as functionaries of the system, treated these ancient traditions as backward and redundant and as an obstacle to the advance of their superior civilization.

The impact of Roman culture on the towns and villages of Galilee was evident in the growing crisis of debt and dispossession among rural peasants at the time that Jesus began his ministry. The land of Israel, gifted by Yahweh

Figure 7.1: Excavations at the site of the city of Sepphoris. Photograph used by permission from David Padfield

and distributed among families and tribes according to rights of inheritance enshrined in the Torah, was being bought up by a privileged and wealthy elite whose identification with the imperial regime was richly rewarded. Horsley and Silberman describe this process as follows:

> Slowly the villages of the Land of Israel – once duly and solemnly distributed by God to the families, clans, and tribes of Israel – were passing into the hands of aristocratic families, who happened to have influence in royal or priestly circles or large reserves of disposable wealth. This was a horrible reversal of the familiar biblical stories of Exodus and the Conquest of Canaan that were read about and talked about in the village assemblies when the scrolls of the Law were taken out to be read on Sabbaths and festival days (Horsley & Silberman 1997: 29).

Once this context is recognized, the picture of a rural Christ whose actions and teaching were so conditioned by the countryside as to offer little or no guidance to his later followers in urban situations becomes impossible to sustain. Consider, for example, a key moment in Luke's description of Jesus' ministry at which he himself read from the scroll of the prophecy of Isaiah in his native village of Nazareth. The text has Yahweh's servant announcing the arrival of 'the year of the Lord's favour', bringing good news to the poor, freedom to prisoners and all who are oppressed, and sight to the blind (Luke 4:18–19). Not surprisingly, this reading, and Jesus' statement that the prophecy was at that very moment being fulfilled in the hearing of those present, electrified his peasant audience. However, the text of Isaiah (61:1–3) has a clear *urban* reference, relating these promises to 'those who grieve in Zion' and predicting the renewal of 'ruined cities that have been devastated for generations' (61:4). Even more significant is the fact that the Old Testament prophet associates this urban renewal with a radical redistribution of the 'wealth of nations' (61:6) and the extension of Yahweh's just rule to 'all your brothers, *from all the nations*' (Isa. 66:20, emphasis added). This pregnant phrase was used in imperial literature and propaganda to describe the universal reach of Rome's rule. For example, Virgil's *Aeneid* predicted that 'glorious Rome' would 'extend her empire to earth's ends', controlling the whole world and bringing all the nations 'under its sway in peace' (Lopez 2008: 78). Seen in this light, the opening words of Jesus' public ministry in Galilee contain both an implied challenge to Roman hegemony and the promise of a new community in which economic resources, instead of being sucked into the imperial centre, would be redistributed in a manner that reflected Yahweh's intention to bring justice for 'all the nations'.

It is surely clear that when, later in the first century, the followers of Jesus living in the cities of the ancient world heard this narrative read, his actions and words must have connected powerfully to the context in which their lives were lived, providing guidance and inspiration as they confronted the ideology of an urban empire which increasingly demanded not only their submission, but also their worship. The narratives contained in the Gospels, including the specific teaching of Jesus, were relevant to the lives and witness of these urban disciples because the Christ they describe had revealed an alternative kingdom to the one within which they lived and, in many cases, suffered.

Once the context we have outlined above is taken into account, many aspects of Jesus' ministry and teaching can be seen to have clear significance in relation to urban situations. Matthew's Gospel contains no less than twenty-seven occurrences of the term *polis*, and makes frequent use of urban imagery. We may wonder whether when Jesus likens his new community to 'a city on a hill' which 'cannot be hidden' (Matt. 5:14) he had the view of Sepphoris, clearly visible from his native Nazareth, in mind? More to the point, the frequent references to the desolating problem of debt, including the linkage between the reception of God's forgiveness and the remission of the debts owed to the disciple (Matt. 6:12), mirror a context within which 'the land-grabbing of the rulers' and the heavy burden of taxation was opening a chasm between rich and poor and driving small farmers, day labourers, fishermen, shepherds, widows and orphans into absolute poverty and despair (Stegemann & Stegemann 1999: 134). When the familiar language of the Sermon on the Mount is heard within this context, it becomes clear that, by contrasting the ethics and spirituality of the kingdom of God with a culture in which the urban elite were addicted to wealth and accumulation, Jesus is repudiating an alien worldview which creates an insatiable and idolatrous appetite for money and possessions (Matt. 6:32–34).

However, Jesus does more than merely teach; the reign of God is demonstrated by acts of power and deliverance in which the victims of evil and oppression are liberated and given new life. In one of the most dramatic of all the stories concerning Christ's ministry, Mark records how Jesus and his disciples 'went across the lake' into the region the evangelist describes as Gerasa (or 'the region of the Gerasenes', Mark 5:1). There are problems with this statement in that the city of this name was some distance from the scene of the action which the evangelist proceeds to describe, but the intention may be to indicate that Jesus was entering territory which lay outside Galilee and was populated by Gentiles. In other words, the description of the movement across the lake does more than simply chart geographical progress from west to east, but rather indicates the crossing of religious, cultural and political boundaries, so taking Jesus into new and challenging territory. That territory, also identified as the Decapolis (the 'ten cities'), was a Hellenized area which 'represented the eastern frontier of the Roman empire, beyond which lay the Arabian steppes' (Myers 1988: 190). Thus, in crossing the lake and demonstrating the power of the kingdom of God *beyond* the limits of Galilee, Jesus clearly displays the universal reach of his message and mission and, in this process, challenges the power of Rome in a region in which its dominance appeared to be absolute.

The conflict is dramatically played out through the encounter with a possessed and broken man who runs to meet Jesus the moment his feet touch the soil of the Decapolis (Mark 5:2–5). At the heart of the narrative Jesus asks this tragic person his name and receives the reply, 'My name is *Legion*' (5:9). Despite the fact that, as Myers points out, this word had only one meaning in Mark's social world, signifying a troop of Roman soldiers, commentators frequently ignore this fact and overlook the presence of military imagery throughout the passage. While Josephus's description of the scorched earth policy of the Romans in this very area relates to a later period, it serves to illustrate the sort of actions for which the legions were notorious, compelling

us to ask whether the name proffered by this dehumanized person suggests a
connection between the incidence of demon possession in this area (Matthew
indicates the presence of *two* possessed men among the tombs of Gadara) and
Roman military violence?

> Vespasian . . . sent Lucius Annius to Gerasa with cavalry and a considerable number
> of foot soldiers. After taking the town by assault, he killed a thousand of the young
> men who had not escaped, took their families captive, and allowed his soldiers to
> plunder the property. . . . Those who were able-bodied fled, the weak perished, and all
> that was left went up in flames (Josephus, quoted in Myers 1988: 191).

The climax of Mark's story is reached when, having heard the report of Jesus'
deliverance of the possessed man, crowds come out from 'town and countryside' to investigate. They discover to their utter amazement that the former
demoniac is now 'sitting, dressed and in his right mind' (5:15). There cannot
be a more beautiful description of the healing power of Christ than this any-
where in the Gospels, but we should not allow that beauty to divert our attention from the fact that the response of the populace is one of *fear* bordering
on sheer terror, reflected in their pleading with Jesus to 'leave their region'
(5:16–17). If we are justified in suspecting that the demoniac's name reflects
some connection between his tragic, broken life and the brutal violence with
which the Roman legions established and maintained their iron grip on power
in this region, then an explanation of the terror the local population felt when
faced with Jesus' liberating action is to hand. For these people the disturbance
of the status quo (which the fate of the pigs in this story suggests has serious
economic implications) involves a price too high to meet when it brings the
threat of intervention by those same legions to re-establish Roman authority
and control. The citizens of the Decapolis know instinctively that the release
of marginalized people whose tragic biographies constitute living evidence
of Roman injustices is likely to result in renewed acts of repression, and as a
result Christ and his kingdom are refused.

In a final twist to the story, Jesus declines the liberated man's impassioned
plea to be allowed to follow him back across the lake with the instruction to
'Go home' and tell his family 'how much the Lord has done for you'. As a
result the 'Ten Cities' become the context for his witness, and Mark concludes
with the comment that 'all the people were amazed' (5:18–20). We are left to
ask not only what an incident like this tells us concerning the response of Jesus
to the increasingly urbanized culture which he encountered on both sides of
Lake Galilee, but also how Mark's Gospel itself would have been heard and
understood a generation later by a largely urban church facing the renewed

threat of persecution and suffering as the direct consequence of its witness to Christ? So far as Galilee in the 20s and 30s is concerned, Ben Witherington rightly comments,

> The image of Jesus as a gentle shepherd sitting in verdant pastures teaching enjoyable but inoffensive parables to audiences who all loved him, is far from an accurate assessment of the situation. . . . One must remember that in Jesus' world politics and religion were always intimately intertwined, even if one was not part of a zealot movement or a political appointee of a Roman ruler, like the high priest (Witherington 2001: 32).

With regard to the first hearers of Mark's Gospel, if we adopt the traditional view that his initial audience consisted of Christians in the city of Rome in the mid- to late-60s, after the fire of Rome and Nero's decision to make the followers of Jesus within the imperial city the scapegoats for the consequences of his own evil actions, the narrative we have just discussed begins to resonate in powerful ways in precisely such a context. It is not hard to imagine how a relatively small group of Christ-followers, most of whom were of low status and living in difficult conditions at the very heart of the empire, would have heard this narrative as good news: Jesus had entered Gentile, Roman territory and confronted and overcome demonic evil there; he had demonstrated God's love and liberating power to someone who had been brutalized and confined to the absolute margins of respectable society, and he had commissioned his new follower to remain where he was, not fleeing the difficult context, but bearing witness to his own family and neighbours. There is thus, a connection between the social setting of Jesus' ministry in Galilee (and in the Decapolis) in the 30s, and the context of Mark's hearers in Rome in the 60s, *so that the members of an urban church in the imperial city would hear the stories of Jesus' teaching and miracles as absolutely relevant to the context within which they found themselves.* As Witherington says,

> Both were volatile settings for religious Jews and perhaps especially for the Jesus movement, whose members were not seeking solitude and the avoidance of controversy, but rather, by being involved in a movement to radically reform early Judaism, were the center of controversy in the 30s, and then, as a visible and openly evangelistic group in the 60s, were the victims of Nero's reprisals after the fire (ibid.: 31).

The fact that we have spoken above of a *conflict* between Jesus and the urban culture of the imperial power which controlled Palestine does *not* lead to the conclusion that Jesus should be understood as locating the source of personal and social evils in the city as such. Jesus cannot be enlisted in the cause of anti-urbanism. As we have seen, his 'manifesto' in the synagogue at Nazareth clearly echoes the prophetic anticipation of a salvation which results in urban *renewal* and the restoration of devastated cities. As we have repeatedly stressed, the issue at stake concerns underlying worldviews, and Christ's message – his summons to repentance, the conflict with demonic forms of evil, and the announcement of the in-breaking of the reign of God – can provide the foundation for a new vision of urban life.

Indeed, it is important to notice the connections between the Jesus movement in its earliest phase and people who may be classified as urban dwellers who, because of their access to significant financial resources, were in a position to provide material support for the emerging movement. This includes the wealthy tax collectors who joined the movement and who, like Zaccheus, renounced the rule of mammon and deployed their considerable fortunes in line with the new values of the kingdom of God (Luke 19:8–10). While this particular example involves an act of reparation in which ill-gotten gains were distributed among the poor, in other cases the financial resources of high-status followers of Jesus are clearly used to provide for his own support and that of his disciples. The key text is Luke 8:1–3 which describes how Jesus travelled 'from one city and village to another, proclaiming the good news of the kingdom of God' accompanied by the Twelve '*and also some women who had been cured of evil spirits and diseases*'. Three of these women are named: 'Mary, called Magdalene . . . Joanna the wife of Chuza, *the manager of Herod's household*' and Susanna. But Luke then adds that there were 'many others' and that this large group of female followers was 'helping to support' the Jesus movement 'out of their own means'. This same group later reappears at the cross of Christ, so that having 'followed him *from* Galilee' they became key witnesses of both his death and resurrection (Luke 23:49; 24:10. See Matt. 27:55–56; Mark 15:40–41). Once again, Mary of Magdala and Joanna, whose marriage placed her close to the very heart of royal power in Galilee, are singled out for mention and appear to be closely associated with each other.

Who were these women? And what exactly was the significance of the role they played in the ministry of Jesus, both before and after his execution at Golgotha? The fact that they possessed resources which they were free to deploy in constant support of Jesus and his disciples suggests that these were wealthy people who, unlike the peasant population referred to above, operated within the new urban culture, exploiting the opportunities which it provided for people with 'an eye for business'. As we have seen, the entire region of Galilee, including the towns along the shores of the lake which were

being transformed by the impact of the new city of Tiberius, was becoming 'an international commercial hub for the promotion of agribusiness
and industrial expansion' (Sawicki 2000: 134). It is especially significant that
Mary's home town of Magdala had undergone dramatic changes as the fishing
on Lake Galilee ceased being a seasonal occupation of farmers in the slack
period between sowing and harvest and became a highly profitable business.
Once Roman control of the area had been established, new techniques for
the salting and pickling of fish were developed, resulting in the growing com-
mercialization of the fishing enterprise, the massive expansion of the market
for the resultant fish products, and the growth of the entire process 'on
something approaching an industrial scale' (Horsley & Silberman 1997: 25).
The spicy fish sauce called *garum* and fish stews known as *salsamentum* became
familiar to urban populations across the Roman Empire, so much so that
Josephus called Magdala, *Tarichaeae,* a word signifying factories for the salting
of fish, or the processing of food for international markets.

The transformation of Magdala provides another example of the deepening of social and economic divisions to which attention has been drawn earlier
in this chapter. The new techniques and methods for manufacturing fish
products and the marketing of them across the empire required a massively
increased yield of fish from the lake, a development which changed the lives
of the adjacent farming population even as it turned a once sleepy, lakeside
town into a commercial centre. In the words of Horsley and Silberman,

> This was an industry that apparently brought great wealth to some and great misery
> to others: the Magdala excavations have revealed a complex pattern of narrow urban
> streets, reservoirs, and buildings where the town's putrid business was conducted –
> and at least one spacious private villa whose owner proudly announced the source of
> his fortune with a mosaic depiction of a boat and large fish installed on the floor of
> his entrance courtyard (ibid.).

So how did Mary of Magdala obtain the wealth that enabled her to become
one of the sponsors of the Jesus movement? And how did a sophisticated
women like Joanna manage to retain her position within the court of Antipas
while apparently helping to fund the journeys of Jesus and his disciples,
frequently accompanying them on these missions? While caution is needed
when drawing inferences from brief statements in the Gospel records, the
role of these women as described by Luke appears to have been of considerable significance, and it is beyond dispute that the message of Jesus was
heard and believed at the very heart of urban power in the court of Herod
Antipas. Whether we can go further and follow Marianne Sawicki's proposals

regarding the likely links between these two women is debatable, but her fascinating reconstruction, including the suggestion that the extensive trading links
of such women could have played a crucial role in the rapid post-resurrection
spread of the gospel, may shed new light on the earliest history of the Jesus
movement. Sawicki writes:

> Joanna, as the wife of a high-ranking officer of the Herodian court was an important
> and powerful personage. It is likely that her responsibilities included providing
> hospitality for guests at the palace in Tiberius. Plausibly, in that capacity she dealt
> with suppliers of food and entertainment from the local region. I have suggested that
> the Mary who was known as 'Mary of Magdala' may have represented a purveyor
> of fresh fish, salt fish, and fish sauce in that town, which was a few miles north of
> Tiberius (Sawicki 2000: 180).

Whether or not these two women met each other in this kind of situation,
what is beyond dispute is that, along with many others, they experienced
the healing and delivering power of Jesus, becoming his devoted followers
from *within* the Roman-Herodian urban culture we have described above.
We might wonder whether the diseases and spiritual disorders from which
all these women suffered were connected to their experience of a privileged
and prosperous life within the new cities? Were they, like their sisters in the
urban world two thousand years later, experiencing the Roman city as 'gendered space' and paying the price for this in the shape of various debilitating
disorders and diseases? The fact that they found release and healing through
their encounters with Jesus of Nazareth demonstrates that the salvation he
offered crossed both the gender gap and what would today be called the class
divide. The extraordinary diversity of the male followers of Jesus within the
apostolic band has often been noted; what is perhaps even more remarkable
is the bringing together of those men, most of whose social and economic
circumstances had been profoundly disrupted by the revolutionary changes
on and around the Lake of Galilee (see Matt. 4:18–22), with women who had
profited financially from this situation. The message of the kingdom of God
was clearly 'good news to the poor' and it brought 'release to the oppressed',
whether that oppression took structural form and condemned peasant communities to debt and servitude, or whether, by contrast, it was a form of
bondage resulting from a guilty conscience and a crisis of meaning in the lives
of those who made enormous material gains from their identification with the
dominant, colonial culture.

We may draw two conclusions from this survey of the relationship between
Jesus and the city as we have outlined it above. The first concerns the *substance*

of his message and mission, while the second has to do with what may be called his *methodology*. As to Jesus' message, while it contained a revolutionary newness, it was also shaped in continuity with the history of biblical Israel as this has been discussed in the previous chapter, especially the revelation of God in the narratives of creation, exodus and the gifts of land and freedom; the ethical demands of Yahweh as these were contained in the Torah; and both the critiques of unfaithfulness and corruption, and the persistent vision of a coming age of *shalom*, which found expression in Israel's classical prophets. John V. Taylor has said that when Jesus appeared preaching the message of the kingdom of God, 'he was opening up to the entire world that Kingdom of right relationships which long ago God had invited one special nation to enjoy' (Taylor 1975: 52). However, as with Isaiah, Micah and Jeremiah, the context within which Jesus' ministry took place, in which an urban empire filled the horizons, meant that his message was inescapably political and controversial. In contrast to the dualism of modern, Western culture (a dualism which has profoundly shaped Christianity in Europe and North America and results in serious misreadings of the biblical texts), Jesus' ministry integrated religious, political and economic concerns, placing all of them within the sphere of the reign of God. This was bound to precipitate a clash with an empire which made idolatrous claims for itself and operated on the basis of a worldview which justified a form of domination based on the use of violence, and then used its power in ways that created widening socio-economic divisions as large numbers of people were driven into poverty and despair.

When, after the resurrection, the stories of Jesus' ministry were recorded, the evangelists recognized the radical nature of the words and deeds of Christ in the very act of describing their accounts as 'Gospels'. This terminology signals the fact that the claims made by and for Jesus were profoundly subversive of an empire which used this same language to announce its 'imperial gospel'. Roman propaganda in the form of public announcements, inscriptions on coinage, as well as monumental art placed on prominent display in cities, presented the Caesars as 'saviours of the world' and declared the births of their sons and heirs as 'good news' for the whole earth. Thus, when Mark introduces his narrative with the words, 'The beginning of the *gospel* about Jesus Christ, the Son of God' (Mark 1:1), he is challenging the blasphemous pretensions of Rome and its collaborators and 'taking dead aim at Caesar and his legitimating myths' (Myers 1988: 124).

The dangers of reading the Gospels with the dualistic lenses supplied to us by the Enlightenment lie in two directions; we may either *spiritualize* the message of Jesus and ignore his socio-political impact, or we end up *politicizing* him in a manner that overlooks the theological and religious foundation of his message and work. The radical political challenge of the gospel must not be divorced from the central announcement of the coming of the kingdom of heaven, since it is precisely this message which shapes Jesus' critique of an urban culture which has substituted idols in place of the worship of the Living God. In doing so it has become a culture of injustice, despair and death.

What is more, Jesus detected forces at work in this situation which cannot be reduced to conventional politics but, as we have seen, involved the realm of the spiritual and the demonic. So, for example, his constant warnings concerning the dangers posed by money are underpinned by the knowledge that what might seem to be a neutral medium of economic exchange, can in fact become imbued with such spiritual power that it enslaves and blinds human beings, driving barriers between them and becoming the exclusive preoccupation of their lives. The stark warning, 'You cannot serve both God and money' (Matt. 6:24), had a particular resonance in the ancient world, and it remains as a fundamental challenge today in an urban world in which money is too often seen as a universal remedy for the human condition, while the spiritual perils that accompany it are suppressed and ignored in ways that reflect the activity of hidden powers (see Witherington 2010).

What then, secondly, does this survey teach us concerning Jesus's *methodology* with regard to the urban culture of his time? Marianne Sawicki describes how Christ avoided 'urban interior space' as a protest against 'Roman disruption of traditional Galilean village networks through establishment of urban centers'. His distribution of 'free fish and bread' was, she suggests, a refusal of 'imperial economic disruptions of local-market commodities circulation'. The actions of Jesus were thus resistant to, and subversive of, Roman ideology and practice, undermining 'its perceived reasonableness' and challenging its 'hegemonic ability to appear to offer the superior rationale for organizing human activities' (Sawicki 2000: 173–174). However, the reign of God announced by Christ could not exist outside of this world in some kind of free-standing, ahistorical context, but rather appears *within* the existing socio-political situation. Thus, as we have seen, the signs of the kingdom become evident where they might be least expected, including *within* the court of Herod Antipas. For those followers of Jesus whose discipleship was expressed through supportive roles during preaching trips in rural Galilee, and back at home *within* the city, where both family and business responsibilities demanded their presence, Jesus' metaphors concerning salt, light and leaven offered encouragement and direction. In Sawicki's words, they expressed 'a theology of digging in and staying put, an ecclesiology of infiltration rather than escape and conquest' (ibid.: 155).

In contrast to the thesis of Dieter Georgi, which we noticed at the beginning of this chapter, it now becomes clear that the post-resurrection urban mission of the followers of Christ throughout the Roman world was not an innovation unconnected to the historical Jesus, but was entirely consistent with his own response to the city. The earliest disciples 'had to figure out how to live in a landscape compromised by colonial oppressions' and so to 'seek and find the kingdom of God *in the midst of that*' (ibid., emphasis added). And in the metaphors of salt, light and leaven, Jesus already pointed the way toward a missionary engagement with the city which would allow the urban population to 'see your good deeds and praise your Father in heaven' (Matt. 5:13–16). It should be stressed, finally, that allowing these metaphors to shape Christian witness in an urban world is far from being either a soft option, or an escape from the radical demands of the gospel of Christ. On the contrary, Christians who are determined to take this path must be prepared for suffering and even death as the outcome of their witness to God's reign, because – as we shall see later – there is a price to be paid for living a life in imitation of Jesus which exposes the reality of urban corruption and darkness from within and points to an alternative way of being human which demands both the rejection of the reigning urban myths and the complete reconstruction of life together in the city.

The tragedy of Jerusalem

We turn now to the particular city which had unique significance for Christ and which, according to all four Gospels, he confronted directly at the climax of his ministry. In the previous chapter we traced the history of the city of Jerusalem from the time of its capture and transformation as the capital of the united kingdom of Israel during the reign of David, to its utter destruction by the Babylonians in 587 BC. Following the return from exile, the city was rebuilt during the Persian period (538–333 BC), as indicated in the Old Testament books of Nehemiah and Ezra. Jerusalem later came under the control of Alexander the Great, and the resultant Hellenization of the city sparked revolt and subsequent redevelopment during the Maccabean period. However, the city to which Jesus came had, since 63 BC, fallen under the control of the imperial power of Rome, being reshaped once again by ideas and values which stood in stark and disturbing contrast to Israel's ancient faith.

The Roman model of urbanization which, as we have seen, was introduced into Palestine through the massive building projects of the Herodian dynasty, was applied to the development of Jerusalem, transforming it into a city of such magnificence and splendour that an observer from the metropolitan centre, Pliny the Elder, could describe it as 'by far the most famous of the cities of the East'. Herod the Great introduced a festival modelled on the Olympic Games, called the Actium Games, and constructed a hippodrome, an amphitheatre and a theatre within Jerusalem for this purpose. Roman-style entertainments were thus introduced to the 'holy land', including chariot races, athletic competitions in which naked men wrestled with each other, dramas and gladiatorial contests. The latter involved the spectacle of lions and other powerful beasts fighting to the death with each other and with condemned criminals. The amphitheatre was built at some distance from the centre of the city since the forms of 'entertainment' which took place there were profoundly offensive to Jewish sensibilities, as were the lavish decorations, including inscriptions praising the conquests of Augustus, and shields, breastplates, helmets, swords and lances arranged artistically on the walls (Perowne, 1960: 134).

The 'Romanization' of Jerusalem in the time of Jesus extended to the building of Herod's Temple. He doubled the size of the site on which the previous temple had stood, making the building larger than the Acropolis in Athens and creating a structure of 'unprecedented magnificence'. The Jewish historian, Josephus, marvelled at the sight of the temple, which literally glowed as the result of the gold lavished upon it; even the spikes on the roof of the porch designed to ward off birds were covered in gold! Josephus reported that the golden adornment of Jerusalem's iconic buildings was so abundant that after the Roman destruction of the city in 70 AD the value of this precious metal throughout the province of Syria was halved, causing the gold market to collapse (Jeremias, 1969: 25).

The resident population of Jerusalem in the time of Jesus was about 25,000, but this was augmented during the annual festivals by a vast inflow of pilgrims from across the empire. Luke's description of the languages spoken by visiting pilgrims within the city at the festival of Pentecost indicates that these people had travelled to Jerusalem from every part of the known world (Acts 2:9–11). This information is confirmed from secular sources, as when Philo cites a letter written to Caligula which describes the locations of the Jewish diaspora as including Egypt, Syria, Europe, Babylonia and 'lands beyond the Euphrates', stretching into Asia. So great was the flow of visitors and so significant their potential economic impact that, as we noticed above, Herod Antipas attempted to divert the streams of people from the well-trodden routes to the west and east of Galilee in order to siphon into his own treasury some of the financial and material benefits resulting from the pilgrim trails. The needs of such huge numbers of people for basic services like accommodation and food, not to say 'financial services' such as the exchange of currency, resulted in the development of 'a flourishing commercial life', reflected in the growth of 'the luxury trade' among Jerusalem's wealthy residents (Jeremias 1969: 29–30).

How then did Jesus respond to the 'holy city' of Jerusalem? It is important to recognize that the temple was not only the focal point of religious devotion and worship but that it had become a central and powerful political and economic institution. The High Priest was appointed by the Roman governor and the temple staff were responsible for the collection of tribute to Rome. Richard Horsley describes the scribes and Pharisees as representatives of the temple-state and notes that when such people came to Galilee from Jerusalem, Jesus resisted and condemned them as violators of the Torah. Their appeal to the sacredness of the temple in justification of the demand for the payment of tithes concealed acts of oppression against vulnerable people and broke the core commandment to honour father and mother (see Mark 7:9–13; 12:38–40). Thus, well in advance of his final journey to Jerusalem, Jesus had recognized the ideological nature of the religion centred on the temple and saw clearly that this was the antithesis of the message of the kingdom of God which he both announced and embodied.

Ideological religion always results in the oppression of its victims while working to the advantage of its advocates. There is clear evidence that those who defended the compromise with Rome and gave it concrete form by embedding a form of syncretism within the structures of temple religion and worship, profited from this arrangement. The high-priestly families lived in elegant villas overlooking the temple, as described by Horsley and Silberman:

> Ever since the vast expansion of the Temple structures and institutions, these high-priestly families and families of priestly officers in charge of the Temple's treasury, workshops, storerooms, and supply facilities had amassed considerable fortunes. . . . In spacious structures unhesitatingly dubbed 'mansions' by the archaeologists who uncovered them in the 1970s, we can get a glimpse of a lavish life in mosaic-floored reception rooms and dining rooms with elaborate painted and carved stucco wall decoration and with a wealth of fine tableware, glassware, carved stone tabletops and other interior furnishings, and elegant peristyles (Horsley & Silberman, 1997: 78–79).

Little wonder then that Jesus, in the tradition of Isaiah and Jeremiah, weeps over this city. While the urban culture of Sepphoris or Tiberius could be resisted as an alien intrusion into Galilee, the tragedy of Jerusalem was that this city, chosen in ancient times as the dwelling place of Yahweh and intended to model an urban society shaped by the law and covenant, had once again abandoned its calling and been co-opted by a pagan culture of death. The Jesus movement had offered an alternative in the shape of the summons to repentance and the recovery of a unique destiny which would both heal the land of Israel and bring God's promised *shalom* to the nations. But the offer was refused and the attempt of Jesus to gather and protect its people 'as a hen gathers her chicks under her wings' was resisted. This remarkable language, reported by Luke, goes beyond the metaphors of the prophets who had likened Jerusalem to an adulterous bride, by suggesting that since the city's own children have been removed from the love and care of their true Father, Jesus seeks to act as their 'mother', protecting them from harm and reconciling them to the forgotten Father (Luke 13:34–35). As Walker says, 'the false parent' did not take kindly to this offer and when Jesus entered the city, the conflicting voices of his followers ecstatically praising God for the arrival of the messianic king, and the outrage of the Pharisees who, afraid of the consequences of this breach of public order, demanded that he silence his disciples, caused Jesus to weep over Jerusalem and to utter a profoundly moving lament (Luke 19:37–44). The city had failed to recognize the true source of its peace (*shalom*) and, by perpetuating its compromise, idolatry and collusion with oppression and injustice, would drive the growing numbers of zealous nationalists into ever more violent reaction, so precipitating a conflict which would end in the terrible tragedy of the destruction of Jerusalem. Commenting on Jesus' lament over the city, Fred Craddock writes,

> A lament is a voice of love and profound caring, of vision of what could have been and of grief over its loss, of tough hope painfully releasing the object of its hope, of personal responsibility and frustration, of sorrow and anger mixed, of accepted loss but with energy enough to go on (Craddock 1990: 229).

The climax of Christ's ministry, involving the journey to Jerusalem and the confrontation which took place there, leading to his arrest, trial and crucifixion, is recorded in each of the four Gospels. In the Fourth Gospel we find two accounts of Jesus in Jerusalem, one of which is placed at the very outset of his ministry, so presenting us with a Christ who challenges power and corruption in the city from the very beginning. Commenting on John's description of the city, Peter Walker suggests that, beneath the external veneer of sacredness, Jerusalem had become 'like any other city' and that when the Jewish leaders are described as declaring before Pilate, 'We have no king but Caesar' (John 19:15), they were revealing that Jerusalem had so far imitated Roman models that it was 'no different from any other city in the Empire' (Walker 1996: 181). This affirmation of loyalty to Caesar represented an act of apostasy in which the liberating God of the exodus was effectively renounced through a return to the enslaving and oppressive patterns of sacred kingship from which ancient Israel had been set free. In this context Jesus' institution of a new passover within the city (Mark 14:12–26) had radical implications, both for his immediate disciples and for later hearers of the Gospels scattered in the imperial cities of the Empire. A new passover clearly presaged a new salvation and implied that *'even in Jerusalem* the people of Israel were still in Egypt and in "slavery"' (ibid.: 14). Walker points out that the language Mark uses to describe Jesus' journey toward Calvary clearly echoes that used elsewhere in the New Testament in connection with the 'leading out' of ancient Israel from the bondage in Egypt (Mark 15:20, compare Acts 7:36; 13:17). The path to the cross was thus the way to a new and greater liberation, an exodus which in its spiritual depth and geographical reach would fulfil the visionary hopes of the prophets for the arrival of the age of God's *shalom*.

Death and resurrection

Of course, the perception of the cross as the means of a new and greater exodus from bondage and oppression was far from being immediately apparent to the followers of Jesus. Indeed, Mark records that when Jesus was arrested 'everyone deserted him and fled' (Mark 14:50). And in the beautiful Lukan narrative of the journey to Emmaus we are given an example of the state of mind of two of these retreating disciples (Luke 24:13–35). They are broken, terrified people whose dreams have died and whose faith now trembles on the verge of absolute collapse. Elsewhere I have discussed this story in detail and have suggested that every aspect of Luke's account points to the conclusion that the fleeing disciples were people 'for whom hope is exhausted and life itself begins to teeter on the brink of the abyss of meaninglessness' (Smith 2007: 6). If we are to understand why this was so we need to cut through the fog created by the sentimental language often used to describe Jesus' death in Christian devotional literature and see his execution for what, on the historical plane, it was: a brutal act of Roman-sponsored terror which branded its victim as a threat to imperial order and rule. In the words of Horsley and Silberman,

> The stench, the screams, the horrible sights of the public places of execution on the outskirts of every Roman city offered a grotesque counterimage to the elegance and architectural splendor of the temples, forums, and plazas within. The cross and the Corinthian column were the two sides of the Roman experience. One offered shade and shelter to all those who would accept the Roman world's logic and structures of power, the other systematically transformed anyone branded as an enemy of

the Roman order from a living, breathing person into a bruised, bloated, almost unrecognizable corpse (Horsley & Silberman 1997: 86).

When the crucifixion of Jesus is seen within this historical perspective it is little wonder that his followers, tainted by guilt through association with an enemy of the state and suffering the almost unbearable trauma arising from the violent and humiliating end of the prophet-messiah to whom they had devoted their lives, should either make their exit from the city or retreat in paralyzing fear behind locked doors within it (John 20:19). The rejection of Christ and his death outside the city walls, together with the subsequent flight to the suburbs by his followers, provides one possible paradigm for a Christian response to the urban world. A later New Testament writer drew attention to the fact that Jesus had been crucified 'outside the city gate' and concluded that all who wished to identify with him would, therefore, have to do so *outside* the worldly city, 'bearing the disgrace he bore'. He added that Christians have no 'enduring city' on earth but, instead, 'are looking for the city that is to come' (Heb. 13:12–14). This suspicion of urban culture as inherently hostile to faith and dangerous to ethical behaviour shaped by the values of the kingdom of God surfaces at different points in the New Testament writings, including James's warning to Christian traders who had allowed quintessential Roman, urban values to compromise their faith as they moved from city to city to 'carry on business and make money' (Jas 4:13). In similar vein, the final book in the Bible contains a description of urban churches in various stages of compromise with Roman ideology and values, and issues the explicit injunction to 'come out' of the worldly city in order to avoid sharing 'in her sins' (Rev. 18:4).

However, the great irony of the gospel is that the foundations of an entirely new city, the new Jerusalem, were actually laid in the terrible events that took place at Calvary. As N. T. Wright has said, Jesus himself viewed his cross as symbolic 'not merely of Roman oppression, but of the way of love and peace which he had commended so vigorously'. The cross became the sign, not of the victory of Rome, 'nor of those who would oppose Caesar with Caesar's methods', but of *the victory of God* (Wright 1996: 610). The discovery that what had seemed to be a crushing defeat was in fact the means of the divine victory over sin and death came as the result of the belief that Christ had been raised from the dead. Dieter Georgi traces the growth of 'a new attitude to urban reality' among the first followers of Christ to what he calls a series of 'extraordinary experiences', or what we may describe as the epiphanies of the risen Jesus, in and around Jerusalem (Georgi 2005: 55). The broken disciples on the road to Emmaus are so utterly transformed by an encounter with the risen Jesus that they retrace their steps in the darkness of the night to re-enter the violent city, convinced of the imperative need to bear their testimony *within* its walls. Thus, the first witnesses of the resurrection, including the large group of women whose surprising role in Jesus' ministry we have noted earlier, returned to, and remained within, the city where, Georgi observes, their testimony was eventually heard by Hellenistic Jews who subsequently moved 'into the urban culture of the Mediterranean, including large cities such as Antioch' (ibid.: 59).

Urban Christianity in the Roman Empire

The story of the spread of the Jesus movement across the Roman Empire and its initial penetration of key urban centres is told in the second volume of Luke's work, known to us as the book of Acts. We cannot repeat that story here, neither is it possible to examine in detail all of the specific texts elsewhere in the New Testament which may be thought to have particular significance for an urban theology. It is clear both from Luke's account and from modern scholarly research (reflected in the quotation at the head of this chapter) that the primitive Christian church took root and flourished in the great cities of the ancient world such as Antioch, Ephesus, Corinth and Rome itself. Writing in a now classic work, Wayne Meeks observed that Pauline Christianity was entirely urban and that it was in the cities of the Roman Empire that Christianity 'had its greatest successes until well after the time of Constantine'. The apostle Paul was 'a city person' whose very language was shaped by urban culture. According to Meeks, Paul's world consisted, 'practically speaking, only of the cities of the Roman Empire' and his missionary strategy was 'to plant small cells of Christians in scattered households in some of the strategically located cities of the north-east Mediterranean basin'. Meeks concludes that 'the mission of the Pauline circle was conceived from start to finish as an urban movement' (Meeks 1983: 8–10).

Given that this is the case, it stands to reason that the literature which we know as the New Testament, including the Gospels, the letters and the Apocalypse, reflects the context of the urban empire of the first century and that its primary purpose must have been to communicate the story of Jesus within that context and to provide teaching, nurture and pastoral support to groups of Christ-followers scattered in Graeco-Roman urban settings. Strangely, this seemingly obvious conclusion has been largely overlooked by Western Christians, whose approach to this literature has been influenced by the Christendom experience which placed the church at the *centre* of political power, rather than at its margins, and for many centuries operated within a predominantly *rural* culture, far removed from the urban context of the apostolic churches. As a result, the New Testament as a whole, and specific documents within it, such as the letter to the Romans, have been read as time-less, abstract statements of truth with little or no reference to their immediate historical context within the urban empire of Rome. Dieter Georgi writes that the primitive churches 'integrated and radicalized the principles of urban culture in a critical fashion' and that the expanding Christian movement remained an urban religion until the barbarian invasions of the continent of Europe introduced a radically new cultural setting for the Christian faith. 'Then the people from the backwoods took power, and Christianity turned into a rural and small-town religion and has remained so until today' (Georgi 2005: 67).

With the passing of the Christendom phase of history and the arrival of the urban world which we have discussed in the earlier part of this book, there is an urgent need for a rereading of the New Testament, granting full recognition to the urban setting of the earliest period of the Christian mission. Once this context is recognized, texts which we thought we understood may explode with unanticipated meanings and are likely to be seen as possessing powerful, even revolutionary, significance for both the church and the world in the century ahead.

The crucial question we must face here concerns the manner in which the early disciples of Christ related their confession of his lordship to the ideology of the Roman Empire and the veneration of the Caesars. Were the cities of the Empire sites of inevitable and irreconcilable conflict between the worshipers of the crucified and risen Christ and those who held political power within the Roman system? As we have seen, the story of Jesus related in the Gospels had a clear resonance for his later disciples in precisely such situations and his fate within Jerusalem might suggest that faithful discipleship would be inseparable from conflict and suffering. It might also lead to the conclusion that Christian existence was bound to involve withdrawal, political passivity and non-engagement in the life of the city. On the other hand, Christians believed that the resurrection represented the victory and vindication of their Lord, and that this was authentic good news for all nations. The victory of Christ over the powers of sin and death was understood to be an event of universal significance and therefore had to be announced among all peoples. For the New Testament writers the cross was no mere cultic symbol, but the means of healing, forgiveness and reconciliation for *the whole world* (see 1 John 2:2). The metaphors employed by Jesus that we noted above, implying that his followers were to act as salt, light and yeast *within* an urban world, are clearly paralleled in the New Testament literature by apostolic exhortations to live out the values of the kingdom of God in ways that would first puzzle, then attract outsiders. By creating 'contrast societies' of love and sharing, the Jesus movement presented the pagan, Roman world with an enigma intended to provoke curiosity and investigation. All of which suggests that, as we have argued earlier, there was no single approach to the challenge presented by an urban Empire, but rather a range of possibilities and responses which could depend on variables such as specific local conditions and the varieties of personal and social backgrounds of the disciples themselves.

It has often been observed that the book of Acts describes the spread of the Christian movement in a manner that clearly focuses on the geographical progress of the gospel. The narrative moves from Jerusalem to the heart of the empire in Rome by way of a series of urban missions, including the highly significant encounter with Greek philosophy in Athens. The pattern of Paul's journeys to various cities as described in Acts, and the manner in which believing assemblies were established and then related to each other, reflects pre-existing ideas and structures within the Hellenistic world, leading Laura Nasrallah to suggest that Paul's urban mission is 'best understood in light of contemporaneous political and cultural discourses about Greek cities under Rome' (Nasrallah 2008: 534). For example, the Graeco-Roman concept of the empire as a confederation of cities linked through their *people's assemblies* is echoed (or perhaps mimicked) by the use of the term *ekklesia* to describe the community of Jesus' followers. This word, which has important parallels within the Old Testament, was used in everyday secular Greek to describe the congregation, or assembly, of free citizens in a Hellenistic city. Thus, it appears that by opting for this concept to designate the nature and character of the Christ movement, the 'People of The Way', as they are frequently called by Luke (see Acts 19:9, 23; 22:4; 24:14, 22), avoided language that would have suggested they were yet another religious sect and opted instead for an identity involving an open, world-affirming mission within the empire. The crucified and risen Jesus was, in their eyes, the rightful Lord of the world and by designating their movement with a secular term freighted with considerable social and political significance, the early Christians affirmed at one and the same time the 'worldwide urban society', and 'the urban as well as political character of the Christ community, locally and ecumenically' (Georgi 2005: 63).

Of course, such a move was bound to be controversial since it implied that the small, scattered communities of believers, followers of an obscure Jewish prophet who had been executed as an enemy of the state, possessed the secret of human freedom and communal well-being which the Greeks had long sought. A modern parallel might be found in the furore which followed the decision of British Muslims to found an organization bearing the name,

'The Muslim *Parliament* of Britain'. The implications of this were immediately obvious: the much-vaunted claims made for the centuries-old system of democratic politics based on the Houses of Parliament at Westminster were implicitly challenged by the Islamic co-option of this term to designate a religious body whose prayers and practice possessed deep socio-political significance. The first Christians clearly took a similar risk since the identification of their groups as the '*ekklesia* of Christ' implied the falsity of the ideological claims of Roman propagandists to have brought 'salvation' wherever their imperialist rule had been extended.

It will be recalled that at the beginning of the previous chapter we noted the significance of the frequently overlooked Table of Nations in Genesis 10 and the way in which this list of the earth's peoples and their cities signalled God's concern for all nations, so providing us with a detailed map of the peoples of the world who were to be blessed by Father Abraham's obedience. This text is alluded to at certain key moments in the story of the early church's mission. Luke's statement that the crowds of pilgrims present in Jerusalem at Pentecost came 'from every nation of the world' echoes the Genesis passage, and his subsequent description of the effect of the gift of miraculous powers of communication through which these scattered peoples heard about 'the wonders of God in our own tongues' has often been interpreted as a reversal of the confusion and scattering of Babel (Acts 2:1–13). Even more significant though is Paul's explicit reference to the promises of universal blessing made in the seminal texts of Genesis when he addresses an audience of philosophically-inclined Greeks at the Areopagus in Athens. The narrative has already made clear that Paul's mission was to take the good news to the nations (Acts 9:15 and see Gal. 1:15–16) and here, at the urban heart of the Hellenist world, he traces the origin of all peoples back to the creative act of God and his determination of 'the exact places where they should live'. In other words, all peoples are the objects of divine concern and mercy and their local histories and cultures contain clear indications of God's desire that they should 'reach out for him and find him' (Acts 17:24–28). Davina Lopez discerns in Paul's language echoes of the Genesis passages, of Jeremiah's call to be a 'prophet to the nations' (Jer. 1:5), and of Isaiah's vision of Israel's mission to be a light to those same peoples, bringing them the good news of divine mercy, justice and reconciliation (Isa. 42:1). The revelation of the risen Christ to Paul had led him to the conviction that he was born to 'proclaim Christ among the nations', so becoming the agent of the fulfilment of the promises made first to Abraham, amplified through Israel's classical prophets, and now brought to fruition through the life, death and resurrection of Christ. Lopez concludes that the salvation of Israel and the nations, peoples who 'have been conquered and assimilated into Roman rule', is linked 'to the common genealogical heritage of all the nations from God in Genesis 10 and the blessing of Abraham as the "father of many nations" in Genesis 12' (Lopez, 2008: 134–135).

The mention here of nations that were 'assimilated into Roman rule' alerts us once again to the colonial and hegemonic rule of the Empire and its negative impact on the lives of vast numbers of people at the very point at which the gospel of Christ was being preached during the first century. While it is important to hold in mind the facts noted above which indicate that the early Christians made a critical appropriation of certain features of the Hellenistic world, this process of cultural adaptation and translation cannot disguise the plain fact that the ideology which underpinned the urban empire of Rome involved claims to supremacy and inviolability which were bound to be challenged by a message declaring a crucified Galilean as Lord of the world. Lopez describes the imperial cult as 'a tool for the affirmation for the world-wide reach of Roman power' and she indicates how buildings, monuments and altars promoting that cult 'served to write Rome and Roman ideas into the fabric of an eastern city and its public life'. She writes,

> Such messages, incorporated into the plans and decorations of buildings, promoted specific ideas about social and cosmic order. Here myth and history were presented in tandem to legitimize and, to a large extent, naturalize Roman world domination. In other words, if Roman rule is seen not just as a continuation or highjacking of Greek mythology, but as ordained from the very beginning of time, then the predestined aspect of Roman domination cannot be questioned – it is presented as the logical culmination, fufillment, and purpose of the 'fundamental principles of the world' (Lopez 2008: 96).

The extent to which Roman ideology gave form and shape to the cities of the ancient world is evident from the writings of various well-known Roman historians, apologists and philosophers. For example, Tacitus describes the manner in which his father-in-law, Agricola, had pacified recalcitrant Britons, overcoming their hostility and resistance to Roman ways and transforming them into enthusiastic consumers of a civilized way of life:

> In order that a people dispersed and uncivilized, and proportionately ready for war, might be tamed by comfort to quiet and leisure, he would exhort persons, help communities, to build temples, fora, and houses; he praised the quick, rebuked the lazy, and the competition for his compliments took the place of coercion. . . . As a result, those who rejected the Latin tongue began to aspire to eloquence; further, the wearing of our clothing became an honor, and the toga came into fashion, and little

by little they went astray into alluring vices: to the portico, the bath, and the elegant dinner-party (quoted by Lopez 2008: 164).

For many people in the globalized, urban world of the twenty-first century this statement will sound disturbingly familiar. Tacitus describes an imperial strategy through which the benefits of the *Pax Romana* came to outweigh the defence of traditional values as the material advantages of the colonialist's urban culture provided local elites with a comfortable way of life. This same pattern was repeated wherever the Roman armies established control, including, as we have seen, in the Palestine of Jesus, so that another historian, Pliny the Elder, could claim that 'the wonders of our own city' had provided an exportable model through which 'by our architecture we have vanquished the whole world' (ibid.: 165).

Romans: a letter to an urban church

A first-century letter addressed to 'all in Rome who are loved by God and called to be saints' (Rom. 1:7) is self-evidently directed to believers living in the greatest city the world had then known. It is a letter addressed to an urban *ekklesia* at the very heart of the Empire and, although he had not personally visited this city, Paul was clearly well informed about both the physical and socio-economic conditions in which his hearers lived their lives, and the religious and moral challenges which they faced in Rome. The opening greeting is enough on its own to indicate the absurdity of contextless readings of Romans, and it suggests that any interpretation of the letter which ignores the actual situation of its recipients is bound to mislead us with regard to Paul's message and purpose.

Earlier in this chapter we noticed the significance of the term *gospel* when used to describe the evangelists' accounts of the birth, life, death and resurrection of Jesus, and Paul pointedly employs this word twice in the opening sentence of his letter to Rome (Rom. 1:1–2). Indeed, it recurs throughout his writing and he expresses an unusual eagerness 'to preach the gospel also to you who are at Rome' (1:14). Neil Elliott points out that the Greek word *euangelion* was used in an inscription honouring the emperor Augustus on his accession to power, and that by describing himself as an appointed messenger (*apostolos*) of a 'lord' (*kyrios*) whose imminent arrival (*parousia*) was expected, Paul intended his hearers to catch the echo of 'a diplomatic herald speaking of an approaching conqueror (Caesar was also regularly hailed as *kyrios*), preparing the cities of a province for a coming change in regime' (Elliott 2008b: 98).

We cannot discuss the complex questions concerning the interpretation of this letter which have preoccupied, and sometimes vexed, New Testament scholars. Paul deals with some very big issues and is anxious that the Christ-followers at the urban heart of the Roman Empire should have a clear and detailed exposition of 'the gospel of God'. The letter wrestles with the question of the position of Israel and the nations in the light of the Christ event, addressing both those people whom scholars are now inclined to describe as 'Judeans', and 'Gentile' believers, or those belonging to 'the nations'. This discussion occurs in a context in which social and ethnic tensions, so characteristic of urban life, were increasingly present within the disciple-community and threatened to compromise their unity and love. The Roman believers faced multiple pressures: some arose from the culture of Roman society in which the attribution of *honour* to those whose status demanded respect might blunt the radical edge of the gospel; other pressures came from the overarching ideology of the empire which included claims that, from the perspective of Christ, had to be regarded as both idolatrous and blasphemous; while there was also the relentless, grinding pressure of sustaining life, health and moral integrity in a city noted for obscene contrasts between the lives the rich and those of the poor.

Who were these people in the imperial city who knew themselves to be 'loved by God' and were called to live their lives, individually and communally, in a distinctive and counter-cultural manner? Studies of the social structure of the Roman Empire suggest that the elite segment, including the members of the imperial families within Rome and leading officials there and in other regions and cities, consisted of a mere 3% of the total population. Below them some merchants, artisans and military veterans possessed a moderate wealth, but a staggering 90% of the population existed at or near subsistence level. Within this huge mass of people the great majority struggled to sustain life and very many existed below subsistence: widows, orphans, the disabled, beggars, and so on. Ekkhard and Wolfgang Stegemann summarize the economic structure of the empire as one in which enormous power and wealth was concentrated 'in the relatively small upper class in the urban centres' while the 'great mass of the population' existed in a state of poverty from which there was little prospect of escape (Stegemann & Stegemann 1999: 37).

In a pioneering study of Paul's letter to the Romans, read in relation to the likely socio-economic context of its original hearers, Peter Oakes uses archaeological evidence from the ruins of Pompeii to construct a model Roman house-church whose members would have been among the original recipients of Paul's letter. Oakes describes a likely craftworker house-church meeting in one of Rome's tenement blocks, and considers how Paul's language in this letter would have been heard by, among others, a slave bath-stoker, a poor stone worker, a sexually exploited slave girl, and the house-church host himself. Paul would have been aware that most of the people to whom he offered the assurance that they were 'loved by God' lived on the edge of poverty in housing that was both overcrowded and dangerous. In the words of Philip Esler:

> Because of Rome's huge population, settled on a comparatively small area, there was always a shortage of land for housing it. While the elite lived in their atrium-style *domus*, the rest of the population generally made do by renting apartments in the numerous tenement blocks called *insulae*, often built many stories high over narrow streets. . . . The standard of the accommodation decreased in the upper levels, where the rents were lower and the poor rented rooms. The poorest made do with miserable garrets at the tops of dirty stairs. For everyone rents were high, and falling into debt to pay them was a common problem for the urban poor, and even for wealthy tenants (Esler 2003: 82).

Oakes's model house-church is composed of people who are non-elite and exist close to subsistence level. This is an urban church of the poor and, as such, is representative of early Christianity in Rome. This does not mean that the people who made up such groups lived at identical social and economic levels; within the broad category of the non-elite there were distinctions of status and access to resources, as is implied by the fact that one of the families is in a position to host meetings of Jesus' followers within their apartment, or perhaps in a workshop. How would these people have heard and applied Paul's letter? Oakes discusses Romans 12 against this background, observing that the apostle's injunction not to 'think of yourself more highly than you ought' (12:3) would challenge values based on honour and shame, so undermining the status system which divided the wealthy from the poor and created competition within the non-elite sector for recognition of one's superiority over the poorer neighbour. Paul's teaching, apparently so innocuous when read in a modern democratic society, contains a radical, even revolutionary, challenge since it suggests that a community reflecting God's undeserved grace in Jesus Christ will learn to value people by quite different criteria from those practiced in Rome. Similarly, the subsequent exhortation to love sincerely, being 'devoted to one another' and in brotherly love *honouring* 'one another above yourselves' (12:9–10), challenges deeply embedded cultural values and practices and involves a radical levelling in which those of high status are humbled, while the lowly are lifted up. As Oakes says, even among the non-elite life was structured by formal relationships in which people were expected to act consistently with their assigned societal role, so that the demand for 'love without play-acting' implied a new way of relating to others 'that would produce a range of major changes for all of the types of people in our model house church' (Oakes 2009: 108).

When read within this context, Romans becomes a very different book from the abstract theological treatise familiar to many Western Christians; it is suddenly alive with relevance in relation to issues concerning human identity, ethnic conflict, justice and mercy in a world dominated by unprincipled power and the worship of money and status. And it challenges many of our assumptions about the nature of the church and what it means to follow the way of Jesus Christ in a pagan society. For example, one of Oakes' house-church members is Iris, a slave girl who works for a bar owner who expects her to sleep with customers when this service is requested. Lacking freedom over her own body, she faces 'the tension of a prostitute's existence', to which has been added the pressure of Christian teaching concerning purity and love. How did Paul's ethical teaching relate to the existence of sexually-exploited slaves like Iris whose bodies were not their own and were used to prosper the bar owners, *as well as to keep themselves, and probably their children, from starvation?* This question is not easily answered but Oakes reads Paul's 'significant rhetoric about the body' in the light of it and concludes:

> Much of the freeing of the body is yet to come. A sexually exploited slave such as Iris recognizes this well. An 'over-realized' eschatology, which views the current life as a full enjoyment of God's blessings, would cut little ice with her, as with many situations since then (Oakes 2009: 149).

We cannot fail to be struck at this point by the parallels between the context of the majority of Paul's first hearers in Rome and the situation facing millions of Christians across the Global South today. The urban slums to which reference has been made earlier in this book are the sites of massive Christian growth as churches of the poor multiply in conditions that are an affront to human dignity. *Yet Paul's letter to the Romans was addressed to followers of Christ in similar circumstances to these.* The elegance and sophistication of the Roman city, which was the source of pride and celebration among Roman intellectuals, was only one side of the picture; beyond the iconic buildings and open plazas, the mass of the population lived in overcrowded and insanitary conditions much like those described by Mike Davis on our 'planet of slums' today (Davis 2006). It has been calculated that the density of the urban population of Roman Antioch, for example, *was greater than that in modern Calcutta, and that in Rome itself, with its limited space for expansion, between 200 and 300 persons were crammed into every acre!* The few members of the privileged and obscenely wealthy elite might enjoy the benefit of systems of sanitation and waste disposal which were not to be found in cities again until modern times, but the masses had to make do with open ditches running down the centre of narrow alleyways, into which rubbish and human waste was routinely dumped. The same contrasts in the urban experience of the rich and the poor applied in relation to the supply of water; while the extraordinary aqueducts for which the Romans are justly famous fed clean water to the homes of the elite, the poor had to carry what they could from public cisterns in which the water often became polluted and undrinkable. As a result, sickness became highly visible on the streets of poor areas, with observers reporting that 'swollen eyes, skin rashes, lost limbs' became a feature of the urban scene (Stark 2006: 28).

This picture of Rome, revealing the underside of the city so far removed from the glory and splendour of the classical metropolis, will seem familiar to millions of Christians who belong to the churches of the poor in the Global South today. Consider for instance, the experience of Alex Zanotelli, a Catholic missionary who describes his 'insertion' into the slum of Korogocho in Nairobi, where the limitations of his theology, spirituality and Bible knowledge were cruelly exposed by the realities of the lives of some of the poorest people on earth. Zanotelli testifies that in these conditions he learned to read the Bible in a completely fresh way, hearing the text 'from the underside of history' and discovering that his previous concepts of theology and morality fell apart. In a passage which bears a striking similarity to Oakes's description of the ethical problems facing the imagined slave girl, Iris, in ancient Rome, Zanotelli writes:

> When I try to dissuade young girls from going to town for prostitution, they tell me there is no other way to survive. 'But you are sure to get Aids!' I insist. 'It's OK! Die of Aids or die of hunger, what's the difference? Or maybe there is! You have a chance of longer life with Aids'. I understood that what I had held as morality is, to a large extent, middle class morality (Zanotelli 2002: 15).

In such contexts Paul's assurance in the first lines of his letter, that believers in the slums of Rome were 'loved by God', and the subsequent emphasis on that unconditional love, as when he writes that 'God has poured out his love into our hearts by the Holy Spirit' (5:5), was obviously profoundly meaningful. But there are a host of statements and themes in this letter that suddenly leap from the page when heard from the perspective of the underside of urban society – then and now. The injunction to reject 'the pattern of this world' and to allow a renewed mind to produce personal and social transformation

(12:2) becomes a call for an understanding of the social and structural causes of the distress and tragedy which destroy the lives of millions of people, and for the complete submission of the mind to the lordship of the crucified Christ. Again, Peter Oakes confesses that reading Romans through the eyes of someone like his imagined slave girl resulted in his realization that the subject of God's justice and *judgment* must be seen 'as part of the gospel' (2:16). For the poor and oppressed the discovery of God's mercy and free grace does not lessen the importance of the news that this same God is just and will 'judge the world, setting it to rights', a process already set in motion through Jesus Christ (Oakes 2009: 176).

In these and a multitude of other ways, the literature of the New Testament can be illumined when heard within the context of urban realities as these are daily experienced by the poor. As Oakes says, while we should not bypass the academic study of Paul's greatest letter, 'there is also a place for thinking about how it sounds to people at ground level' (Oakes 2009: 179). And 'ground level' will include places like the Korogocho slum in Nairobi where poor Christians, living at or below subsistence level in a globalized world, may be able to inform their rich and privileged brothers and sisters just what Paul would have sounded like to his first hearers in the over-crowded alleyways of ancient Rome.

While Paul's letter to the Romans provides the most obvious example of the way in which understanding the urban context of the first followers of Jesus Christ can assist the interpretative task, the same principle applies elsewhere in the New Testament since all of this literature was produced against the background of the religio-political claims made for the Empire and its rulers. In a famous debate held in the coastal town of Priene in the province of Asia, a law was passed establishing a festal day to celebrate the 'gospel (*euangelia*) of Caesar', described as follows:

> It is hard to say whether the birthday of the most divine Caesar is to be observed more as an event of joy or of salvation . . . since he has brought into full shape everything that had decayed and had been corrupted. He has given a new face to the universe . . . Therefore everyone may look to this day as the beginning of his own life, too. . . . It means the end and the limit of any feeling of being burdened now that he has been born (quoted in Georgi 2005: 81).

Whichever urban *ekklesia* Paul happened to be writing to he could not fail to present Christ in a manner that challenged idolatrous claims of this kind. The familiar words of Galatians 4:4, for example, that 'when the time had fully come, God sent his Son, born of a woman, born under the law', have a fresh resonance when read in relation to the Priene statement just quoted. Or consider Paul's exhortation to the Thessalonians in which he quotes people who 'are saying "Peace and safety"' (1 Thess. 5:3) – a phrase familiar to his hearers as a slogan for the promotion of the *Pax Romana*. Paul derides the Roman claim to have established true peace and predicts that *destruction* will come upon those responsible for this falsehood! Against this, he urges the humble members of the congregation in this city to 'take over the role of gods and human heroes' and so to become, in Christ, the agents of nothing less than the 'turning of the ages'. As Georgi says, they were to do this 'not by means of violence and triumph but through the everyday features mentioned in the beginning of the letter: faith, love, and hope' (ibid.: 85).

Examples of this kind could be multiplied many times over. The Corinthian correspondence was directed to a church in a city which had particularly close connections with Rome and had quite deliberately copied the imperial capital in its public art, architecture, urban planning and organization. Little wonder then that Paul felt impelled to stress the *power* of the cross of Christ, notwithstanding its apparent foolishness to those whose image of success had been defined by the Roman obsession with victory achieved through the exercise of violence; or that in a city known for ethnic, racial and social tensions, he should need to insist on the abolition of such distinctions within the new community of faith; or that he was required to address a series of moral and ethical problems in a manner that can only be understood as the social context in the city of Corinth is taken into account (Gordon 1997: 59–98). Or consider the letter to the Colossians, which has been described as 'an explosive and subversive tract in the context of the Roman empire', especially on account of the great poem celebrating the supremacy of Christ in 1:15–20, which unambiguously asserts that Jesus, the crucified one, bears the exact image of the invisible God and must have 'the first place in everything' (Col. 1:18, NRSV). Against the background of the imperial 'gospel' this passage appears treasonable since it 'subverts every major claim of the empire' and declares Christ to be 'the Creator, Redeemer and Lord of all creation, including the empire' (Walsh & Keesmaat 2004: 84).

What, finally, of the non-Pauline literature, which often seems to be overshadowed and neglected, as though letters like those of Peter, John, James and Jude constitute a kind of appendix following the definitive exposition of the Christian gospel provided by Paul? A contemporary Mexican theologian points out that the situations addressed in this literature bear remarkable similarities to the contexts within which many humble Christians across the Global South live their lives today, struggling to discover and practice patterns of faithful discipleship as people living at the margins of an unjust world.

Peter, James and John understood that their hearers confronted a dominant model of social life to which they were tempted to respond either through a process of assimilation, which threatened to destroy the unique message of Christ, or by retreating into a ghetto-like isolation which seemed to provide a kind of security, but at the cost of ceasing to function as light, salt and leaven within the wider social world. The issues raised in these letters reflect exactly this kind of dilemma:

> ... what to do in order to distinguish oneself from the groups that, supported by a specific ideology, fomented anarchy or rebellion; how to show that the subversive force of the Christian life does not necessarily reside in confronting the authorities just because they are authorities, but rather in believing in the possibility of ferment from within the social structures, in such a way that there is more and more space for the personal and social novelty that the kingdom came to bring (Rodriguez 1997: 198).

In this connection, the letter of James is especially significant. Throughout the modern era, people on the underside of industrialized cities have found in James' explicit critique of the Roman rich and powerful, especially in 4:13 – 5:6, a biblical basis from which to challenge those who professed faith while actually serving money. Groups like the Chartists in the great industrial cities of nineteenth-century England based their demands for justice, including fair wages and the recognition of their human dignity, on their reading of the gospel and the specific warnings of James directed to those who foolishly hoard wealth in 'the last days' (5:3). Far from being a letter which is marginal to the central concerns of the New Testament, James actually connects us directly to both the Jewish prophetic heritage which we have explored in the previous chapter, and to the life and ministry of Jesus, known to the author as both brother and Lord. The writer knows very well the dangers that lie in wait in cities for those whose faith is merely theoretical and conceptual and he insists on an organic connection between belief and practice; faith must *work*, it must be a living, dynamic power which results in change and transforms both individuals and communities. Without such a holistic faith the confession that there is one God becomes a mere slogan, little better than the knowledge possessed by demons! As Robert Wall observes, this neglected letter sounds a sharply prophetic note, 'critical of business-as-usual values' and inviting the repentance of the rich and comfortable. The perceived tension between this message and that found in the Pauline literature should not be too hastily resolved in a process of forced harmonization, but rather embraced as a divine gift to Christians inclined to become over-spiritual, providing them with a way to re-imagine 'a more inclusive understanding of "normative" Christianity' (Wall 1997: 2–4).

We may sum up the significance of the non-Pauline literature briefly discussed here in the words of Raul Rodriguez, who says that the kind of instructions contained within these letters encourage humble believers by reminding them that 'resistance is achieved in simple everyday things, not in those that are extraordinary and make waves'. These writers do not demand great heroism but rather a commitment to faithfulness and perseverance when confronted with the seemingly invincible power of the world which can so easily result in discouragement, conformity and despair. Peter, John, James and their fellow writers, teach us to value 'the numerous small accomplishments of our communities' and to practice a holistic faith within a community sustained by prayer, hope and mutual love (Rodriguez 1997: 205).

The new Jerusalem

All that has been said above concerning the crucial importance of understanding the context of the New Testament literature applies in a special way to the last book in the Bible. Here we deal with a work that can be described as urban from first to last: it begins with letters addressed to seven churches located in cities across Asia Minor, ends with a remarkable vision of the new Jerusalem and, in between, describes in graphic detail the ultimate fate of 'Babylon', used as a code word for the city of Rome.

The problems of growing nominalism and the cooling of the original ardour of faith which we have already noted in the letter of James, loom even larger in this final book of the Bible. The majority of the urban churches addressed in Revelation 2 – 3 were at various stages of decline and apostasy on account of the increasing prosperity enjoyed by Christians who had found ways of harmonizing their confession of Jesus Christ with an active and profitable involvement in the economic and social life of the Roman Empire. The church at Ephesus which, according to Luke, had come to birth in an extraordinary spiritual movement which provoked an urban riot on account of the economic impact of the gospel on certain trades, had now cooled off, settled down and developed a more respectable form of faith (Rev. 2:1–7). In Laodicea the situation was even worse; the accommodation of Christians with the Roman system here was far more advanced and material prosperity within the congregation was accompanied by a form of delusion which blinded this church to the reality of its spiritual compromise and bankruptcy (3:14–22). This letter in particular makes uncomfortable reading for Western

Christians in the twenty-first century since many of them enjoy the fruits of economic globalization while being unaware of the deadening of conscience which accompanies their prosperity and distorts both their knowledge of the world and of themselves. Harry Maier confesses that as a first-world, white, privileged male, he is forced to ask where else he can find himself in the Apocalypse if not in this letter to Laodicea, 'rich, not needing anything, neither hot nor cold, but lukewarm – the typical citizen of a reigning order that keeps the majority of the planet's inhabitants in servitude to service me and my comforts?' (Maier 2002: 38).

In this context we might say that John of Patmos uses shock tactics to arouse churches in danger of the sleep of death, bombarding them with a stream of vivid, disturbing images intended to deconstruct their comfortable view of the world and jerk them into a new consciousness in which reality comes to be seen from the perspective of the throne of God. Thus, no sooner has the prophetic message been delivered to the apostate church at Laodicea than John finds himself summoned to exit the phenomenal world, a realm of madness, violence and rampant injustice, and to pass through 'a door standing open in heaven' (4:1). Once through that door, everything changes; the standard of values which dominated the Empire and seemed so universal as to permit no alternatives, is exposed as false and dehumanizing, and the glory of Rome becomes dross in the light that streams from the throne of God. Richard Bauckham has said that the effect of the visions which make up the bulk of the book is to *expand the hearers' world*, opening it up to divine transcendence. 'The bounds which Roman power and ideology set to the readers' world are broken open and that world is seen as open to the greater purpose of its transcendent Creator and Lord' (Bauckham 1993a: 7). This means that to a greater extent than even with the Gospels or the letter of Paul to the Romans, this document was controversial and dangerous; there are no half measures here as the followers of Jesus are summoned to deep repentance and to a discipleship that brooks no compromise with idolatry and deception. Revelation, Bauckham says, contains a radical critique of the system of Roman power and is 'the most powerful piece of political resistance literature from the period of the early Empire' (ibid.: 38).

How does John's Apocalypse achieve its purpose? First, the book operates at the level of the *imagination*, providing followers of Christ in urban settings which were saturated with images and symbols designed to reinforce the Roman worldview, with an alternative and subversive symbolic world. Davina Lopez has drawn attention to the enormous significance of visual imagery in the Roman world and has shown how statues, inscriptions, coinage and architecture were all designed to embed the official ideology of the Empire in the consciousness of peoples who had been forcibly incorporated within it. The power of such symbols is immense in contexts in which the vast majority of the population are not literate, so that written texts are scarce and designed to be *performed* rather than read by solitary individuals. In such a situation, the worldview of the powerful and privileged comes to be internalized and regarded as inevitable and universal; it is simply 'the way the world is' and cannot therefore be critiqued or challenged. However, Lopez points out that this dominant way of viewing reality can be questioned from below on the part of people who experience a sharp dissonance between the official story and their actual experience of life; such people are able to *imagine* a different kind of world. As Lopez says,

> Imagination arises from a position of hope among the disenfranchised; it is the ability to envision a different world when that task seems overwhelming, implausible and forbidden. Imagination is, in a sense, an often-coded revenge of the margins and the borders; it is often only vaguely familiar or intelligible to [those holding power] while at the same time shattering [their] totalizing grip (Lopez 2008: 18).

This was precisely the situation of John of Patmos, a 'companion in the suffering and kingdom and patient endurance' in Jesus while confined at a Roman penal colony 'because of the word of God and the testimony of Jesus' (1:9). However, John's concern, as we have seen, was to awaken Christian communities which were in danger of being seduced by the propaganda of the Empire, and were no longer listening to the voice of the Spirit (2:7, 11, 17, etc.). What was urgently required was the purging and refurbishment of the Christian *imagination*, and thus Revelation tackles peoples' imaginative response to the world, 'which is at least as deep and influential as their intellectual convictions' (Bauckham 1993b: 159).

It is more than half a century since the American writer Vance Packard published his ground-breaking study of modern advertising, *The Hidden Persuaders*, in which he showed how modern psychology was employed by marketing experts to create needs, hungers and desires within the American public that would transform them into consumers of goods which, while previously unknown, would come to be regarded as indispensable to their human well-being and happiness. Packard noted that while most people thought of themselves as rational human beings who controlled their own choices and decisions, the 'hidden persuaders' had a very different view of the public: 'they see us as bundles of day-dreams, misty hidden yearnings, guilt complexes, irrational emotional blockages.' These high priests of an economistic culture regarded the masses within the cities of America as 'image lovers' who might easily be persuaded to engage in impulse buying and who, under the increasing barrage of carefully targeted advertising campaigns, would display 'growing docility in responding to their manipulation of symbols that stir us to action' (Packard 1957: 14).

In the decades since Packard wrote this his predictions have proved remarkably accurate and a commercial culture equipped with a staggering array of persuasive techniques has come to dominate the modern world. With globalization this culture has spread around the world, so that even in the poorest and most deprived of urban settings in Africa, Latin America and Asia, illuminated billboards placarding the symbols of a consumer culture indicate the hegemonic intent and universal reach of the market system. As Jeremy Seabrook has observed, this culture is extremely difficult to resist because it seeps into every aspect of life, invading both public space with its glittering symbols, while also penetrating to the sub-conscious levels of human beings with its false promises of happiness and well-being. Where an occupying colonial power might be clearly identified and resisted through organized struggles for political freedom, this colonization of heart and mind is much more serious since 'the adversaries are impalpable, dissolving and regrouping all the time, *the better to take the citadels of faith and custom from within*' (Seabrook 2004: 24, emphasis added).

In an age like this, urban theology can only meet the challenge of the world we have described if it recognizes the crucial importance of the realm of the imagination and provides the materials which would enable a refurbishing of Christian imaginative worlds. The Revelation of John, with its profusion of visual imagery and dramatic symbolism, so bewildering to readers unable to access the codes which unlock the book's meaning, created exactly such an alternative symbolic world with the Creator God at its heart, and so enabled the followers of Jesus to resist the idols of Rome and maintain their vision and hope for a different kind of world.

The second feature of this extraordinary book which enables John to achieve his purpose concerns his vision of the destiny and calling of the nations. According to Roman imperial mythology, the destiny of the nations was that they were to be discovered, pacified and incorporated within the Empire in line with the mandate issued by Jupiter which promised Rome 'empire without end, without limits on space or time'. John subverts Rome's self-image as a liberating and civilizing force by depicting her as a prostitute seated 'on many waters' (17:1). Later it is explained that these waters represent 'peoples, multitudes, nations and languages' and that the woman is a symbol for 'the great city that rules over the kings of the earth' (17:15–18). However obscure aspects of this symbolism may be, it is clear that John sees Rome both as benefiting economically from its dominance over the nations, and as exercising force to control the threat of chaos which was always present where rebellious movements surfaced. The seas were vital for transportation, thus facilitating the movement of goods to the centre, but were also sites of great threat and danger which again and again brought death and destruction. In other words, the vision depicts the *Pax Romana*, proclaimed as a universal blessing for all peoples, but here exposed as a cover for a world order in which the nations were exploited in Rome's interests as their produce and wealth flowed into the imperial centre *like many waters*. Justo Gonzalez, in a stimulating study which the bears the subtitle, *The Book of Revelation in an Age of Cultural Conflict*, comments that cultural encounters 'do not take place in abstraction of economic and political systems' and that when 'the rivers of wealth flow in one direction, it is only natural for the population to flow in the same direction' (Gonzalez 1999: 83).

John's vision of the future for the nations of the world is utterly different from that of Rome. He is asked at one point to consume a scroll which initially tastes as sweet as honey, but then becomes sour in his stomach. This action is followed by a command to 'prophesy again about many peoples, nations, languages and kings' (10:9–11). Like Paul, John is clearly aware of the biblical traditions concerning the future of the nations to which we have made repeated reference in this present book. And also like Paul, he sees the promises to Abraham and the Old Testament prophets concerning the nations as now fulfilled in Jesus Christ, so that the destiny of the peoples of the earth is not that which was so arrogantly declared by Rome, but rather is to find their true freedom through Christ, the Lamb of God. Gonzalez suggests that the sweet-and-sour scroll consumed by John, which results in his commission to 'prophesy *about* many peoples' indicates that he must speak to largely Jewish congregations and challenge them concerning God's liberating, saving purpose for the peoples who, like them, were suffering under Roman imperial domination. This bitter-sweet experience of John is replicated in the urban world of today in which increasingly multi-cultural cities challenge forms of Christianity which remain associated with a single culture or, even worse, are so deeply identified with an economically dominant society as to betray God's liberating purpose for all peoples. John's vision is of a church in which every culture is respected under the lordship of the crucified and risen Christ (5:9–10; 7:9; 21:24). As Gonzalez puts it,

> The vision which John the Jew has is a vision of a Gentile church, a church where Gentiles, the nations, *ta ethne*, the *goyim*, will come and take their place right next to Israel, and all together will claim the ancient promise made to the people of Israel,

that they would be a kingdom of priests. That is a vision sweet as honey, for it
shows the fullness of the mercy of God; but it is also a vision bitter to the stomach,
because it shows that no people, no tribe, no language, no nation, can claim a
place of particular honor in that fullness. And it is bittersweet because it involves
radical change in the very congregations where John has served and which he loves
(ibid.: 92).

The third and final way in which John achieves his purpose in this
book concerns the culminating vision of a city that is yet to come, the new
Jerusalem which comes down to earth from heaven. As we have seen, the
book of Revelation is addressed to urban Christians and it takes for granted
the context of an urban world. The fact that it culminates with a utopian urban
vision demonstrates that nothing in this book should be read as reflecting
an anti-urban bias, but it is equally clear that John recognizes that the urban
ideal has been fatally corrupted by the ideology which underpinned the city
of Rome and shaped urban structures and societies throughout the Empire.
In Rome, the city built on 'seven hills' (17:9), the worldly spirit that had previously been manifest in ancient Babylon, had reappeared and taken such a
powerful and pervasive form as to result in the corruption of all the cities
which fell under its influence and control.

Thus, the second half of Revelation is dominated by the contrast between
Babylon and New Jerusalem and the destruction of the former appears to
be the pre-condition for the arrival of the latter. The collapse of the worldly
city is described in terrifying detail in chapter 18, with a particular focus on
three classes of people: the *kings* of the earth who, like the Herodian dynasty,
had been the local agents of Roman power and beneficiaries of its system;
the *merchant class,* who would lament the loss of an empire which provided
them with profitable trading opportunities; and *sea captains and sailors,* whose
vessels had transported goods to the imperial city from across the seas (18:9,
11, 17). These people were key players in the extension of Roman power and
economic control around the known world, and close examination of the
extraordinary list of products traded by the merchants reveals the extent of
this system. The places of origin of the items described in 18:12–13 have been
identified as including Spain, Egypt and North Africa, Syria, the Persian Gulf,
India, Ceylon, Indonesia and China. The achievement of Rome in establishing this worldwide system was celebrated by the orator Aelius Aristides in
extravagant language:

Here is brought from every land and sea all the crops of the seasons and the produce
of each land river and lake . . . so that if someone should wish to view all these things,

he must either see them by travelling over the whole world or be in this city. ... It is possible to see so many cargoes [in Rome] . . . that one imagines that for the future the trees are left bare for the people there and that they must come here to beg for their own produce if they need anything (quoted in Bauckham 1993b: 375).

Aristides' final comment, apparently made without irony or regret, highlights precisely why John of Patmos, viewing the entire enterprise from the perspective of those peoples whom Rome reduced to beggary and worse, prophesied and celebrated the ultimate destruction of Rome. The extent to which the author of this book viewed the empire from its underside is vividly illustrated by a statement at the end of the list of cargoes bought and sold within this market system: '. . . *and bodies and souls of men*' (18:13). Here is the ultimate deconstruction of Roman propaganda as John of Patmos reminds his readers that the slaves whose labour sustained the system were 'not mere animal carcasses to be bought and sold as property', but human beings made in the image of God. In this one pregnant phrase John has exposed 'the inhuman brutality, the contempt for human life, on which the whole of Rome's prosperity and luxury' rested (Bauckham 1993b: 370–371).

What then is the alternative? John summons the followers of Jesus to 'come out' of Rome so that they 'will not share in her sins' (18:4), but that withdrawal can only take place if there is an alternative vision of urban life which offers hope to the oppressed, and inspiration to those who had much to *lose* by abandoning Rome. The eschatological vision of the new Jerusalem in chapters 21 – 22 presents John's hearers with the divine alternative: a city which comes down from heaven to earth and, as Bauckham says, 'represents the true fulfilment of the ideal of the city, a city truly worth belonging to' (Bauckham 1993a: 130). However, the question that immediately arises here is whether, in sober truth, this brilliant vision is not simply a pipe dream? Is this merely another form of religious escapism by means of which those who currently suffer injustice and poverty are offered the false comfort of post-mortem compensation?

There are two ways of responding to these questions. First, it may be recalled that we earlier suggested that the *foundations* of the city of God were actually laid in the events which took place outside Jerusalem when the crucifixion of Jesus was revealed to be the means of the *victory of God*. John of Patmos is absolutely aware of this fact; indeed, the book begins with a revelation of the Christ who declares, 'I was dead, and behold I am alive for ever and ever! And I hold the keys of death and Hades' (1:17–18). The same crucified and risen Jesus, the Lamb appearing 'as if it had been slain', is declared to be alone worthy to break the seals of the scroll which symbolizes the unfolding of human history, and so to be entrusted with 'power and wealth and wisdom and strength' (5:6–14). In other words, the city of God which descends from heaven in the closing visions of Revelation is not an eschatological reality which belongs entirely to the future, *but the culmination of the process by which, from Pentecost onwards, the alternative city of God has been under construction, built on the foundations laid in the salvation of the world brought about by Christ.* As Pablo Richard has observed, the fundamental reality of this book is 'the resurrection of Christ in the present history of our world' and it is this which makes Revelation a book of 'hope and joy because Christ has risen *and this good news changes the meaning of present history*' (Richard 1995: 171, emphasis added). Babylon and New Jerusalem thus exist in the present, the one frequently dominant while the other often remains hidden, but the message of the Apocalypse is that the future lies with the City of God.

The second thing to say in response to the critical questions raised above is that the culminating vision of the triumph of God in the coming of New Jerusalem, casts its light and hope *backwards* across history, providing inspiration and practical guidance to those who resist the spirit and values of Babylon wherever they appear, and work to build God's alternative city in the knowledge that, because Christ has risen, their labours 'in the Lord are not in vain' (1 Cor. 15:58). A detailed study of John's final visions (which lies beyond the scope of this present book) would show the many ways in which they contain 'concrete and constructive suggestions for real churches, for the city as a central reality, and for a sane urban world' (Georgi 2005: 161).

Conclusion

It remains for us to notice certain features of God's alternative city that are significant for the construction of an urban theology in the context of the twenty-first century. The vision with which the Bible closes is one in which the life of the entire world has become urban. Were this vast city, shaped as a massive cube (the symbol of perfection), extending 1,500 miles in every direction, to be imposed on the actual map of the world it would cover the entire Mediterranean area. Or as Catherine Gonzalez puts it, the area covered by New Jerusalem 'would make the Boston-New York-Philadelphia-Baltimore-Washington complex look like a small town!' Its height would reduce New York's skyscrapers (or for that matter the soaring towers of Dubai) to such insignificance they would appear as small cabins! (Gonzalez & Gonzalez 1978: 107). What is more, the kings of the nations of the world, now liberated from the oppressive power of Babylon, are converted and 'bring their splendour' into the city of God (Rev. 21:24). In other words, while New Jerusalem comes *down* from heaven, all of human labour, politics, art and culture which contributed toward the establishing of the reign of justice and mercy which is God's will, carries over into the heavenly city and has eternal value. As Darrell Cosden has noticed, John's vision is one in which 'God is pleased to gather up, transform, and include not just his "pure" creation, but also the genuine additions to the created reality that we have brought about through creation-transforming actions' (Cosden 2006: 75).

The new Jerusalem is a place which is both filled with light (21:23) and in which culture and nature are in total harmony (22:1–2). The presence of God within the city is the source of its illumination, while the description of the 'river of the water of life' which flows down its great, broad street and irrigates 'the tree of life', bearing crops every month of the year, echoes and greatly extends the Genesis narratives describing the Garden of Eden. In Bauckham's words, this is an urban vision which insists upon 'that harmony of nature and human culture to which ancient cities once aspired but which modern cities have increasingly betrayed' (Bauckham 1993b: 135). The ancient aspiration for such harmony was especially evident as we have seen, within the Old Testament, but it can also be found among the Greeks. Thus, Dieter Georgi has argued that each of the details we have mentioned, the ever-present 'brightness and clarity', and the reconciliation of nature and civilization, correspond to the ideals of the Hellenistic city, so that in John's vision 'Hellenistic city planning and architecture has been brought to perfection' (Georgi 2005: 177).

Can we say the same thing with regard to other urban visions? Earlier in this book we noted the parallels between these biblical texts and the dreams of visionary urban planners like Ebenezer Howard and Le Corbusier, and we may ask whether their inspirations, which, despite the defects we have discussed, resulted in garden cities and urban centres filled with light, contained at least some intimations of God's intention for the city, now perfected, purified and fulfilled in the new Jerusalem? Will the leaves of the tree that 'are for the healing of the nations' (Rev. 22:2) be applied to all our imperfect endeavours to build the city, purging the evil and negative features which blighted our efforts, while sanctifying and perfecting those aspects of our work that, whether consciously or not, conformed to the Creator's blueprint?

At the end of the nineteenth century, reflecting on the condition of the industrial cities of Britain and noting the beginnings of a serious loss of regular worshippers in the Victorian churches, Henry Drummond was struck by two 'very startling' aspects of John's vision of the city of God: the nearest thing to *heaven* that John could imagine was *a city*; and it was a city that *contained no church building!* John, he said, 'combines these contradictions in one daring image, and holds up to the world the picture of a City without a Church as his ideal of the heavenly life' (Drummond 2008: 11). The reference is to the prophet's announcement that he could 'not see a temple in the city' (21:22). For Drummond, this provided the basis for a withering critique of British churches since, in flat contradiction to John's vision, they had alienated masses of urban people from Christ by confining him behind altar rails and leaving the daily life of the city, its work, business and leisure, utterly devoid of the light that comes from New Jerusalem. Drummond's challenge to Christians still remains, but so too does the challenge to our urban world which arises from a vision in which the well-being of the city is inseparable from the presence within it of 'the Lord God almighty and the Lamb'. It is that divine nearness which renders the temple redundant and abolishes forever the distinction between the sacred and the secular. In other words, the biblical understanding of the city is fundamentally theological, which leads us to our final chapter and the attempt to relate theology to the urban world around us.

8. THEOLOGY FOR AN URBAN WORLD

[T]he future of human cities and their meaning is one of the most critical spiritual issues of our time. . . . [W]hat is so often missing from contemporary concerns about cities is precisely a vision. And vision or perspective, rather than some kind of definitive conclusion, is a primary theological task (Sheldrake 2005: 67).

It will be recalled that earlier in this book we indicated the intention to attempt to lay the foundation for an urban theology, first, by engaging in dialogue with scholars working in a range of academic disciplines concerned with urbanization and second, by surveying the biblical narratives with particular reference to the urban contexts within which they were written, specifically the great urban empires of the ancient world, from Assyria to Rome. Having now completed these tasks, the challenge which remains to be faced is that of seeking to construct an interpretative bridge between these very different worlds in order to discover whether, and in what ways, the texts of the Bible might relate to the context of the urban world of today. Given that this is a context shaped by modern worldviews and that it has been transformed through technological and social revolutions beyond the imagination of the biblical authors, it is clear that we need an approach which eschews naïve and simplistic uses of the Bible, even as it strives to readdress the biblical texts 'as illuminating and revelatory in contemporary contexts' (Brueggemann 2000a: 18).

The necessity and urgency of this task is highlighted by two aspects of our current situation. First, for many millions of poor people in the cities of the Global South, the Bible is a living, authoritative text which shapes their response to the urban context within which they find themselves, providing them with hope in situations of suffering, injustice and violence. The crucial question in these contexts is precisely *how* the biblical texts are being preached and heard? Do they act as the 'opium of the people', offering escape from the harshness of an unjust world through the promise of spiritual reward in a sphere which lies entirely outside of history, or do these ancient texts expose and unmask the forces responsible for the suffering of the oppressed, and so energize them in resistance to injustice and in action to bring about social and economic change? Carlos Gallardo, commenting on Matthew's Gospel within its concrete first-century setting, describes it as a message of 'good news for the persecuted poor' and demonstrates how, when this text is allowed to speak into the world of the poor today, it is heard in the *favellas* as a call 'to become agents of the kingdom', bearers of the light of the glory of God through a new praxis of justice, resulting in 'the reordering of relationships with God, with men and women, with the world, and with oneself' (Gallardo 1997: 190). Clearly, the construction of hermeneutical bridges between the world of the Bible and the context of the urban world of today can result in these texts exploding with fresh relevance in Latin American, African and Asian cities.

In the second place, we have noticed that many urbanist scholars write about the contemporary world in almost apocalyptic language, fearing for the future of our fragile planet as well as for the physical, psychological and spiritual well-being of its inhabitants as long as an unrestrained market system continues to be the engine propelling the global rush toward the cities. The literature on this subject reverberates with sober warnings of the impossibility of continuing as we are:

- from *analyses of consumerism*, as involving the replacement of ethical norms with artificially created needs, so releasing individuals from the restraints imposed by traditional social bonds and substituting these with the ephemeral experiences of personal pleasure associated with the culture of shopping (Bauman 2001b);
- to warnings from experts in *public health* that while medical science has made huge strides in reducing mortality through the control of the diseases that devastated the populations of the first industrial cities, it has 'provided few solutions to emergent social pathologies' which are the consequence of precisely the ideology of consumerism just mentioned (Hanlon *et al.* 2010);

- and finally, the constant assertion that no mere technical fixes can address the crisis of our times because what is demanded is a sustained, critical examination of *the values and worldview assumptions* which underpin the way of life of the modern world. As Jonathan Watts puts it at the conclusion of his detailed study of the growth of Chinese cities: 'A step back can be progress. Before we retool our economies, *we need to rethink our values*' (Watts 2010: 392, emphasis added).

In such a situation the importance of the biblical perspectives we have outlined in the two previous chapters might seem to be self evident. Indeed, it is not unusual to discover scholars employing biblical imagery when discussing the converging crises of the twenty-first-century urban world. For example, in a monumental study of what he called 'the world revolution of Westernization', by which a minority of the world's population 'imposed its own accomplishments as a universal standard to which all others, however reluctantly, had to submit', Theodore Von Laue describes the cultural chaos and psychological misery experienced by millions of people on the receiving end of this process. Acknowledging that the global rivalry for wealth and power has resulted in 'an unprecedented rise in material prosperity', Von Laue argues that it has also produced 'a global metropolis remarkably uniform in appearance and standards' but 'crammed full with deadly fears and explosive anger'. He describes the dilemmas confronting the urban world, and discovers an analogy with the Old Testament text we have discussed in chapter 6 when he writes that, 'the global confluence thus far has produced not a shiny global city but a Tower of Babel' in which 'all subtle distinctions between right and wrong, good and evil, worth and worthlessness' are being undermined. Almost a quarter a century ago Von Laue identified the fundamental issue as one concerning ethical values: 'Where in this global Babylon do we find the transcendent moral absolutes that can restrain the rising penchant for violence?' (Von Laue 1987: 3–8).

Idols of our time

In seeking to apply the insights of the Bible to this situation, we need to keep in mind the dialectic between the prophetic critique of urban societies, on the one hand, and the surfacing of hope for the coming of a new and different world, on the other. We have tracked these two lines of tradition through the Old and New Testaments and in holding them in tension together we may move beyond the sterile anti- and pro-urban positions which have characterized so much discussion of the phenomenon of urbanization. The Bible, we might say, is against the-city-for-the-city; it contains the most searching and profound critical reflections on urban life (insights which, whether consciously or not, have shaped contemporary social criticism, including that of Karl Marx), while it also offers an alternative vision of an urban society shaped by justice and mercy, and characterized by love, community and joy. When one of these themes is isolated from the other we end up with a distorted and seriously unbalanced perspective which results in either a deeply pessimistic view of the city, or a shallow optimism which fails to reckon with the reality of the forces of evil which often threaten the very survival of cities.

The prophetic critique of the cities of the ancient world is never limited to external forms and structures, but is concerned with deep-level foundations in relation to the fundamental beliefs and values at the core of human cultures. For example, the Babel narrative to which reference has just been made is more than a simple metaphor illustrating the human condition; it takes us beyond a surface level analysis to uncover the roots of the tragic condition of human beings in the shape of their *alienation* from the true source of life and *shalom*. When we apply this perspective to the analysis of contemporary cities in which life is increasingly reduced to possessing material things, or to the quest for sensations which distract from existential reality, we are bound to conclude that, in so far as cities are the products of alienated human beings they will be devoid of meaning. The towers of iconic buildings may multiply as the earth becomes covered with a network of interconnected and similar cities, but the privatized urban spaces within which people increasingly encounter each other (shopping malls, airport lounges, entertainment or sporting arenas) contain no organic societies and so become, to use anthropological terminology, 'non-places' (Augé 1995). For the biblical writers *the deepest cause of this tragedy is located in the hubris which drives the builders' projects, a pride accompanied by spiritual blindness, by a kind of secular quest for immortality, and an idolatry which condemns them to meaningless, sisyphean labour.*

The mention of idolatry highlights a biblical theme of major importance to this discussion. According to the Hebrew prophets, the urban critique (whether of Babylon or Jerusalem) must include, and may need to commence with, the criticism of religion when this provides an aura of sanctity for unjust political and economic structures, presenting these as divinely ordained and therefore beyond any possibility of challenge. Although idols are clearly human creations, and the prophets relentlessly expose them as such, they come to possess enormous power, dominating and enslaving their devotees and closing off the possibility of social transformation. The relevance of this to the concerns of this book becomes evident if we ask how it has come about that 'market

forces' have assumed a god-like status by which they dictate social and economic policies which shape the lives of practically everyone on this planet? In
chapter 3 we noted the process by which economic activity became divorced
from ethical control, leading eventually to the growth of an *economistic* culture
in which the 'free market' became the source of cultural values. During the
second half of the twentieth century this culture came to dominate the earth
with the result that people across the world 'were forced to abandon socio-
economic systems that had for centuries proved capable of ensuring their survival' (Collier & Esteban 1998: 28). This revolutionary change was presented
as a non-negotiable condition for entering the global market and came with
the promise that it would eventually bring prosperity and increased freedom.
However, while local urban elites certainly enriched themselves in the new era
of globalization, the very survival of masses of ordinary people was threatened
by these changes as traditional skills were devalued, poverty and hunger eroded
ancient communal bonds, and millions of people were reduced to an abject
state of dependency. The startling words of Vinoth Ramachandra allow people
in the northern hemisphere to hear a Christian voice from the Global South
alerting them to the consequences of the veneration of the idols of our time:

> The dominant economic ideology now uncritically promulgated by American and
> European governments and schools of management is that the sole criterion for
> corporate decisions is return on investment capital. . . . Thus, in the name of this
> entrenched ideology, the well-being of millions . . . is destroyed for the putative
> wellbeing of future generations. . . . [C]apitalism, in the form practised in America
> and Europe today and propagated throughout the world, seems to be behaving like
> Stalinism and Maoism did only a few decades ago (Ramachandra 1996: 112).

In biblical terms it is clear that what we face here is an idolatrous elevation
of a humanly-constructed process of economic exchange, around which has
been woven a complex web of modern myths which mystify and conceal
the nature and outcomes of this system. In the words of Bob Goudzwaard,
'Unchallenged economic growth, an idol made by our own hands, has become
a power which forces its will on us' and in the relentless search for greater
material prosperity we have allowed various forces and powers 'to rule over us
as gods' (Goudzwaard 1984: 14).[1] However, idols rarely remain alone, so that

---

1. Note the title of an analysis of the economic crash during the first decade of the
   twenty-first century: *The Gods That Failed: How Blind Faith in Markets Has Cost Us
   Our Future* (Elliott & Atkinson 2008).

the worship of mammon (to use the term found on the lips of Jesus) is invariably accompanied by additional ideologies which further strengthen the dominant system, providing a protective shield for the privileges of the minority
of people who so clearly benefit from it. It will be recalled that Isaiah's great
vision of an alternative city of justice and *shalom*, where resort to the violence
of war has become a distant memory, is immediately followed by the dismal
description of empirical Jerusalem, said to be 'full of silver and gold' *and* full of
horses and chariots (Isa. 2:7–8). The idolatrous pursuit of wealth went hand in
hand with a military build-up which, it was believed, *could secure peace and security
for a city built on greed and injustice.*

The striking relevance of texts like these in relation to the modern world
becomes evident when we consider the way in which the ideologies of endless
economic growth and of security guaranteed through ceaseless military development have become interlocking and mutually reinforcing idols, propelling
humankind on a path which ends in death. While the Bible demands the
practice of justice and love for the neighbour as required by the Torah as a
condition of human freedom and social harmony, the modern world reversed
this order, making peace, security and prosperity into primary goals in the
mistaken belief that justice and freedom would follow as eventual outcomes
of the triumph of this system. By the 1970s this mythology had produced an
unprecedented arms race and a situation in which human beings possessed
the capacity to destroy the earth ten times over, but the promised benefits of
justice, security and well-being for the whole human family had come no closer
in a world which trembled on the brink of mass death. As Walter Wink has
observed, the ancient *myth of redemptive violence* (which we discussed in chapter
3) remains alive and well in the modern world, and contains an account of evil
into which children are socialized through the narratives endlessly depicted
in TV programmes and computer games (Wink 1998: 53–54). The tragedy of
the urban world in the twenty-first century is even greater because these same
ideologies have spread their baleful influence around the globe, with impoverished nations spending obscene amounts of money on armaments and nuclear
weapons proliferating in a context of terror and counter-terror which leaves
no-one secure. Indeed, we now appear to be locked into a spiral in which the
growing despair, anger and violence of the wretched of the earth, caused by the
idol-worshipping system to which we have referred above, triggers responses
of fear on the part of global elites, resulting in what scholars have called a 'new
military urbanism' which anticipates 'permanent and boundless war' and leads
to a growing 'militarization of urban life' (Graham 2010: 60).

In a context like this, the call of the Bible to recognize the destructive
power of idolatry has enormous resonance and demands that Christians

should be in the vanguard of resistance to the dehumanizing forces at work in our world. However, as Goudzwaard noted, too many people who claim to be followers of Christ have, like the believers in the cities of Asia Minor in the time of John of Patmos, 'selected their own goals, delivered themselves over to various ideologies, and thus have unwittingly worshipped demonic powers' (Goudzwaard 1984: 77). Meantime, the voices raised in prophetic protest, reflecting extraordinary courage in challenging the idols of our time, frequently come from outside the Christian tradition. Consider the case of Arundhati Roy who, on the occasion of the national celebrations accompanying the unveiling of India's nuclear weapon, recognized this as a hideous idol which constitutes humankind's most terrible act of blasphemy: it contains, she wrote, a direct challenge to God which is worded: *we have the power to destroy everything you have created* (Roy 1999: 162).

Theology and hope for the city

If the identification and repudiation of the idols which enslave people constitutes one major aspect of the theological and pastoral task of those who worship the God of the Bible, the embracing of an alternative vision which brings the hope of true freedom, equality and peace provides another, complementary and essential perspective. We have discussed the appearance and development of these two interlinking themes throughout the Bible and have seen how the Hebrew prophets offer both a courageous critical analysis of urban life and a hope-filled vision of a renewed and transformed world, promising the arrival of a city of joy in which peace, described as being like 'a flooding stream', would extend to all the inhabitants, including 'all your brothers, from all the nations' (Isa. 66:7–21). With the coming of Christ both these themes undergo significant changes, but the tension between the critical analysis of the urban context in which believers find themselves, and the embracing of the hope for a different kind of world, the nature of which has now been fully revealed and embodied in the person and work of Jesus of Nazareth, remains present. This is clear from Paul's words to Christ's followers in the imperial city of Rome:

> Do not conform any longer to the pattern of this world, but be transformed by the renewing of your mind. Then you will be able to test and approve what God's will is – his good, pleasing and perfect will (Rom. 12:2).

As we have seen in the previous chapter, the 'pattern of this world' for Paul and his first readers found expression especially in the Roman Empire and the cult of the Caesar religion with its claim to be the source of universal peace and salvation. The language of the letter to the Romans indicates very clearly Paul's awareness of the pervasive and subtle nature of the imperial ideology and its ability to control the minds of Roman citizens. His primary concern is that this ideology was being internalized and assimilated by people who made a formal confession of Jesus as Lord. Here, once again, we recognize the power of idolatry and Paul's rejection of it is no less uncompromising than that of the Old Testament prophets. The Caesar cult not only served the city of Rome and the peoples throughout the empire, it 'maintained the welfare of the universe' (Georgi 2005: 149). Paul's response throughout his writings, but especially in Romans, confronts this ideology as a form of idolatry which, in its negative impact on the world and its association with violence and brutality, reveals demonic origins. Thus, the letter to the Romans contains an exposition of the meaning of Christ which presented a head-on challenge to Rome and, by means of what scholars have called a 'hidden transcript', it offered pastoral guidance to a disciple-community of resistance in an urban environment. Dieter Georgi has even suggested that when this letter came to the attention of people within the imperial circle and its deepest meaning was understood, it provided the grounds for Paul's conviction and execution: 'Paul's being killed cannot be explained in any other way' (ibid.).

However, the theme of hope, based on an alternative and radically differ- ent vision, is also present here as those who renounce the idolatry dominant within their social world are reminded of the 'will of God', which consists of contributing to the life of a community characterized by humility and the service of others in love, sharing and mutual support. In other words, as the remainder of Romans 12 makes plain, the rejection of the Roman 'gospel' is but the prelude and condition for the embracing of the way of Jesus Christ and the creation of an alternative urban community. This point is of vital importance for urban theology because it underlines the fact that the critique of an urbanism resting on false foundations and resulting in divided and dehu- manizing cities, *does not imply the rejection of the city*. Indeed, we may go further than this and assert that the critical-prophetic evaluation of urban forms does not preclude either the acknowledgement of positive elements within dys- functional cities, or the recognition that the original vision of planners and builders may have been motivated by a desire to create urban forms capable of fulfilling the dream of the *polis* as the instrument for the creation of the good society.

At this point we are reminded that this positive approach to the urban phenomenon, even when particular cities fall far short of the ideal, is found throughout the biblical narratives; from Jeremiah's exhortation to the exiles to 'seek the good (*shalom*)' of the pagan city of Babylon, to Jesus' own metaphors requiring his followers to enter the cities as salt, light and leaven, and Paul's recognition of the positive elements in the Greek vision of cities in which democracy and genuine community might flourish. In fact, the Roman claim that the Empire was the source of universal blessing rested on a Greek foundation, so that the gift to the world of the *Pax Romana* was interpreted as the fulfilment of the Hellenistic dream of urban freedom and political liberty. The Romans 'interpreted their imperialist expansion as a world mission' and as an authentic application of 'Hellenistic world culture around the Mediterranean and beyond' (ibid.: 62). Paul's response involves *both* the uncompromising rejection of the imperial idolatry, which meant that he was bound to challenge the legitimacy of the Roman claim to have created a world society which marked 'the end of history', *and* the counter-claim that what both Greeks and Romans were searching for *is in fact possible when Christ, the rightful Lord of history, is recognized as both Saviour and God.* Contemporary New Testament scholarship has identified numerous ways in which Paul's concepts and language echo Hellenist ideals, from his understanding of the nature of the *ekklesia*, to his models of organization and leadership, and the insistence that Christ has abolished ethnic, racial and class distinctions, so creating a new kind of human community within a body that is both universal and local. In all of these instances Paul adopts Greek urban ideals which he sees as now made possible in purified and developed forms through Jesus Christ, the true Saviour of the world. In Dieter Georgi's words, Paul's vision of the free heavenly city, which he perceives not as an architectural phenomenon, 'but as an idea of a certain type of human community' clearly reflected Hellenistic urban thinking (ibid.: 64).[2]

The above discussion contains some significant pointers toward the shape of an urban theology in the globalized world of the twenty-first century. There are clear parallels between the claims made for the urban empire of Rome two thousand years ago and the celebratory language employed by the advocates of globalization today. Now as then, faithfulness to the crucified Christ will demand a theological critique of the idolatries which masquerade as neutral political and economic theories. Urban theology in this context will be

---

2. Laura Nasrallah's important article, 'The Acts of the Apostles, Greek Cities, and
    Hadrian's Panhellenion' traces the influence of Hellenistic urban ideals in the
    narrative of Paul's ministry in the book of Acts. She writes that Acts presents a
    new vision of Christian identity which is 'moored in prestigious ancient Israelite
    traditions, but moves easily nonetheless through the Greek cities that begged
    connection with and protection from the Roman Empire' (Nasrallah 2008: 566).

informed and shaped not only by the revelation of God in the crucified Jesus, but also by the cries of millions of members of the Body of Christ who suffer the profoundly negative consequences of the globalization process. For these 'little ones' in the Majority World there are few signs of hope as long as the dominant system continues to be lauded as the only possible route to social and economic well-being. Jean-Marc Ela, one of Africa's most perceptive and articulate Christian voices, describes how, from that continent's huge urban slums to its remotest forests and savannahs, 'men, women and youth, burdened with misery and poverty, thirst for justice and freedom'. Ela's prophetic analysis of the impact of the Western model of economic growth and development offers a challenge which a faithful urban theology dare not ignore:

> We see the cavalier manner in which the city, home of the concentration of modern economic enterprises, ignores the plight of the villages in the bush, abandoning them to malnutrition, infant mortality, illiteracy, and circular indebtedness, forcing the peasants to concentrate on agricultural production for export (for African economies are shaped by the needs of the capitalist world) (Ela 1986: 62–63).

The task of urban theology in such a world cannot be undertaken in the ivory towers of secure, tenured university posts, unless accompanied by the kind of commitment and courage shown by the apostle Paul and a willingness, if need be, to suffer and die in order to confront the idols of our time. A prophetic theology will demand both deep repentance within the wealthy and privileged world, and justice and dignity for the masses of poor people trapped in the slums and villages of the Global South. Such a theology can neither retreat to a ghetto nor become preoccupied with personal religion and the post-mortem salvation of the soul, because the vision of the Bible *is* global; it does extend to all the nations on earth, promising a salvation which brings justice and equity to all peoples. What is more, it envisages an urban world in which the city becomes a place of beauty, healing and great joy. Such a hope provides the basis for an alternative vision of globalization in which the centre of unity is no longer provided by an ideology focused on the pursuit of wealth at the expense of other people and without regard to the destructive impact of that quest on other creatures, but rather by the worship of the God who so loved the world as to enter in Christ into its very depths of despair, abandonment and death. As Justo Gonzalez writes in his brilliant study of the book of Revelation,

> Contrary to what we might expect, and in contrast with much of its later history, the church in the changing society of the first century, rather than simply bemoaning

change, posited and announced an even greater change. Let others complain that Rome has become the cesspool for the scum of the world. Let others seek refuge in their exurban villas. John calls Christians in Ephesus, Smyrna, and the other cities of Asia, to continue living in those cities as those whose citizenship is in the New Jerusalem (Gonzalez 1999: 107).

The gospel for an urban world

Within the limits of this book it is not possible to attempt a detailed study of the articulation and application of the gospel to urban cultures. That being so, we merely suggest at this point some of the specific ways in which the 'Christ event' provides direction and guidance to the urban disciples of Jesus. In the previous chapter we reflected at some length on the manner in which the Gospel accounts of Jesus' ministry in Galilee would have provided a later generation of believers scattered across the Empire with direction, encouragement and challenge. We saw how the horrific and humiliating execution of Christ came to be understood as the means of the *victory* of God, and the preaching of the cross subsequently became central to Paul's gospel. The death of Jesus is a theme which has inspired myriad devotional responses in worship and art and it has exercised devout minds across the centuries in attempts to express its meaning. We notice here, first, that Christ's rejection and cruel execution *demonstrates the strength of evil and its unyielding resistance to the reign of God and the coming of his kingdom of peace and justice.* The crucifixion, which resulted from a mockery of a trial in which justice was subverted in a process rigged to secure a pre-determined outcome, suggests an abnormal level of hatred, fear and wickedness which requires explanation in terms of *demonic* forces. For the New Testament writers the true nature of evil extends beyond the actions for which individuals are responsible and is embedded in the very structures of the social and political world, resulting in forms of domination and oppression which bind and enslave people. Evil in the biblical worldview has a *cosmic* dimension. This degree of wickedness, which is invariably disguised behind the myths of civilization and progress, is exposed and revealed in all its terrible reality at the cross of Jesus Christ. The powers of death and hell, with all their divisive, dehumanizing works, are *broken* at the cross and a path of freedom and healing for alienated human beings is opened up by means of which previous enemies become reconciled in a new community of love and peace (Eph. 2:14–18). However, while the message of the cross announces the victory of God over 'powers and dominions' which must otherwise appear to be invincible, it also contains a sobering reminder

of the reality and depth of evil which continues to be at work in the urban
world, leaving the disciples of Jesus in little doubt that they are called to follow
their Lord on the path of suffering and cross-bearing. Ernst Käsemann wrote
that Christianity would appear incredible if it failed to carry the victory of the
cross into every deepest hole and corner of the world: 'What our world needs
everywhere today is this exorcism of its demons' (cited unattributed on the
title page of McAlpine 1991).

In the second place, the cross of Christ has profound implications for *our
understanding of God and his relationship to the urban world we have described in this book.*
Unfortunately, the symbol of the cross has often been deployed in ways which
have subverted the message of the gospel, turning it into a sign of power and
conquest in a manner which entirely effaced the reality of God's redemptive
love expressed through the weakness and suffering displayed at Calvary. It
is impossible to ignore the presence and activity of precisely those demonic
forces just mentioned in the process by which Christianity was itself so tragically corrupted so that, as Richard Bauckham puts it, the beast of Revelation
'constantly reappeared in ever new Christian guises'. The institutionalization
of the religion beneath the symbol of a dominating cross was certainly not 'the
coming of the eschatological kingdom' (Bauckham 1993a: 151–152).

By contrast, the cross of Jesus reveals a God whose suffering love and
kindness reaches into the deepest recesses of human despair, even as it offers
people who enjoy power and privilege a salvation which shatters their illusions, exposes them to reality in a fallen world, and promises both forgiveness and release from their sinful addictions. This transformation of the
lives of people enslaved by the worship of the idols of our time is gloriously
possible, but it demands genuine repentance and the embrace of the way of
Jesus Christ. The urban world described in this book, a world of deep social
divisions, rising ethnic tensions, and cities in which the will-to-power is too
often divorced from any vision of a good society, offers the global Christian
movement a *kairos* moment in which the true meaning of Christ crucified can
be recovered and may become the means for the healing of our world. The
wise words of Richard Mouw merit extended quotation:

> [E]vangelicals . . . have operated with a restricted view of the redemptive ministry
> of Jesus. They have placed limits on the scope and power of the Cross. In boasting
> of a 'full gospel' they have often proclaimed a truncated Christianity. In speaking
> of a blood that cleanses from all unrighteousness, they have consistently restricted
> the meaning of the word 'all'. The problem might be described in this way: they
> have given full reign to the blood of Christ within a *limited* area. They have seen the
> work of Christ as being a totally transforming power only within individual lives.

They have not shown much interest in the work of the Lamb as it applies to the broad reaches of culture or the patterns of political life, nor as a power that heals racism, ethnocentrism, sexism, and injustice that have for so long poisoned human relationships. To such Christians we must insist that the Lamb is indeed the lamp of the City; just as we must insist to liberal Christians that the light which illuminates the City does indeed issue from the Lamb who shed his own blood as a ransom for sin (Mouw 2002: 111–112).

Third, the cross of Jesus cannot be separated from the apostolic witness that the Crucified One was vindicated and 'declared with power to be the Son of God by his resurrection from the dead' (Rom. 1:4). As we have seen, the appearances of the risen Jesus in and around Jerusalem were of crucial importance to the mission of the early Christian movement in the cities of the Empire. Max Stackhouse has described the resurrection as decisive for the value systems of those involved in the urban ethos and he points out its importance both with regard to the hope of individuals and in respect of its revelation of the necessity of a holistic approach to the human person. With regard to the former, the message of cross and resurrection connects in powerful ways to the crisis of meaning and the loss of hope which increasingly characterizes people in the so-called developed world, where an annihilating boredom erodes the purpose of life and creates the soil within which postmodern urban pathologies germinate and grow.[3] In a context in which a desolating loss of hope is frequently concealed beneath an external jollity and activism, the passion narratives, describing a descent to the depths of betrayal, abandonment, death and hell, and the bursting forth of new life and hope, can indeed come as good news. In respect of the need for a holistic approach, Stackhouse observes that the resurrection of Jesus signals that 'the physical and spiritual life of the person are inseparable' and that this wholeness must be respected in the mission of urban churches. Those who truly believe in the resurrection of the crucified Christ will be people who are willing to enter 'the junk heaps of the cities and free people found in bondage there'.

---

3. Among many studies of the existential crisis facing people in the urbanized Western world, Christopher Lasch's best-selling *The Culture of Narcissism: American Life in an Age of Diminishing Expectations* remains perhaps the most insightful. He writes that Americans 'feel themselves overwhelmed by an annihilating boredom, like animals whose instincts have withered in captivity'. People complain of 'an inability to feel' and so 'cultivate vivid experiences, seek to beat the sluggish flesh to life, attempt to revive jaded appetites' (Lasch 1979: 11).

However, urban mission 'must keep body and soul together in quite literal senses. Massive attacks on spiritual and physical poverty are both legitimate and morally mandatory. But one without the other is merely fatal' (Stackhouse 1972: 100–101).

Fourth, our final comment on the significance of the cross of Jesus for urban theology and mission today concerns the Pentecostal gift of the Spirit and the emergence of the first community of followers of the crucified and risen Christ, which provided, both then and now, a model of the new society in which the promise of God's *shalom* was realized. The description of Peter's Pentecostal sermon in Acts makes clear the connection between Jesus of Nazareth, crucified and raised from the dead, now 'exalted to the right hand of God', and the 'promised Holy Spirit' whose presence with the disciples explains 'what you now see and hear' (Acts 2:22–24, 31–33). The gift of the Spirit then, releasing the very life of God in the form of the transforming power of the risen Christ into human history, is the culminating point in the Christ event, so that those who respond in faith and acknowledge Jesus as Lord are enabled to live in the present as the agents of God's counter-cultural kingdom. The remarkable descriptions of this new community in Acts 2:42–47 and 4:32–37 show how this earliest community displayed, precisely within the urban context of Jerusalem, the transforming power of the risen Lord in lives made new, thus making the values of the kingdom visible and public. These disciples, later described as the 'People of the Way', drew the wondering admiration of fellow-Jews who marvelled at the manner in which the followers of the prophet from Nazareth practiced a way of 'life together' which had a clear resemblance to the vision of urban society enshrined within the Torah. Jürgen Moltmann describes the significance of Pentecost in the following words:

> The Pentecost story is about an experience of God. It is the experience of the Spirit who descends on men and women, permeates them through and through, soul and body, and brings them to a new community and fellowship with one another. In this experience people discover that they are filled with new energies they had never imagined to exist, and find the courage for a new style of living (Moltmann 1983: 130).

Pentecostalism, theology and the urban world

In the statement above, Moltmann not only reflects on the biblical narrative accurately, he might also have been describing the churches of the poor in the slums and *favellas* of the Global South today. Millions of poor Christians who have fled the degraded countryside in a desperate search for economic stability in the city have discovered in the Christ event, including the narrative of Pentecost, the promise of the felt-presence of God through the gift of the Spirit, bringing comfort, hope, and 'new energies they had never imagined to exist'. Christians from privileged and wealthy countries who visit their sisters and brothers in such situations often feel that they have encountered communities which bear an uncanny likeness to the first followers of 'The Way' described in the book of Acts, and they are unlikely ever to forget the encounter. Consider this statement from a group of Christian women in the Nairobi slum of Mukuru-Kayaba:

> [L]ife in the slums is not only full of bad things, but also has its rich side which many people are not aware of. . . . In the slums people are united during trouble and also in good times. . . . Slum-dwellers are very generous. It is rare to see somebody's neighbour going hungry. You will be given at least some *unga* (maize flower) for porridge. . . . Whatever hardships we people face, we do not easily succumb to them. Today your home is razed to the ground and tomorrow a new structure is going up . . . we really fight tooth and nail until we see some hope. . . . We came to the towns to look for money/employment. . . . So *we are here not out of choice but out of necessity*, and we have decided to make the slums a better place (Marenya 2002: 51–57).

An urban theology for the globalized world of the twenty-first century must listen to and learn from voices like these. The growth of non-Western Christianity in contexts of poverty and struggle has been phenomenal, as many observers have noted. For example, Harvey Cox, whose voice we heard long ago at the very start of this book, felt compelled to research the modern Pentecostal phenomenon which, he freely admitted, had taken him by surprise and disproved his earlier assumptions that the urban future of the world was likely to be irreversibly *secular*. The sheer global scale of this movement compelled Cox to recognize that the urban world was witnessing 'a period of renewed religious vitality' which had the potential to bring about massive social change. He described the beginnings of modern Pentecostalism in Los Angeles in 1906 as the point in Western history at which 'the pulsating energy of African American spirituality, wedded by years of suffering to the Christian promise of the kingdom of God, leaped across the racial barrier and became fused with similar motifs in the spirituality of poor white people' (Cox 1995: 99). The movement dismantled the separating wall 'that western civilization had so carefully erected between the cognitive and emotional sides of life' and, in sharp contrast to both the rationalism which stemmed from the

Enlightenment and the acceptance of the privatization of religion by main-stream Christianity, the early Pentecostals discovered, like the first Christian community in Jerusalem two thousand years before, that the coming of the Spirit deepened their experience of reality and fired their imagination with the vision of a different kind of America and a transformed world.

During the past one hundred years Pentecostal forms of Christianity spread rapidly across the Global South as the result of vigorous mission-ary proclamation and these rising streams of fresh spiritual life were further swollen as the result of the appearance of Charismatic phenomena within tra-ditional denominations and the rise of entirely indigenous movements within primal religious contexts. In the case of the latter, the faith of new Christians in Africa, Latin America and many parts of Asia had never encountered the acids of the European Enlightenment, except in the sense that their devo-tion to Jesus was forged in a colonial context in which they suffered on the receiving end of the work of settlers and administrators possessed by a sense of imperial mission and with a predisposition to dismiss ancient traditions as primitive and uncivilized. Within these new, independent churches spiritual gifts similar to those rediscovered among poor blacks in America, including forms of spiritual insight, prophecy and healing which were already part of the religious currency within traditional societies, were offered to the service of Jesus Christ. Armed with such spiritual weapons and inspired by the biblical narratives rendered in local vernaculars, humble believers were able to decon-struct the colonial narrative, recover a sense of human dignity, and demand freedom and justice for their own people. Jean-Marc Ela, himself a Catholic theologian, observes that the rise of such independent churches in many parts of colonial Africa, affirming both their devotion to Christ and their determi-nation to maintain an African identity, formed the 'mainstay of all protest against colonization' and provided 'the locus of the combat for the liberation of the oppressed'. It was within these churches that 'the deep aspirations of colonized Africa and the immense cry of the oppressed' came to expression (Ela 1986: 46–47).

Let us be clear about what is being said here. Pentecostalism, understood very broadly in this discussion, provides no panacea for the ills of our urban world and in the course of the past century it has shown itself to be as vul-nerable to corruption, decline and syncretism as other religious movements. The immensely varied groups classified under this label make up a confus-ingly broad tradition which at times shades into the bizarre and heretical. Cox himself warned that a 'cult of experience' could become a religious form of the postmodern search for 'new sources of arousal and exhilara-tion' and might simply merge into 'New Age self-absorption' (Cox 1995:

313). However, the positive contribution of the Pentecostal-Holiness movements, including many locally initiated congregations among the poor in the
megacities of the Global South, is impossible to deny, and their potential as
agents of personal and social transformation has been recognized by many
observers, Christian and secular alike (see Martin 2002). What is more, these
movements may contain the seeds of hope not only in their immediate, local
contexts but far beyond this, since in our interconnected and highly mobile
world an urban theology which demonstrably expresses itself through love
(Gal. 5:6) may compel the admiration of the watching world in exactly the
same manner as happened at Pentecost, only now on a truly global scale.
The testimonies of humble Christians, like that cited above, bear compelling witness to the power of the gospel in creating hope in desperate situations, *but they may also cut through the coldness and complacence of churches which have
existed so long in contexts of material satiation that they have forgotten the liberative,
life-bestowing power of the gospel.* Cheryl Bridges Johns, in an important study of
Pentecostalism as 'a pedagogy among the oppressed', writes that Western
believers are beginning to learn 'to respect the voices of the oppressed, not
only for their pathos, but also for their logos which has been forged through
suffering' (Johns 1993: 8).

The urban *ekklesia*: evangelical, emerging and catholic

Our study of the New Testament in the previous chapter highlighted the
significance of the *ekklesia* of Christ within the mission of the primitive
Christian movement in the urban empire of Rome. In the subsequent centuries the church has frequently been reshaped, or reformed, as the message of
the gospel entered new cultural and social contexts. It is possible to identify
a series of major transitions, recently described as paradigm shifts, which
occurred as Christianity repeatedly entered and penetrated new cultural settings, becoming reinvigorated in the process. This 'infinite translatability' of
the Christian faith has rightly been seen as an aspect of its peculiar genius,
reflecting the central belief in the incarnation of God in the person of Jesus
Christ, a first-century Jew whose own life was so clearly shaped by a particular
time and place. However, while the translatability of the faith confers a positive value on human cultures and validates a variety of expressions of both
the church and the gospel, it also poses problems in defining those elements
within the tradition which transcend particular cultures and provide the movement across time and space with unity and coherence. Amid all the variety,
what holds the faith together? Or does the recognition of the importance

of local cultures and languages actually mean that, in practice, Christianity becomes a socially divisive force, isolating peoples from each other by granting a kind of sanctity to their ethnic and cultural identities?

The questions raised here are very serious ones, never more so than today when, as the outcome of globalization, human cultures are interacting to an unprecedented extent, sometimes merging, often violently clashing, or when faced with the possibility of extinction, spawning movements of resurgence and revitalization. This complex situation poses entirely new challenges for the church and its mission; the centuries-long process of successively, or serially, translating the gospel within new cultural settings has largely given way to a world in which a multiplicity of cultures may be encountered in the kaleidoscopic settings of the great cities of the twenty-first-century world. As a result, as Dale Irvin has said, the very nature of the city now presents fresh challenges to theology and mission because it has become the visible manifestation of a new global reality, shaped by 'transnational migrations, hyphenated and hybrid identities, cultural conjunctions and disjunctions, and global theological networks or flows' (Irvin 2009: 181).

What kind of *ekklesia* will emerge to meet the challenge of this new context? The missionary transmission of the faith mentioned above has resulted in the extraordinary growth of churches across the Global South, creating what has come to be called 'World Christianity'. This phenomenon has been celebrated as breaking the normative link between the gospel and Western culture, revealing the cultural conditioning of all theology, and providing peoples previously treated as merely receivers of truth with new voices, releasing them to contribute their own rich understanding of Christ and the gospel. But can World Christianity become an *ekklesia* for an urban world, or will it remain merely a disparate collection of culturally conditioned expressions of faith, operating under a common brand name but lacking any sense of organic unity? To put the question in another way: does the global Christian movement presage the appearance of an alternative model for the human family to that now provided by economic globalization, or is such a prospect completely illusory because, beneath a merely nominal unity, the Christian faith in fact *reflects* the socio-cultural divisions of the wider world instead of *transcending* them?

Few questions are more important than these for a credible urban theology and the witness of history will not allow us to make any easy response since its testimony is that the institutional church has as often been a countersign of God's kingdom as it has provided a faithful embodiment of it. Nonetheless, the vision of the triumph of God's *shalom* remains alive and since the Bible chooses to employ the image of a city 'to sum up the perfect life in Christ', we may both hope for, and labour for, an *ekklesia* appropriate to the daunting challenge of the world we have described (Ward 2003: 464).

While it is clearly impossible to describe the shape the church will take in the age which lies ahead, we can make certain fundamental affirmations. In the first place we propose that *an ekklesia able to respond to the challenge of the urban world will be an evangelical community*. This term is not used here in any partisan sense, but rather to emphasize the essentially *missional* character of the Body of Christ. What may be called the evangelical impulse received a tremendous boost through the movements of revival which swept through the modernizing societies of Europe and America in the eighteenth century, but it did not originate there since its presence can be detected in every phase of the history of the Christian movement, including:

- the early Nestorian missionaries who went far to the East, entering ancient China and winning the respect of its rulers;
- the Celtic saints, allowing the 'wind of God' to take them wherever it would;
- Orthodox monks, penetrating the dark, freezing forests of Russia armed only with their icons and an astonishing trust in the power of the risen Christ and the Holy Spirit;
- and prophetic African preachers such as William Wade Harris, traversing thousands of miles in West Africa on foot, speaking of Christ to huge numbers of people, and presenting him as the Saviour of Africa.

In the twenty-first century the *ekklesia* of Christ will need to be evangelical, not in some completely pre-defined sense, but because as it confronts the complex, shifting frontier of the world's burgeoning cities its missionary calling will demand a willingness to innovate in order to ensure that the liberating message of the kingdom can be heard, and the good works which accompany faith may be seen, so providing present and future generations with an opportunity to discover an alternative story to the one which dominates the media, the educational system and the language of modern politics. But if this is to happen, and if the demanding and dangerous task of undertaking this latest translation of the gospel is to be done, certain received presuppositions concerning mission will have to be given up. For example, we may no longer define mission in the city as directed solely to a narrow, deprived segment of urban society. Dale Irvin points out that urban ministry in the United States was fatally limited to the slums and the poor, and so was never conceived as directed to business people 'who worked in the financial district and commuted home to the suburbs'. He continues,

It did not mean ministry to the artists, to the city police officers and firefighters, to the civil servants, to the restaurant owners, or the urban university professors. It did not mean engaging the corporate community, the investment community, or the media or advertising industry (Irvin 2009: 178).

In the urban world of today and tomorrow, the city must be seen as indivisible and the inherited association of mission with ghettos and poverty must give way to the recognition that, while ministry among the poor remains a priority, the most urgent and challenging tasks may be to bring the message of the kingdom of God to bear on those people whose lives are lived in close proximity to the idolatrous systems we have described earlier. How do we articulate the gospel for people who appear to have much to lose from an encounter with the crucified Christ? How might we issue the call to discipleship to those who have prospered precisely because the privatized forms of religion preached in suburban churches have enabled them to separate their business practices from their faith, so closing down any discussion of the ethics of wealth creation from the perspective of the gospel of Christ? Tim Keller, whose Redeemer Presbyterian Church in Manhattan has wrestled boldly precisely with questions like these, describes the relationship of Christians to culture as 'the singular current crisis point for the church' and says that believers are 'called to be an alternate city within every earthly city, an alternate human culture within every human culture, to show how money, sex and power can be used in nondestructive ways' (Keller 2006).

The second affirmation we offer here is that *the* ekklesia *capable of meeting the challenge of the century before us is still in the process of emerging.* This term has provoked considerable discussion in Protestant circles during the past decade, much of it characterized by heat rather than light. However, the assertion that the church of Christ is an emerging phenomenon should occasion no surprise to people familiar with the New Testament and the subsequent history of the Christian movement; it has been so from the very beginning and as a pilgrim community, always on the road and in a continual state of 'becoming', it grows and develops in a process that can only end when its mission is completed. If the church is to respond to the question 'What kind of day is it today?', which the Dutch missionary theologian Johannes Verkuyl said it must always be asking, then change and emergence will be discovered to be the unavoidable consequences of evangelical faithfulness (Verkuhl 1978: 108).

In this book, our answer to Verkuhl's question has focused on one critically important aspect of the present time and we have proposed that the challenge of the *urban day* within which history will unfold in the century before us is paramount. If that challenge is to be met, although there are important lessons

to be learned from every previous era in the history of the church, new forms
of Christian community will be needed which will connect with the social and
cultural realities shaping the cities of our world. As Dale Irvin observes, the
Christian mission has until now tended to relate to forms of culture in rural
settings and contextual theologies and ecclesiologies have assumed the continuing existence and priority of stable, homogeneous cultures. However, this
bucolic world is no more; urban life creates a cultural mosaic in which 'life
on the street and the culture of streets take on intensely new configurations
of inter- and cross-cultural experience and meaning' (Irvin 2009: 179). Quite
obviously, an 'emerging' church cannot be defined in advance of its appearance, but it will be a community of faith which responds to a context in which:

- world Christianity gives visibility to new forms of worship and spiritual
  life which are increasingly present within 'world cities' as the result of
  patterns of migration from South to North;
- other faiths are no longer geographically distant and accessible only
  through text books, but are a living presence and offer, especially in the
  case of Islam, an alternative urban theology. Nicholas Wolsterstorff is
  of the opinion that the manner in which Muslims have applied their
  theology to the building of the city, and especially the *beauty* of the
  Islamic urban form as a reflection of the very essence of God, presents
  us with a profound challenge (Wolsterstorff 1983: 129). Clearly, the
  emerging church in an urban world will need to be in conversation with
  its Muslim neighbours;
- the networked, mobile, 'liquid' nature of life in the postmodern city
  creates new patterns of behaviour and relationships, so placing issues
  concerning the structures of the church, the nature of its leadership, and
  patterns of nurture and fellowship firmly on the agenda. In the words
  of Christopher Baker, it is time for the church to enter into creative and
  critical dialogue with an increasingly hybrid urban culture and to begin
  to build a 'creative connection between new forms of church and new
  forms of urban community' (Baker 2007 2).

Finally, *the evangelical, emerging ekklesia will be catholic.* In fact, it would be
accurate to say that at the time of this writing the emerging church *is* catholic,
in the sense that it is an international movement which straddles the globe
and reflects in the amazing diversity of its membership the Bible's vision of
a numberless multitude worshipping the Lamb of God 'from every nation,
tribe, people and language'. Justo Gonzalez has pointed out that the question
today is not *whether* there will be a multicultural church, but rather, whether

Christians who have always understood faith within the framework of their own, dominant culture 'will be able to participate fully in the life of the multi-cultural church that is already a reality' (Gonzalez 1999: 91).

However, we must also ask whether, in relation to the challenges posed by globalization, the Body of Christ, scattered around the world, shaped by local cultures, but also fragmented by denominational divisions and rivalries, will discover a way to give substance to the ancient confession of belief in 'one, holy, catholic, and apostolic church'? Can World Christianity discover a basis for unity which involves respect for the theological diversity which is the legit-imate outcome of inculturation, so celebrating the experiences and insights of a multicultural church, while at the same time demonstrating to the watch-ing world a visible oneness in Christ the Redeemer? Can Christians discover together what Robert Schreiter has called 'a renewed and expanded concept of catholicity' at the boundaries between 'those who profit and enjoy the fruits of the globalization process and those who are excluded and oppressed by it' (Schreiter 1997: 130)? Such a unity, arising from a fresh understanding of the fullness of faith, in which the biblical theme of the promise of God's *shalom* would offer the global system the ethical values without which it will increas-ingly serve demonic ends, can renew hope for peoples everywhere. What is more, it might bring nearer the answer to the great prayer of Ephesians 3:14–21 which wonderfully combines universality with the affirmation of the local and the particular. At the ecumenical level it glimpses the whole family of believers 'in heaven and on earth', while insisting that only 'together with all the saints' can the fullness of Christ's love can be grasped – then adding that, after all, this love lies beyond comprehension! Can we hope that a church which, for the first time in two thousand years is truly ecumenical in its geo-graphical extent, will discover a catholic unity which would give credibility to its challenge of the idols of our time and would offer the world empirical evidence that the gospel can bring to birth to a human family united in love and the practice of justice?

As long ago as 1981 the Catholic theologian Johannes Baptist Metz argued that there was a need for new forms of the church, for a process of change and transformation which in its reach and impact might justify the claim of being a second Reformation. We conclude this discussion of the urban *ekklesia* with a quotation from *The Emergent Church* in which Metz suggests that the nature of *conversion* will be the issue of critical importance for the future, and that only a Christianity which implants the gospel deep into peoples' lives, in a manner that 'damages and disrupts one's own self-interests and aims at a fundamental revision of one's habitual way of life', can meet the challenge of our age. He wrote:

I want to express the fear . . . that this change of heart is not taking place. . . . The
crisis (or sickness) of life in the church is not just that the change of heart is not
taking place . . . but that the absence of this change of heart is being further concealed
under the appearance of a merely *believed-in-faith*. Are we Christians . . . really changing
our hearts, or do we just believe in a change of hearts and remain under the cloak of
this belief in conversion basically unchanged? . . . Do we show real love, or do we
just believe in love and under the cloak of belief in love remain the same egoists and
conformists we have always been? Do we share the sufferings of others, or do we just
believe in this sharing, remaining under the cloak of belief in 'sympathy' as apathetic
as ever? (Metz 1981: 3).

Here is your God!

In the survey of the Old Testament earlier in this book we noticed the significance of the Book of Comfort which opens the second half of the prophecy
of Isaiah. The context within which that great text appeared has a number of
important parallels with the situation we confront in the urban world of the
twenty-first century. The destruction of Jerusalem, the unchallenged dominance of the pagan system of Babylon, and the seemingly unending humiliation and suffering of both the exiles and the pathetic survivors who remained
among the ruined cities of Judah, conspired together to create a spiritual and
theological crisis which threatened the very survival of the faith of Israel.
Yahweh's apparent distance and inactivity gave birth to a liturgy of complaint
which voiced the fear that the God of the Covenant had retreated to the
margins of the cosmos, leaving the history of the world to be determined by
whichever nation was able to deploy superior, ruthless power in the endless
struggle for dominance and control (Isa. 40:27; 49:14).

In this situation of despair the voice of prophecy is heard again, breaking
into the present with an announcement so stunning, so impossible within the
framework of the existing reality, as to be completely revolutionary. Nowhere
else in the Bible, except in the even darker night which engulfed faith in the
shadow of Calvary, is the power of the prophetic imagination more dramatically demonstrated. At the core of the prophet's message is the summons to
bring good news to broken Jerusalem and to declare to the ruined cities of
Judah, 'Here is your God!' (Isa. 40:9). The urban character of this prophetic
revelation is immediately evident and this remains true throughout the wonderful visions which unfold in the following chapters. As is so often the case,
the positive announcement of good news to the despairing and hopeless has
a polemical aspect with regard to those who benefit from the existing system

so that, while the address to the exiles is one of comfort, expressed with an almost heart-breaking tenderness, the announcement that a *highway* is to be built in the desert as a 'way for the LORD' (Isa. 40:3–4) contains a clear reference to a key feature of the city of Babylon. Ceremonial 'highways' appear prominently in Babylonian hymns, where they are described as roads of 'jubilation' made straight and smooth for the transportation and public display of both the sacred kings and their gods. The 'highway' thus functioned not only as a key site for the celebration of the myths and rituals of Babylonian religion, but it became for the exiles an important symbol of the power and glory of the empire which had overwhelmed their city and now held them within its iron grip. The prophecy takes up this image and wonderfully subverts it, mocking a religion which requires constantly repaired roads in order that the gods carried in procession will not suffer the indignities of toppling over (41:7; 46:1–4). By contrast, Yahweh's glory needs no such ceremonial highway because instead of being represented by a humanly-made image, *he will carry the captives home and free them to rebuild their ruined cities.* As Claus Westermann observes, what reveals the glory of the God of Israel is 'his action in history' (Westermann 1969: 39).

The approach of the prophet to this situation suggests the contribution which Christian theology may make in the context of the crises which face us in the urban world of the twenty-first century. For the demoralized exiles the obvious success of the Babylonian system and its dominance over a vast area of the known world, left no space remaining for an alternative way of thinking based on faith in Yahweh. This kind of situation recurs later in the Bible when John of Patmos reports that the 'whole world' was subdued by, and subjected to, the authority of the imperial power of Rome, so that people from all nations came to *worship* 'the beast', asking in despair: 'Who can make war against him?' (Rev. 13:4). Notice that the imperial claims and the self-image of the ruling elite are again subverted by the language of prophecy, so that the glory of Rome is stripped away to reveal the ugly reality concealed beneath the state propaganda. John understands how the hearts and minds of people have been conditioned to accept Rome's claims, but he dares to say that 'the inhabitants of the earth' have been *deceived* (13:14). The contribution of prophecy in both these cases involves the creation of a language which opens up space within which the dominant worldview can be viewed from a fresh angle, and a radical alternative to it comes into view.

The relevance of this to the concerns of this book can be seen in the fact that many urbanist scholars and commentators, deeply aware of the crisis looming over our world, are tempted to despair because, as sociologist Paul Chatterton says, their dreams of just and equal societies seem blocked by 'a poverty of imagination, and a reluctance to use their work to dream the urban impossible and harvest that future in the present'. Chatterton invents a new term to suggest that in an age dominated by the ideology of market economics, so that all solutions to urban problems must conform to the orthodoxy of that dogmatic system, we need *urban imagineers* who are able 'to create new vocabularies, imaginations and strategies for action that could bring about a radically different city'. Such visionaries, breaking free from the constraints of a worldview which is propelling us toward apocalypse, will dream of a different world to the one we know, 'making real what currently seems impossible, unknown or out of our reach' (Chatterton 2010: 235).

The language used here reminds us of the statement of Philip Sheldrake quoted at the head of this chapter, suggesting that what is urgently required in discussions concerning the future of our cities is fresh *vision*. Sheldrake points out that this is precisely the primary concern of theology which, rooted in a biblically originated, theocentric understanding of the world, offers new vocabularies and fresh imagination. However, urban theology presents its own profound challenge to the growing number of academics and practitioners who despair of the possibility of solutions to our problems in the absence of a radically new way of imagining the future. The distinctive insight it brings to the discussion concerns the need for critical reflection at the deepest, foundational levels of our culture, and the insistence that the new vision of the city we so urgently need cannot come to birth as long as thought and action remain confined within a secular, materialist worldview. The prophetic perspective requires us to hear the announcement that the God whom we have believed to be banished either to edges of the cosmos, or to privatized spaces of the sub-consciousness of individual believers, is *present* within the history of our world, challenging the idols which hold the nations in thrall, and working in ways that transcend our grasp to bring salvation and *shalom* to the world and its cities. As Richard Bauckham has said, the Bible confronts oppression, injustice and inhumanity with an uncompromisingly theocentric vision because only such knowledge is capable of resisting 'the human tendency to idolatry which consists in absolutizing aspects of this world' (Bauckham 1993a: 160).

Our final comment concerns the implications of the prophetic word for the life and witness of the Christian community. The summons to recognize God's *presence* within a world in which ultimate power appeared to belong to whichever nation could deploy the most brutal and overwhelming military force was directed in the first instance to people of faith. They were to hear this liberating word and to recognize the glory of Yahweh who was alone worthy of worship and obedience. The despair expressed in their laments was to give way to a renewed hope and confidence in the light of a fresh, enlarged understanding of the nature of their God and the extent of his purposes of grace and mercy. If the parallels we have suggested between then and now are valid, then the challenge to the Christian community in the urban world of today becomes clear; it is time to *awake,* to move beyond the syncretistic forms of religion in which modernity dictated that faith be confined, within a very restricted area of the personal life, and to catch the vision of a whole world released from a culture of death and the bondage to idols. Perhaps the most critical issue for the church in the urban world concerns the quality of its *worship,* and the extent to which that worship impacts daily life, shaping decisions and choices which may have previously been driven by the values of an economistic culture. As Mark Labberton has said, in the act of worship 'we cast our lives upon the faithful and just power of God' and in doing so 'we oppose all acts of unjust power'. He writes:

> In the gospel, the matchless and invincible heart of God confronts and defeats the heart of darkness and death. In its unexpected, power-inverting way, the sacrificial love of God in 'Christ crucified' (1 Corinthians 1:23–24) recasts all forms of power. That's the work and meaning of the cross. Our worship helps us remember this power realignment so that we can live differently because of it (Labberton 2007: 109–110).

Only as the Christian community across the world hears the prophetic announcement of God's presence within our historical situation and catches a fresh vision of his reign on earth, will it be able to break free from the spiritual paralysis which is the consequence of its acceptance of the limits imposed upon it by the modernist worldview. Such a genuine spiritual renewal would also lead to the discovery of fresh language with which to bear witness to the gospel message of liberation and hope, and would provide credibility as, in humility and love, this community shared its dream of a city with foundations.

BIBLIOGRAPHY

Social science perspectives

ABRAHAM, J. H. (1973), *The Origins and Growth of Sociology*, Harmondsworth: Penguin Books.

ALLEN, JOHN and CHRIS HAMMETT (eds.) (1995), *A Shrinking World? Global Unevenness and Inequality*, Oxford: Oxford University Press.

AMIN, ASH and NIGEL THRIFT (2002), *Cities: Reimagining the Urban*, Cambridge: Polity Press.

ARISTOTLE (1973), 'The Politics', in Abraham, 35–39.

ATKINSON, ADRIAN and KORINNA THEILEN (2008), '"Modernization" and Urbanization in China', *City* 12.2: 154–160.

AUGÉ, MARC (1995), *Non-Places. Introduction to an Anthropology of Supermodernity*, London: Verso.

BARKER, PAUL (2009), *The Freedoms of Suburbia*, London: Francis Lincoln.

BAUMAN, ZYGMUNT (1998), *Globalization: The Human Consequences*, Cambridge: Polity Press.

— (2001a), *Community: Seeking Safety in an Insecure World*, Cambridge: Polity Press.

— (2001b), 'Consuming Life', *Journal of Consumer Culture* 1.1: 9–29.

— (2003), *Liquid Love: On the Frailty of Human Bonds*, Cambridge: Polity Press.

— (2004), *Wasted Lives: Modernity and its Outcasts*, Cambridge: Polity Press.

— (2007), *Liquid Times: Living in an Age of Uncertainty*, Cambridge: Polity Press.

BELL, DAVID and JAYNE MARK (eds.) (2006), *Small Cities: Urban Experience Beyond the Metropolis*, Abingdon: Routledge.

BERLEANT, ARNOLD (2005), *Aesthetics and Environment: Variations on a Theme*, Aldershot: Ashgate Press.

BERMAN, MARSHALL (1983), *All That Is Solid Melts Into Air: The Experience of Modernity*, London: Verso.

— (2010), 'Falling', in Beaumont & Dart (eds.), 123–137.

BEAUMONT, MATTHEW and Gregory DART (eds.) (2010), *Restless Cities*, London: Verso.

BESS, PHILIP (2006), *Till We Have Built Jerusalem: Architecture, Urbanism and the Sacred*, Wilmington, Delaware: ISI Books.

BOWCOTT, OWEN (2008), 'Silk City: Kuwait Plans New £132bn Metropolis', *The Guardian*, 23 July: 22.

BOND, PATRICK (2007), 'Johannesburg: Of Gold and Gangsters', in Davis and Monk (eds.), 114–126.

BOOTH, ROBERT (2008), 'Pitfalls in Paradise: Why Palm Jumeirah is Struggling to Live Up to the Hype', *The Guardian*, 26 April.

BRENNER, NEIL and ROGER KEIL (eds.) (2006), *The Global Cities Reader*, London: Routledge.

BRIDGE, GARY and SOPHIE WATSON (eds.) (2002), *The Blackwell City Reader*, Oxford: Blackwell Publishing.

BRIGGS, ASA (1968), *Victorian Cities*, London: Penguin.

BROUDEHOUX, ANNE-MARIE (2007), 'Delirious Beijing: Euphoria and Despair in the Olympic Metropolis', in Davis and Monk (eds.), 87–101.

BROWN, CALLUM (1981), 'Religion and the Development of an Urban Society: Glasgow 1780–1914', unpublished PhD thesis, University of Glasgow.

— (1988), 'Did Urbanization Secularize Britain?' *Urban History Year Book*: 1–14.

BUNTING, MADELEINE (2009), 'Protestors in Seattle Warned Us What Was Coming, But We Didn't Listen', *The Guardian*, 14 December: 25.

BURDETT, RICKY and DEYAN SUDJIC (eds.) (2008), *The Endless City*, London: Phaidon Press.

BURGESS, ERNEST W. (2002), 'The Growth of the City', in Bridge and Watson (eds.), 244–250.

CASTELLS, MANUEL (1997), *The Information Age: Economy, Society and Culture. Volume II, The Power of Identity*, Oxford: Blackwell Publishing.

— (2002), *Castells Reader on Cities and Social Theory*, ed. Ida Susser, Oxford: Blackwell Publishing.

CHATTERTON, PAUL (2010), 'The Urban Impossible: A Eulogy For the Unfinished City', *City* 14.3: 234–244.

CIFATTE, MARIA CATERINA (2008), 'Women and the Liveability of Cities', *Journal of the European Society of Women in Theological Research* 16: 43–55.

CLARK, DAVID (2003a), *Urban World/Global City*, 2nd ed., London: Routledge.

— (2003b), *The Consumer Society and the Postmodern City*, London: Routledge.

CURITIBA, BRAZIL (n.d.), 'Three Decades of Thoughtful City Planning', <http://www.dismantle.org/curitiba.htm> (accessed 23 March 2009).

DAMER, SEAN (1990), *Glasgow, Going for a Song*, London: Lawrence and Wishart.

DAVIS, MIKE (1990), *City of Quartz: Excavating the Future in Los Angeles*, London: Vintage.

— (2001), *Late Victorian Holocausts: El Nino Famines and the Making of the Third World*, London: Verso.

— (2002), *Dead Cities and Other Tales*, New York: The New Press.

— (2004), 'Planet of Slums', *New Left Review* 26, March-April, <http://www.newleftreview.org/?view=2496> (accessed 18 March 2008).

— (2006), *Planet of Slums*, London: Verso Press.

— (2007), 'Sand, Fear and Money in Dubai', in Davis and Monk (eds.), 46–48.

DAVIS, MIKE and DANIEL BERTRAND MONK (eds.) (2007), *Evil Paradises: Dreamworlds of NeoLiberalism*, New York: The Free Press.

DEAR, MICHAEL J. (2000), *The Postmodern Urban Condition*, Oxford: Blackwell Publishers.

DENISON, EDWARD (2008), 'Building Shanghai: Historical Lessons for China's Gateway', *City* 12.2: 207–216.

DONSKIS, LEONIDAS (1996), 'Lewis Mumford: Mapping the Idea of the City', *Journal of Interdisciplinary Studies* VIII, 1/2: 49–68.

DUANY, ANDRES and ELIZABETH PLATER-ZYBERK (2007), 'The Neighborhood, the District, and the Corridor', in LeGates and Stout (eds.), 192–196.

EADE, JOHN and CHRISTOPHER MELE (eds.) (2002), *Understanding the City: Contemporary and Future Perspectives*, Oxford: Blackwell Publishers.

ELIADE, MIRCEA (1971), *The Myth of Eternal Return: or, Cosmos and History*, transl. W. R. Trask, Princeton: Princeton University Press.

ELIOT, T. S. (1961), *Selected Poems*, London: Faber & Faber.

ELLIOTT, LARRY and DAN ATKINSON (2008), *The Gods That Failed: How Blind Faith in Markets Has Cost Us Our Future*, London: The Bodley Head.

ELLIN, NAN (1999), *Postmodern Urbanism*, rev. ed., New York: Princeton Architectural Press.

— (2006), *Integral Urbanism*, London: Routledge.

ENGELS, FRIEDRICH (2007 [1844]), 'The Great Towns', in LeGates and Stout (eds.), 50–58.

FALOLA, TOYIN and STEVEN J. SALM (eds.) (2004), *Globalization and Urbanization in Africa*, Asmara, Ethiopia: Africa World Press.

FRANK, JOSEPH (1986), *Dostoevsky: The Stir of Liberation – 1860–1865*, London: Robson Books.

FREIRE, PAULO (1972), *The Pedagogy of the Oppressed*, Harmondsworth: Penguin Books.

FURNISS, CHARLIE (2008), 'Future Perfect?' *Geographical* April: 46–49.

GOTTDIENER, MARK and ROY HUTCHISON (eds.) (2006), *The New Urban Sociology*, 3rd ed., Boulder: Westview Press.

GRAHAM, STEPHEN (2004), 'Postmortem City: Towards an Urban Geopolitics', *City* 8.2: 165–196.

— (2010), *Cities Under Seige: The New Military Urbanism*, London: Verso.

THE GUARDIAN (2007), 'Great Modern Buildings: Notre Dame du Haut', 18 October, <http://www.guardian.co.uk/artanddesign/2007/oct/18/architecture3> (accessed 07 January 2011).

GUGLER, J. (ed.) (2004), *World Cities Beyond the West: Globalization, Development and Inequality*, Cambridge: Cambridge University Press.

GULICK, JOHN (1989), *The Humanity of Cities: An Introduction to Urban Societies*, Granby, Massachusetts: Bergin & Garvey.

HALL, PETER (1996), *Cities of Tomorrow: An Intellectual History of Urban Planning in the Twentieth Century*, updated ed., Oxford: Blackwell Publishers.

HANLEY, LYNSEY (2007), *Estates: An Intimate History*, London: Granta.

HANLON, PHIL *et al.* (2010), 'New Wave: The next revolution in society. 1/1 Four Waves of Public Health', < http://www.afternow.co.uk/papers/3-new-wave-the-next-revolution-in-society/15-four-waves-of-public-health> (accessed 25 July 2010).

HARDOY, JORGE, DIANA MITLIN and DAVID SATTERTHWAITE (2001), *Environmental Problems in an Urbanizing World*, London: Earthscan.

HODIN, J. P. (1972), *Edvard Munch*, London: Thames and Hudson.

HUNT, TRISTRAM (2005), *Building Jerusalem: The Rise and Fall of the Victorian City*, London: Phoenix.

ISMAIL, SALWA (2000), 'The Popular Movement Dimensions of Militant Islam: Socio-Spatial Determinants in the Cairo Urban Setting', *Journal for the Comparative Study of Society and History* 42.2: 363–393.

JACOBS, JANE (1993 [1961]), *The Death and Life of Great American Cities*, New York: The Modern Library.

— (2005), *Dark Age Ahead*, New York: Vintage Books.

JENCKS, CHARLES (2006), 'The Iconic Building Is Here To Stay', *City* 10.1: 3–20.

JOWIT, JULIETTE (2010), 'At Least a Quarter of Flowers May Face Extinction', *The Guardian*, 7 July: 5.

KAIKA, MARIA and KORINNA THIELEN (2006), 'Form Follows Power: A Genealogy of Urban Shrines', *City* 10.1: 59–69.

KATODRYTIS, GEORGE (2005), 'Metropolitan Dubai and the Rise of Architectural Fantasy', *Bidoun* 4, Spring: 42–46.

KING, ANTHONY D. (2002), 'Urbanism, Colonialism and the World Economy', in Bridge and Watson (eds.), 524–535.

KISHLANSKY, MARK, PATRICK GEARY and PATRICIA O'BRIEN (1993), *The Unfinished Legacy: A Brief History of Western Civilization*, New York: Harper Collins.

KOOLHAAS, REM (1994), *Delirious New York*, New York: The Monacelli Press.

KOTHARI, MILOON and SHIVANI CHAUDRY (2010), 'Unequal Cities Mean Unequal Lives', *Urban World* 1.5: 12–17.

KOTKIN, JOEL (2005), *The City: A Global History*, London: Weidenfeld & Nicolson.

KRANZFELDER, IVO (1998), *Edward Hopper: 1882–1967 – Visions of Reality*, Borders Press.

KUMAR, KRISHNAN (1986), *Prophecy and Progress: The Sociology of Industrial and Post-Industrial Society*, Harmondsworth: Penguin Books.

KUNSTLER, JAMES HOWARD (2001a), *The City in Mind: Notes on the Urban Condition*, New York: The Free Press.

— (2001b), 'Godmother of the American City', *Metropolis*, <http://www.metropolismag. com/html/content_0301/jac.htm> (accessed 22 March 2006).

— (2005), *The Long Emergency: Converging Catastrophes of the Twenty First Century*, London: Atlantic Books.

LASCH, CHRISTOPHER (1979), *The Culture of Narcissism: American Life in an Age of Diminishing Expectations*, New York: W. W. Norton.

LAWTON, GRAHAM (2004), 'Urban Legends', *New Scientist* 18 September: 32–35.

LE CORBUSIER (2002 [1971]), 'The City of Tomorrow and Its Planning', in Bridge and Watson (eds.), 20–29.

— (2007 [1929]), 'A Contemporary City', in LeGates and Stout (eds.), 322–330.

LEGATES, RICHARD T. and FREDERICK STOUT (eds.) (2007), *The City Reader*, 4th ed., London: Routledge.

LUBECK, PAUL M. and BRYANA BRITTS (2002), 'Muslim Civil Society in Urban Public Spaces: Globalization, Discursive Shifts and Social Movements', in Eade and Mele (eds.), 305–335.

MA, JIAN (2008), 'Viewpoint: The Forbidden Beijing', <http://news.bbc.co.uk/today/ hi/today/newsid_7522000/7522105.stm> (accessed 28 July 2008).

MARTIN, DAVID (2005), *On Secularization: Toward A Revised General Theory*, Aldershot: Ashgate Publishing.

MARTINE, GEORGE ET AL. (2008), *The New Global Frontier: Urbanization, Poverty and Environment in the 21st Century*, London: Earthscan.

MARX, KARL and FRIEDRICH ENGELS (1986 [1848]), *Manifesto of the Communist Party*, Moscow: Progress Publishers.

MARENYA, NEDDY (ed.) (2002), 'The Voice of the Women from the Slums', in Pierli & Abelado (eds.), 50–58.

MASSEY, DOUGLAS S. (1996), 'The Age of Extremes: Concentrated Affluence and Poverty in the Twenty-First Century', *Demography* 33.4: 395–411.

McGRATH, JAMES (2006), 'The Glasgow Story: Early Times to 1560', <http://www. theglasgowstory.com/index.php> (accessed 10 March 2006).

McNEILL, DONALD (2006), 'Globalization and the Ethics of Architectural Design', *City* 10.1: 49–58.

MILES, MALCOLM (2006), 'Garden Cities and City Gardens', in David Bell and Mark Joyce (eds.), *Small Cities: Urban Experience Beyond the Metropolis*, 135–150, London: Routledge.

MILUN, KATHRYN (2007), *Pathologies of Modern Space: Empty Space, Urban Anxiety and the Recovery of the Public Self*, Abingdon: Routledge.

MINTON, ANNA (2009), *Ground Control: Fear and Happiness in the Twenty First Century City*, London: Penguin Books.

MITCHELL, DON (2003), *The Right to the City: Social Justice and the Fight for Public Space*, London: The Guildford Press.

MÜLLER-KARPE, MICHAEL (2003), 'The Temple of Gareus, Uruk, Iraq', in Charlotte Trumpler (ed.), *The Past From Above*, 281, 320, London: Francis Lincoln.

MUMFORD, LEWIS (1966), *The City in History: Its Origins, Its Transformations, and Its Prospects*, Harmondsworth: Penguin Books.

MURRAY, SEAN (2008), 'Life of Poverty Amid Abuja's Wealth', <http://news.bbc. co.uk/1/hi/world/africa/6355269.stm> (accessed 15 August 2008 [29 December 2010]).

NICHOLSON, ADAM (2006), 'Dubai: the new capital of the world', *The Guardian*, 13 February: 6–11.

OBERAI, A. S. (1993), *Population Growth, Employment and Poverty in Third World Mega-Cities*, Basingstoke: Palgrave.

OWEN, DAVID (2009), *Green Metropolis: Why Living Smaller, Living Closer and Driving Less Are The Keys to Sustainability*, New York: Riverhead Books.

PACIONE, MICHAEL (1995), *Glasgow: The Socio-spatial Development of the City*, Chichester: John Wiley.

— (2005), 'City Profile: Dubai', *The International Quarterly on Urban Policy* 22.3: 255–265.

PACKARD, VANCE (1957), *The Hidden Persuaders*, Harmondsworth: Penguin Books.

— (1960), *The Waste Makers*, Harmondsworth: Penguin Books.

PEARMAN, HUGH (2006), 'Design for Living', *New Humanist* 121.2: 20–23.

PEÑALOSA, ENRIQUE (2008), 'Politics, Power and Cities', in Burdett and Sudjic (eds.), 307–319.

— (2010), 'Why cities must build equality', *Urban World* 1.5, 8–11.

RABB, THEODORE (2006), *The Last Days of the Renaissance and the March to Modernity*, New York: Basic Books.

RABINOVITCH, JONAS (1992), 'Curitiba: towards sustainable urban development', *Environment and Urbanization* 4.2, 62–73.

RADOKI, CAROLE (ed.) (2001), *The Urban Challenge of Africa: Growth and Management of Large Cities*, Tokyo: United Nations University Press.

READER, JOHN (2004), *Cities*, London: Heinemann.

ROBERTS, BRYAN R. (1995), *The Making of Citizens: Cities of Peasants Revisited*, London: Arnold.

ROBINSON, JENNIFER (2004), 'A World of Cities', *British Journal of Sociology* 55.4: 569–578.

ROY, ARUNDHATI (1999), *The Cost of Living*, London: Flamingo.

RUBIN, H. J. (2005), *Renewing Hope Within Communities of Despair: The Community Based Development Model*, Albany: State University of New York.

RUSKIN, JOHN (1997 [1862]), *Unto This Last and Other Writings*, London: Penguin Books.

SADOWSKI, YAHYA (1987), 'Egypt's Islamist Movement: A New Political and Economic Force', *Middle East Insight* September: 37–45.

SANDERCOCK, LEONIE (1998), *Towards Cosmopolis: Planning for Multicultural Cities* Chichester: Basil Wiley.

SASSEN, SASKIA (2009), 'The Urban Map of Terror', *The Guardian*, 28 May: 32.

SAUNDERS, DOUG (2010), *Arrival City: How the Largest Migration in History is Reshaping Our World*, London: Heinemann.

SCITOVSKY, TIBOR (1992), *The Joyless Economy: The Psychology of Human Satisfaction*, New York: Oxford University Press.

SEABROOK, JEREMY (1988), *The Race for Riches: The Human Cost of Wealth*, Basingstoke: Marshall Pickering.

— (2003), *A World Growing Old*, London: Pluto Press.

— (2004), *Consuming Cultures: Globalization and Local Lives*, Oxford: New Internationalist Publications.

SIMMEL, GEORG (2002 [1903]), 'The Metropolis and Mental Life', in Bridge & Watson (eds.), 11–19.

SMITH, DAVID M. (2000), *Moral Geographies: Ethics in a World of Difference*, Edinburgh: Edinburgh University Press.

— (2002), 'Social Justice and the South African City', in Eade and Mele (eds.), 66–81.

SOUTHALL, AIDAN (2000), *The City in Time and Space*, Cambridge: Cambridge University Press.

SPERBER, DANIEL (1998), *The City in Roman Palestine*, New York: Oxford University Press.

STEEL, CAROLYN (2008), *Hungry City: How Food Shapes Our Lives*, London: Chatto & Windus.

SUDJIC, DEYAN (2005), *The Edifice Complex: How The Rich and Powerful Shape the World*, London: Penguin Books.

TAWNEY, R. H. (1936), *Religion and the Rise of Capitalism*, London: John Murray.

— (1961), *The Acquisitive Society*, London: Collins/Fontana.

TAYLOR, STEVE (2005), *The Fall: The Evidence for a Golden Age, 6,000 Years of Insanity, and the Dawning of a New Era*, Winchester: O Books.

TONNIES, FERDINAND (1973), 'Community and Society', in Abraham (ed.), 244–264.

UN-HABITAT (2003), *The Challenge of the Slums: Global Report on Human Settlements*, London: United Nations.

— (2008), *State of the World's Cities, 2008/09 – Harmonious Cities*, London: Earthscan.

— (2010), *State of the World's Cities*, London: Earthscan.

URBAN HABITAT (2006), 'Curitiba's Bus System is Model for Rapid Transit', *Race, Poverty and the Environment*, 12.1; <http://urbanhabitat.org/node/344> (accessed 23 March 2009).

UNITED NATIONS ENVIRONMENT PROJECT (UNEP) (1997), <http://www.unep.org/geo/geo1/fig/fig4_4.htm> (accessed 15 March 2006).

VIDAL, JOHN (2003), 'Every Third Person Will be a Slum Dweller Within 30 Years, UN Agency Warns', *The Guardian* 4 October: 17.

VIDLER, ALEX (2001), *Warped Space: Art, Architecture and Anxiety in Modern Culture*, Massachusetts: The MIT Press.

VON LAUE, THEODORE (1987), *The World Revolution of Westernization. The Twentieth Century in Global Perspective*, New York: Oxford University Press.

WATTS, JONATHAN (2006), 'Invisible City', *The Guardian* G2, 15 March: 8–13.

— (2010), *When A Billion Chinese Jump: How China Will Save Mankind – Or Destroy It*, London: Faber and Faber.

WEBER, MAX (1958), *The City*, New York: The Free Press.

— (1985), *The Protestant Ethic and the Spirit of Capitalism*, London: Unwin Paperbacks.

WHILE, AIDAN (2005), 'A Manifesto for What Cities Might Be: Leonnie Sandercock and Cosmopolis', *Crucible*, October-December: 6–10.

WHYTE, IAIN (2006), *Scotland and the Abolition of Black Slavery, 1756–1838*, Edinburgh: Edinburgh University Press.

WRIGHT, LLOYD (2004), 'Reclaiming Public Space: The economic, environmental and social impacts of Bogotá's transformation', The Fifth International Conference on Walking in the 21st Century, 9–11 June 2004, Copenhagen, Denmark, < http://www.walk21.com/papers/Copenhagen%2004%20Wright%20Reclaiming%20public%20space%20the%20econmic%20env.pdf > (accessed 04 December 2008).

ZIGROSSER, CARL (ed.) (1969), *Prints and Drawings of Käthe Kollwitz*, New York: Dover Publications.

Biblical/theological perspectives

ALBRIGHT, WILLIAM FOXWELL (1957), *From Stone Age to Christianity: Monotheism and the Historical Process*, 2nd ed., New York: Doubleday Anchor Books.

ANDERSON, BERNHARD W. (1967), *Creation Versus Chaos: The Reinterpretation of Mythical Symbolism in the Bible*, Philadelphia: Fortress Press.

— (1978), *The Living World of the Old Testament*, 3rd ed., London: Longman.

BADER-SAYE, SCOTT (2006), 'Improvising Church: An Introduction to the Emerging Church Conversation', *International Journal for the Study of the Christian Church*, 6.1: 12–23.

BAKER, CHRISTOPHER (2005), 'Religious Faith in Exurban Community: A Study of Faith Communities in Milton Keynes', *City* 9.1: 109–123.

— (2007), *The Hybrid Church in the City: Third Space Thinking*, Aldershot: Ashgate Publishing.

BAKER, DEREK (ed.) (1979), *The Church in Town and Countryside*, Studies in Church History, vol. 16, Oxford: Blackwell.

BATEY, RICHARD A. (1991), *Jesus and the Forgotten City: New Light on Sepphoris and the Urban World of Jesus*, Grand Rapids: Baker Bookhouse.

BAUCKHAM, RICHARD (1993a), *The Theology of the Book of Revelation*, Cambridge: Cambridge University Press.

— (1993b), *The Climax of Prophecy: Studies in the Book of Revelation*, Edinburgh: T & T Clark.

— (1999), 'Response to Ernest Lucas: The New Testament Teaching on the Environment', Unpublished Papers of a Theological Consultation for the John Ray Initiative, Brunei Centre, University of London: 1–4.

BEDEWES, CHRISTINE (2005), *Parish Transformation in Urban Slums: Voices of Kibera, Kenya*, Nairobi: Paulines Publications.

BENJAMIN, DON C. (1983), *Deuteronomy and City Life: A Form Criticism of Texts with the Word CITY ('ir) in Deuteronomy 4:41–26:19*, New York: University Press of America.

BESSENECKER, SCOTT (2006), *The New Friars: The Emerging Movement Serving the World's Poor*, Milton Keynes: Authentic Media.

BREWIN, KESTER (2004), *The Complex Christ: Signs of Emergence in the Urban Church*, London: SPCK.

BRIGHT, JOHN (1976), *Covenant and Promise: The Prophetic Understanding of the Future in Pre-Exilic Israel*, Philadelphia: Westminster Press.

— (1981), *A History of Israel*, 3rd ed., Philadelphia: Westminster Press.

BROWN, PETER (1969), *Augustine of Hippo: A Biography*, London: Faber & Faber.

BROWN, P. and JOHN T. CARROLL (2000), 'The Garden and the Plaza: Biblical Images of the City', *Interpretation* January: 3–11.

BRUEGGEMANN, WALTER (1978), *The Prophetic Imagination*, Philadelphia: Fortress Press.

— (1982a), *Genesis: Interpretation – A Bible Commentary for Teaching and Preaching*, Atlanta: John Knox Press.

— (1982b), *Living Toward a Vision*, New York: United Church Press.

— (1986), *Hopeful Imagination: Prophetic Voices in Exile*, Philadelphia: Fortress Press.

— (1987), *Hope Within History*, Atlanta: John Knox Press.

— (1993), *Using God's Resources Wisely: Isaiah and Urban Possibility*, Louisville: Westminster John Knox Press.

— (1997a), *Theology of the Old Testament: Testimony, Dispute, Advocacy*, Minneapolis: Fortress Press.

— (1997b), *Cadences of Home: Preaching Among Exiles*, Louisville: Westminster John Knox Press.

— (2000a), *Texts That Linger, Words That Explode*, Minneapolis: Fortress Press.

— (2000b), *Deep Memory, Exuberant Hope*, Minneapolis: Fortress Press.

— (2007), *Mandate to Difference: An Invitation to the Contemporary Church*, Louisville: Westminster John Knox Press.

— (2009), *Divine Presence Amid Violence: Contextualizing the Book of Joshua*, Eugene, Oregon: Cascade Books.

— (2010), *Journey to the Common Good*, Louisville: Westminster John Knox Press.

BRUEGGEMANN, WALTER (ed.) (2001), *Hope For The World: Mission in a Global Context*, Louisville: Westminster John Knox Press.

BUBER, MARTIN (1949), *The Prophetic Faith*, New York: Macmillan.

BUONFINO, ALESSANDRA and GEOFF MULGAN (eds.) (2006), *Porcupines in Winter: The Pleasures and Pains of Living Together in Modern Britain*, London: The Young Foundation.

CALLAHAN, ALLEN DWIGHT (2009), 'Babylon Boycott: The Book of Revelation', *Interpretation* January: 48–54.

CAREY, GREG (2008), 'The Book of Revelation as Counter-Imperial Script', in Horsley (ed.), 157–176.

CARROLL R., M. DANIEL (2010), 'A Biblical Theology of the City and the Environment: Human Community in the Created Order', in Toly and Block (eds.), 69–89.

CARTER, WARREN (2010), 'Matthew's People', in Horsley (ed.), 138–161.

CHALMERS, THOMAS (1995 [1821, 1823, 1826]), *The Christian and Civic Economy of Large Towns, vols. 1–3*, London: Routledge/Thoemmes Press.

COLLIER, JANE and RAFAEL ESTEBAN (1998), *From Complicity to Encounter: The Church and the Culture of Economism*, Harrisburg: Trinity Press International.

CONN, HARVIE (1992), 'Genesis as Urban Prologue', in Greenway (ed.), 13–33.

COSDEN, DARRELL (2006), *The Heavenly Good of Earthly Work*, Milton Keynes: Paternoster Press.

COX, HARVEY (1968a), *The Secular City*, Harmondsworth: Penguin Books.

— (1968b), *On Not Leaving It To The Snake*, London: SCM Press.

— (1995), *Fire From Heaven: The Rise of Pentecostal Spirituality and the Reshaping of Religion in the Twenty-First Century*, Reading, Massachusetts: Addison-Wesley Publishing.

COWPER, WILLIAM (n.d.), *The Poetical Works of William Cowper*, London: Frederick Warne.

CRADDOCK, FRED (1990), *Luke, Interpretation: A Bible Commentary for Teaching and Preaching*, Louisville: John Knox Press.

DAVEY, ANDREW (2001), *Urban Christianity and the Global Order: Theological Resources for an Urban Future*, London: SPCK.

— (2007), 'Faithful Cities – Locating Everyday Faithfulness', *Contact* 152: 8–20.

— (2008), 'Better Place: Performing the Urbanisms of Hope', *International Journal of Public Theology* 2: 27–46.

DAWN, MARVA J. (2001), *Powers, Weakness and the Tabernacling of God*, Grand Rapids: Eerdmans.

DEVER, WILLIAM G. (2003), *Who Were the Early Israelites and Where Did They Come From?*, Grand Rapids: Eerdmans.

DRANE, JOHN (2006), 'Editorial: The Emerging Church', *International Journal for the Study of the Christian Church* 6.1: 3–11.

DRUMMOND, HENRY (2008 [1893]), *The City Without A Church*, Radford: Wilder Publications.

ELA, JEAN-MARC (1986), *African Cry*, New York: Orbis Books.

— (2001), *My Faith as an African*, Nairobi: Acton Publishers.

ELIZONDO, VIRGIL (1988), *The Future is Mestizo: Life Where Cultures Meet*, Bloomington: Meyer Stone Books.

ELLIOTT, NEIL (2008a), *The Arrogance of Nations: Reading Romans in the Shadow of Empire*, Minneapolis: Fortress Press.

— (2008b), 'The Apostle Paul and Empire', in Horsley (ed.), 97–116.

ELLUL, JACQUES (1970), *The Meaning of the City*, Grand Rapids: Eerdmans.

ESLER, PHILIP (2003), *Conflict and Identity in Romans: The Social Setting of Paul's Letter*, Minneapolis: Fortress Press.

FRETHEIM, TERENCE (1984), *The Suffering of God: An Old Testament Perspective*, Philadelphia: Fortress Press.

FRITZ, VOLKMAR (1995), *The City in Ancient Israel*, Sheffield: Sheffield Academic Press.

GALLARDO, CARLOS BRAVO (1997), 'Matthew: Good News for the Persecuted Poor', in Vaage (ed.), 173–192.

GEORGI, DIETER (2005), *The City in the Valley: Biblical Interpretation and Urban Theology*, Atlanta: Society for Biblical Literature.

GOETZ, DAVID (2003), 'Suburban Spirituality', *Christianity Today* July: 31–37.

GOLDINGAY, JOHN (1989), 'The Bible in the City', *Theology* XCII.745: 5–15.

GONZALEZ, JUSTO (1990), *Manana: Christian Theology From A Hispanic Perspective*, Nashville: Abingdon Press.

— (1999), *For the Healing of the Nations: The Book of Revelation in an Age of Cultural Conflict*, New York: Orbis Books.

GONZALEZ, CATHERINE and JUSTO GONZALEZ (1978), *Vision At Patmos: A Study in the Book of Revelation*, Nashville: Abingdon Press.

GORDON, J. DORCAS (1997), *Sister or Wife? 1 Corinthians 7 and Cultural Anthropology*, Journal for the Study of the New Testament Supplement Series 149, Sheffield: Sheffield Academic Press.

GORNIK, MARK (2002), *To Live in Peace: Biblical Faith and the Changing Inner City*, Grand Rapids: Eerdmans.

GORRINGE, T. J. (2002), *The Theology of the Built Environment: Justice, Empowerment, Redemption*, Cambridge: Cambridge University Press.

GOTTWALD, NORMAN (1979), *The Tribes of Israel: A Sociology of the Religion of Liberated Israel, 1250–1050*, New York: Orbis Books.

— (2008), 'Early Israel as an Anti-Imperial Community', in Horsley (ed.), 9–24.

GOUDZWAARD, BOB (1984), *Idols of Our Time*, Downers Grove: InterVarsity Press.

GOWAN, DONALD E. (1975), *When Man becomes God: Humanism and Hybris in the Old Testament*, Pittsburg: The Pickwick Press.

— (1988), *From Eden To Babel: Genesis 1–11*, Edinburgh: The Handsel Press.

GRAHAM, FRED W. (1978), *The Constructive Revolutionary: John Calvin and His Socio-Economic Impact*, Atlanta: John Knox Press.

GREENWAY, ROGER (ed.) *Discipling The City: A Comprehensive Approach to Urban Mission*, Grand Rapids: Baker Bookhouse.

GUTHRIE, THOMAS (1857), *The City – Its Sins and Sorrows. Being a Series of Sermons from Luke xix.41*, New York: Robert Carter & Brothers.

HAMLIN, JOHN E. (1983), *Inheriting the Land: A Commentary on the Book of Joshua*, Grand Rapids: Eerdmans.

HEIDEL, ALEXANDER (1949), *The Epic of Gilgamesh and Old Testament Parallels*, Chicago: University of Chicago Press.

— (1951), *The Babylonian Genesis*, 2nd ed., Chicago: University of Chicago Press.

HILLIS, PETER (2007), *The Barony of Glasgow*, Edinburgh: Dunedin Academic Press.

HORSLEY, RICHARD A. (2008a), *Jesus in Context: Power, People and Performance*, Minneapolis: Fortress Press.

— (2008b), 'Jesus and Empire', in Horsley (ed.), pp. 75–96.

— (2010), 'Introduction: Unearthing a People's History', in Horsley (ed.), 1–20.

HORSLEY, RICHARD A. (ed.) (2008), *In The Shadow of Empire: Reclaiming the Bible as a Faithful History of Resistance*, Louisville: Westminster John Knox Press.

— (2010), *A People's History of Christianity. Volume 1, Christian Origins*, Minneapolis: Fortress Press.

HORSLEY, RICHARD A. and NEIL ASHER SILBERMAN (1997), *The Message and the Kingdom: How Jesus and Paul Ignited A Revolution and Transformed The Ancient World*, Minneapolis: Fortress Press.

HOWARD-BROOK, WES and ANTHONY GWYTHER (1999), *Unveiling Empire: Reading Revelation Then and Now*, New York: Orbis Books.

HUBBARD, MOYER V. (2010), *Christianity in the Greco-Roman World: A Narrative Introduction*, Peabody, Massachusetts: Hendrickson Publishers.

IRVIN, DALE T. (2009), 'The Church, the Urban, and Global Mission: Mission in an Age of Global Cities', *International Bulletin of Missionary Research* 33.4: 177–182.

JACOBSEN, ERIC J. (2003), *Sidewalks in the Kingdom: New Urbanism and the Christian Faith*, Grand Rapids: Brazos Press.

JEREMIAS, JOACHIM (1969), *Jerusalem in the Time of Jesus: An Investigation Into Economic and Social Conditions During the New Testament Period*, Philadelphia: Fortress Press.

JOHNS, CHERYL BRIDGES (1993), *Pentecostal Formation: A Pedagogy Among the Oppressed*, Sheffield: Sheffield Academic Press.

KELLER, TIM (2006), 'A New Kind of Urban Christian', *Christianity Today*, <http://www.christianitytoday.com/ct/2006/005/1.36.html> (accessed 12 June 2006).

KITCHEN, K. A. (1977), *The Bible in its World: Archaeology and the Bible Today*, Exeter: Paternoster Press.

KOCH, KLAUS (1983), *The Prophets: Volume One – The Assyrian Period*, Philadelphia: Fortress Press.

KOESTER, CRAIG R. (2009), 'Revelation's Visionary Challenge to Ordinary Empire', *Interpretation* January: 5–18.

LATVUS, KARI (2007), 'The Bible in British Urban Theology: An Analysis by a Finnish Companion', in West (ed.), 133–140.

LABBERTON, MARK (2007), *The Dangerous Act of Worship: Living God's Call to Justice*, Downers Grove: InterVarsity Press.

LEE, NANCY C. (2010), *Lyrics of Lament: From Tragedy to Transformation*, Minneapolis: Fortress Press.

LIND, MILLARD C. (1980), *Yahweh Is A Warrior: The Theology of Warfare in Ancient Israel*, Scottdale: Herald Press.

LOPEZ, DAVINA C. (2008), *Apostle To The Conquered: Re-imagining Paul's Mission*, Minneapolis: Fortress Press.

MAIER, HARRY O. (2002), *Apocalypse Recalled: The Book of Revelation After Christendom*, Minneapolis: Fortress Press.

MAIER, FATHER JOE (2005), *Welcome to the Bangkok Slaughterhouse: The Battle for Human Dignity in Bangkok's Bleakest Slums*, Bangkok: Asia Books.

MARTIN, DAVID (2002), *Pentecostalism: The World Their Parish*, Oxford: Blackwell Publishers.

MASON, REX (1997), *Propaganda and Subversion in the Old Testament*, London: SPCK.

MATTHEWS, JOHN (2006), 'Ruchill: A Glasgow Housing Scheme', in Buonfino and Mulgan (eds.), 37–43.

MCALPINE, THOMAS H. (1991), *Facing The Powers: What Are The Options?*, Monrovia, California: MARC.

MCKECHNIE, PAUL (2001), *The First Christian Centuries: Perspectives on the Early Church*, Leicester: Inter-Varsity Press.

MCLEOD, HUGH (1984), *Religion and the Working Class in Nineteenth Century Britain*, London: Macmillan.

— (ed.) (1995), *European Religion in the Age of Great Cities*, London: Routledge.

MEEKS, WAYNE (1983), *The First Urban Christians: The Social World of the Apostle Paul*, New Haven: Yale University Press.

MENDENHALL, GEORGE E. (1962), 'The Hebrew Conquest of Palestine', *The Biblical Archaeologist* XXV.3: 66–87.

— (1973), *The Tenth Generation: The Origins of the Biblical Tradition*, Baltimore: The John Hopkins University Press.

METZ, JOHANN BAPTIST (1981), *The Emergent Church: The Future of Christianity in a Postbourgeois World*, New York: Crossroad.

MEYERS, ELEANOR SCOTT (2000), 'The Church in the City: Past, Present and Future', *Interpretation* January: 23–35.

MOELLER, BERND (1979), 'The Town in Church History: General Presuppositions of the Reformation in Germany', in Baker (ed.), 257–268.

MOLTMANN, JÜRGEN (1983), *The Power of the Powerless*, London: SCM Press.

MOUW, RICHARD J. (2002), *When The Kings Come Marching In: Isaiah and the New Jerusalem*, Grand Rapids: Eerdmans.

MURPHY, FREDERICK J. (1998), *Fallen is Babylon: The Revelation to John*, Harrisburg: Trinity Press International.

MYERS, CHED (1988), *Binding The Strong Man: A Political Reading of Mark's Story of Jesus*, New York: Orbis Books.

NASRALLAH, LAURA (2008), 'The Acts of the Apostles, Greek Cities, and Hadrian's Panhellenion', *Journal of Biblical Literature* 127.3: 533–566.

NETZER, EHUD and ZEEV WEISS (1992), 'New Mosaic Art From Sepphoris', *Biblical Archaeology Review* 18.2: 37–78.

OAKES, PETER (2009), *Reading Romans in Pompeii: Paul's Letter at Ground Level*, London: SPCK.

O'CONNOR, KATHLEEN (2002), *Lamentations and the Tears of the World*, New York: Orbis Books.

OZMENT, STEVEN (1980), *The Age of Reform: 1250–1550 An Intellectual and Religious History of Late Medieval and Reformation Europe*, New Haven: Yale University Press.

PEROWNE, STEWART (1960), *The Life and Times of Herod the Great*, London: Arrow Books.

PICKETT, RAY (2010), 'Conflicts at Corinth', in Horsley (ed.), 113–117.

PIERLI, FRANCESCO and YAGO ABELADO (eds.) (2002), *The Slums: A Challenge to Evangelization*, Nairobi: Paulines Publications.

PITKÄNEN, PEKKA (2004), 'Ethnicity, Assimilation and the Israelite Settlement', *Tyndale Bulletin* 55.2: 161–182.

— (2010), *Joshua*, Apollos Old Testament Commentary, Nottingham: Apollos; Downers Grove: InterVarsity Press.

RAMACHANDRA, VINOTH (1996), *Gods That Fail: Modern Idolatry and the Christian Mission*, Carlisle: Paternoster Press.

RICHARD, PABLO (1995), *Apocalypse: A People's Commentary on the Book of Revelation*, New York: Orbis Books.

RODRIGUEZ, RAUL HUMBERTO LUGO (1997), '"Wait For the Day of God's Coming and Do What You Can to Hasten It..." (2 Peter 3:12): The Non-Pauline Letters as Resistance Literature', in Vaage (ed.), 193–206.

ROGERSON, J. W. and JOHN VINCENT (2009), *The City in Biblical Perspective*, London: Equinox.

SANCHEZ, DAVID A. (2008), *From Patmos to the Barrio: Subverting Imperial Myths*, Minneapolis: Fortress Press.

SAWICKI, MARRIANE (2000), *Crossing Galilee: Architectures of Contact in the Occupied Land of
Jesus*, Harrisburg: Trinity Press International.

SCHREITER, ROBERT J. (1997), *The New Catholicity: Theology Between The Global and the
Local*, New York: Orbis Books.

SCOTT, JAMES M. (1995), *Paul and the Nations: The Old Testament and Jewish Background of
Paul's Mission to the Nations with Special Reference to the Destination of Galatians*, Tubingen:
JCM Mohr (Paul Siebeck).

SHELDRAKE, PHILIP (2001), 'Reading Cathedrals as Spiritual Texts', *Studies in Spirituality*
11: 187–204.

— (2005), 'Cities and Human Community', in Walker (ed.), 67–89.

— (2007), 'Placing the Sacred: Transcendence and the City', *Literature and Theology* 21.3:
243–258.

SHORTER, AYLWARD (1991), *The Church in the African City*, London: Geoffrey Chapman.

SMITH, DAVID (2003), *Mission After Christendom*, London: Darton, Longman & Todd.

— (2007), *Moving Toward Emmaus: Hope in a Time of Uncertainty*, London: SPCK.

SMITH, JAMES K. A. (2004), *Introducing Radical Orthodoxy: Mapping a Post-Secular Theology*,
Grand Rapids: Baker Academic.

STACKHOUSE, MAX L. (1972), *Ethics and the Urban Ethos: An Essay in Social Theory and
Theological Reconstruction*, Boston: Beacon Press.

STARK, RODNEY (2006), *Cities of God: The Real Story of How Christianity Came to be An
Urban Movement and Conquered Rome*, New York: Harper Collins.

STEGEMANN, EKKHARD W. and WOLFGANG STEGEMANNN (1999), *The Jesus Movement:
A Social History of Its First Century*, Edinburgh: T & T Clark.

TAYLOR, JOHN V. (1975), *Enough Is Enough*, London: SCM Press.

TOLY, NOAH J. (2010), 'Cities and the Global Environment', in Toly and Block (eds.),
47–68.

TOLY, NOAH J. and DANIEL BLOCK (eds.) (2010), *Keeping God's Earth: The Global
Environment in Biblical Perspective*, Downers Grove: InterVaristy Press; Nottingham:
Apollos.

VAAGE, LEIF E. (ed.), (1997), *Subversive Scriptures: Revolutionary Readings of the Christian
Scriptures in Latin America*, Valley Forge: Trinity Press International.

VAN LEEUWEN, AREND TH. (1964), *Christianity in World History: The Meeting of the Faiths of
East and West*, London: Edinburgh House Press.

VERKUYL, JOHANNES (1978), *Contemporary Missiology: An Introduction*, Grand Rapids:
Eerdmans.

VINCENT, JOHN (ed.) (2006), *Mark Gospel of Action: Personal and Community Responses*,
London: SPCK.

WALKER, ANDREW (ed.) (2005), *Spirituality in the City*, London: SPCK.

WALKER, P. W. L. (1996), *Jesus and The Holy City: New Testament Perspectives on Jerusalem*, Grand Rapids: Eerdmans.

WALL, ROBERT W. (1997), *Community of the Wise: The Letter of James*, Valley Forge: Trinity Press International.

WALSH, BRIAN J. and SYLVIA KEESMAAT C. (2004), *Colossians Remixed: Subverting Empire*, Downers Grove: InterVarsity Press.

WANDEL, LEE PALMER (1990), *Always Among Us: Images of the Poor in Zwingli's Zurich*, Cambridge: Cambridge University Press.

WARD, GRAHAM (2000), *Cities of God*, London: Routledge.

— (2003), 'Why is the city so important for Christian theology?', *Cross Currents* 52: 462–473.

WENHAM, GORDON J. (1987), *Genesis 1–15*, Word Biblical Commentary vol.1, Milton Keynes: Word Publishing.

WEST, GERALD O. (2007), *Reading Otherwise: Socially Engaged Biblical Scholars Reading With Their Local Communities*, Atlanta: Society for Biblical Literature.

WESTERMANN, CLAUS (1969), *Isaiah 40–66 – A Commentary*, Philadelphia: Westminster Press.

— (1984), *Genesis 1–11 – A Commentary*, Minneapolis: Augsburg Publishing.

WINK, WALTER (1992), *Engaging The Powers: Discernment and Resistance in a World of Domination*, Minneapolis: Fortress Press.

— (1998), *The Powers That Be: Theology for a New Millennium*, New York: Doubleday.

WINTER, BRUCE W. (1994), *Seek The Welfare of the City: Christians as Benefactors and Citizens*, Grand Rapids: Eerdmans.

WITHERINGTON III, BEN (2001), *The Gospel of Mark: A Socio-Rhetorical Commentary*, Grand Rapids: Eerdmans.

— (2010), *Jesus and Money*, London: SPCK.

WOLSTERSTORFF, NICHOLAS (1983), *Until Justice and Peace Embrace*, Grand Rapids: Eerdmans.

WRIGHT, NIGEL (2003), *A Theology of the Dark Side: Putting the Power of Evil in its Place*, Carlisle: Paternoster Press.

WRIGHT, N. T. (1996), *Jesus and the Victory of God*, London: SPCK.

ZANOTELLI, ALEX (2002), 'A Grace Freely Given', in Pierli and Abelado (eds.), 13–19.

INDEX OF NAMES

Abraham, J. H. 56, 70, 74
Aelius Aristides 210–211
Agricola 196
Albright, William Fox 137
Alexander the Great 49, 186
Amin, Ash 76, 84, 85
Anderson, Bernard W. 54
Aristotle 56–57, 58
Atkinson, Adrian 87, 93, 97
Atkinson, Dan 219
Augé, Marc 218
Augustine of Hippo 24–25, 26, 43, 58, 69, 87

Baker, Christopher 235
Batey, Richard 174
Bauckham, Richard 124–125, 163, 206, 207, 211, 213, 226, 239
Baudrillard, Jean 85
Bauman, Zygmunt 81, 155, 216
Benjamin, Don C. 133
Berleant, Arnold 48
Berman, Marshall 83, 161–162
Bess, Philip 30, 32, 84, 96
Bond, Patrick 34
Booth, Robert 24
Bowcott, Owen 37

Bridge, Gary 40
Bright, John 134–135, 149, 156
Britts, Bryana 99–101
Broudehoux, Anne-Marie 37
Brown, Callum 25, 26, 111, 112
Brown, Peter 121, 131, 140, 142
Brueggemann, Walter 46, 132, 135, 139, 142–143, 146, 148, 149, 151, 153, 155, 156, 160, 162, 166, 171–172, 215
Buber, Martin 145, 152
Bunting, Madeleine 164
Burgess, Ernest W. 69
Burns, Robert 109

Cadbury family 78
Calvin, John 62–63
Carroll, John T. 121, 131, 140, 142
Castells, Manuel 18
Charles, Prince 96
Chatterton, Paul 238–239
Churchill, Winston 137
Cifatte, Maria Caterina 60
Clark, David 31, 69, 85
Collier, Jane 85, 219
Conn, Harvie 123
Cosden, Darrell 213

Cowper, William 22, 40–41
Cox, Harvey 17, 229, 230
Craddock, Fred 189

Damer, Sean 109, 113
Davey, Andrew 18, 30
Davis, Mike 24, 36, 45, 90, 96, 127, 129,
    137–138, 200
Denison, Edward 93
Dever, William G. 135
Dickens, Charles 39
Dominic 61
Donskis, Leonidas 65
Dostoevsky, Fydor 68, 76
Drummond, Henry 213–214
Duany, Andreas 95–96
Durkheim, Emile 72, 74

Edward I, King 106
Ela, Jean-Marc 136, 224, 230
Eliade, Mircea 129
Eliot, T. S. 29, 86
Ellin, Nan 91
Elliott, Larry 219
Elliott, Neil 197
Ellul, Jacques 121–122, 125, 126
Engels, Friedrich 73, 74, 110
Esler, Philip 199
Esteban, Rafael 85, 219

Francis of Assisi 60
Frank, Joseph 68
Fretheim, Terence 154–155
Fritz, Volkmar 140–141, 144
Furniss, Charlie 91

Gallardo, Carlos 216
Georgi, Dieter 172, 185, 191–192, 193, 194,
    202, 203, 212, 213, 222, 223
Gilson, Etienne 65
Goldingay, John 127, 132, 146
Gonzalez, Catherine 212
Gonzalez, Justo 55–56, 174, 209–210, 212,
    224–225, 235–236
Gordon, J. Dorcas 203
Gottwald, Norman 125, 136
Goudzwaard, Bob 219, 221
Gowan, Donald 126, 169
Graham, Stephen 62, 138, 220
Gropius, Walter 77
Gulick, John 70–71

Guthrie, Thomas 112

Hall, Peter 81
Hamlin, John 133, 137, 140
Hanlon, Phil 216
Harris, William Wade 233
Haruna, Dayyabu 90
Heidel, Alexander 50, 51–52, 53
Herod Antipas 174–175, 182, 187
Herod the Great 174, 187
Hillis, Peter 110
Hodin, J. P. 66
Holbein, Hans 65
Hopper, Edward 73
Horsley, Richard A. 104, 173–174, 175, 176,
    182, 188, 190–191
Howard, Ebenezer 78, 79, 213

Ibn Khaldun 56
Irvin, Dale 232, 233–234, 235

Jacobs, Jane 83, 92–93
Jacobsen, Eric 95, 96–97
Jencks, Charles 103, 116
Jeremias, Joachim 187, 188
Joanna 181
Johns, Cheryl Bridge 231
Josephus 178, 182, 187
Jowit, Juliette 164

Kaika, Maria 105, 107, 108–109, 111, 113,
    115–116
Käsemann, Ernst 226
Katodrytis, George 36
Keesmaat, Sylvia 203
Keller, Tim 234
King, Anthony D. 89
Kishlansky, Mark 59, 60
Kitchen, K. A. 124
Knox, John 63, 107
Koch, Klaus 147–148
Kollwitz, Käthe 73
Koolhaas, Rem 84
Kotkin, Joel 59
Kranzfelder, Ivo 73
Krier, Leon 96
Kumar, Krishnan 20–21, 67
Kunstler, James Howard 83, 91–92, 93

Labberton, Mark 240
Lang, Fritz 36, 39, 85

Lasch, Christopher 227
Lawton, Graham 50
Le Corbusier 80–81, 82, 83, 84, 91, 114, 115, 138, 213
Leverhulme, Lord 78
Logue, Ed 83
Lopez, Davina 177, 195–196, 197, 207
Lubeck, Paul M. 99–101

McAlpine, Thomas H. 226
McNeill, Donald 116
Maier, Harry 206
Marenya, Neddy 229
Martin, David 104–105, 231
Marx, Karl 23, 45, 74, 151, 218
Mason, Rex 52–53, 54, 55
Massacio 64–65
Massey, Douglas S. 38–39, 41
Meeks, Wayne 192
Mendenhall, George E. 130, 131, 134
Metz, Johannes Baptist 236–237
Miles, Malcolm 96
Milun, Kathryn 81, 85–86, 86, 87, 94
Moeller, Bernd 58
Moltmann, Jürgen 228
Monk, Daniel Bertrand 24, 127
Moses, Robert 83, 87, 114
Mouw, Richard 226–227
Müller-Karpe, Michael 50
Mumford, Lewis 19–20, 53, 56, 58, 60, 61, 69, 74–75, 79
Munch, Edvard 65–66, 73
Mungo (Kentigern), St 106
Murray, Sean 81, 90
Myers, Ched 178–179, 184

Nasrallah, Laura 194, 223
Nebuchadnezzar, 22, 181
Nero 180
Newton, John 40
Nicholson, Adam 36
Ninian 106

Oakes, Peter 198, 199–200, 202
O'Connor, Kathleen 159, 160, 161
Oostuizen, G. 45
Ozment, Steven 61, 62

Pacione, Michael 106, 107–108, 110, 114, 116
Packard, Vance 207–208
Padfield, David 176

Pearman, Hugh 77, 79
Peñalosa, Enrique 98, 99
Perowne, Stewart 187
Pitkänen, Pekka 135
Plater-Zyberk, Elizabeth 95–96
Plato 56, 57
Pliny the Elder 186, 197

Rabb, Theodore 60
Rabinovitch, Jonas 98
Ramachandra, Vinoth 219
Richard, Pablo 212
Roberts, Bryan 88, 89–90
Robinson, Jennifer 44
Rodriguez, Raul Humberto Lugo 204, 205
Rogerson, J. W. 173
Rowntree, Joseph 78
Roy, Arundhati 221
Ruskin, John 76–77

Sadowski, Yahya 101
Sandercock, Leonie 86, 94–95
Sassen, Saskia 138
Sawicki, Marianne 175, 182, 183, 185
Schreiter, Robert 236
Scott, James 128, 166
Seabrook, Jeremy 86, 208
Sheldrake, Philip 215, 239
Shorter, Aylward 87–88
Silberman, Neil Asher 176, 182, 188, 190–191
Simmel, Georg 71–72, 73
Smith, David 190
Smith, David M. 29, 41–42, 44–45, 102
Southall, Aidan 61
Spence, Basil 114
Stackhouse, Max 227, 228
Stanley, H. M. 88
Stark, Rodney 201
Steel, Carolyn 37–38, 78, 79
Stegemann, Ekkhard W. 171, 178, 198
Stegemann, Wolfgang 171, 178, 198
Sudjic, Deyan 116–117

Tacitus 196–197
Tawney, R. H. 63, 108
Taylor, John V. 184
Taylor, Steve 21
Thielen, Korinna 87, 93, 97, 105, 107, 108–109, 111, 113, 115–116
Thrift, Nigel 76, 84, 85
Tonnies, Ferdinand 70

UN-HABITAT 45, 97, 98

Vaage, Leife E. 137
van Leeuwen, Arend 126, 129
Verkuhl, Johannes 234
Vidal, John 38
Vidler, Alex 66, 79–80
Vincent, John 173
Virgil 177
Von Laue, Theodore 217

Walker, Peter 189–190
Wall, Robert 204–205
Walsh, Brian J. 203
Wandel, Lee Palmer 63, 98
Ward, Graham 233
Watson, Sophie 40
Watts, George Frederick 76

Watts, Jonathan 38, 217
Weber, Max 66–67, 68
Wenham, Gordon J. 124, 125, 126
Westermann, Claus 128, 238
Whyte, Iain 108
Wilkinson, John 121
Wink, Walter 220
Wirth, Louis 73
Witherington, Ben 180, 185
Wolterstorff, Nicholas 235
Woodrow, Robert 108
Wright, Lloyd 98
Wright, N. T. 191

Zanotelli, Alex 201
Zigrosser, Karl 73
Zwingli, Huldrych 63

INDEX OF SCRIPTURE REFERENCES

OLD TESTAMENT

Genesis
1 – 11 *124, 125*
1:3 *82*
1:26–28 *123*
1:27 *127*
1:31 *19, 25*
3:9 *127*
4:16–17 *125*
4:17 *49*
4:17–24 *127*
10 *138, 165, 166*
10:10–12 *49*
10:19 *49*
11:1–4 *49*
11:1–9 *126*
11:4–5 *126*
12 – 50 *128*
18:16–33 *128*
19:1–29 *128*
19:28 *128*
41:41–45 *129*
47:20–24 *129*
47:25 *130*

Exodus
1:11 *129*
3:1–15 *131*
12:31 *130*
19:3–6 *131*
31:1–10 *130*

Numbers
13:26–33 *133*

Deuteronomy
1:26–28 *133*
4:5–8 *131*
4:20 *152*
6:4–9 *131*
6:5 *152*
6:10–12 *131–2*
7:9 *152*
12:4–14 *142*
15:1–11 *132*
15:7–8 *132*
16:11–12 *136*
16:18–20 *132*
19:10 *140*
24:19 *132*

26:16 *152*

Joshua
1:6–9 *135*
2:8–11 *134*
2:24 *134*
11 *138*
11:1–5 *135*
11:4–5 *139*
11:6 *139*
20:1–9 *140*

1 Samuel
8:11–17 *141*

2 Samuel
5:9–10 *141*
5:11 *141*
5:13 *141*
12:9–10 *144*

1 Kings
8:12–61 *145*
9:11 *167*
11:11 *146*

2 Kings
22:8–13 *156*

1 Chronicles
1 – 2 *166*

Psalms
8:1 *166*
9:8 *166*
9:19 *166*
19:4 *166*
20:7 *139*
22:27–28 *166*
24:1 *166*
33:16–19 *139*
46:4–7 *142*
46:9 *140*
46:9–10 *138*
46:10 *166*
47:5–9 *142*
47:7 *143*
48:1 *142*
48:1–8 *148*
48:8 *142*
48:11 *143*
55:9–11 *144*
56:8 *160*
66:7 *166*
67:4–5 *166*
74:1 *146*
74:9 *146, 147*
76:6–7 *139*
79:3 *147*
87:4–6 *166*
107:4–9 *143*
107:35–36 *143*
137:4 *161*
147:10–11 *139*

Proverbs
21:30–31 *139*

Ecclesiastes
2:4 *145*
2:8 *145*
2:10 *145*
4:1–4 *145*
5:8–9 *145*

Isaiah
1:9–10 *128*

1:10–15 *150*
1:21 *143*
1:26 *160, 164*
2:1–4 *164*
2:4 *140*
2:5 *47, 165*
2:6–8 *164*
2:7–8 *220*
8:16–17 *156*
10:7 *140*
14:3–6 *167*
14:5–8 *168*
19:18–25 *168*
24:4–5 *163*
24:13 *163*
25:6–8 *164*
26:13–18 *153*
28:14–19 *156*
28:21 *156*
29:13 *152*
30:15–16 *139*
31:1 *139*
40 *161*
40 – 55 *160*
40:1–2 *161*
40:3–4 *238*
40:9 *237*
40:27 *161, 237*
41:7 *238*
42:1 *195*
42:4 *161*
43:16–17 *139*
46:1–4 *238*
47:7–8 *168*
49:14 *161, 237*
55:2 *147*
61:1–3 *177*
61:4 *165, 177*
61:6 *177*
65:17–25 *165*
65:20 *165*
65:25 *165*
66:7–21 *221*
66:18 *165*
66:19 *166*
66:20 *165, 168, 177*
66:23 *165, 168*

Jeremiah
1:5 *195*
3:3 *153*

4:19 *157*
4:23–26 *163*
6:15 *153*
7:5–8 *150*
8:12 *153*
8:18 *158*
9:20–21 *159*
11:19 *157*
12:1–2 *157*
12:6 *157*
15:10 *157*
16:1–4 *157*
20:7–8 *151*
20:9 *158*
22:15–16 *157*
23:13–14 *128*
26:7–11 *150*
29:4–7 *168*
29:7 *162*
39:11–12 *168*
42:10 *161*

Lamentations
1:1 *158*
1:2 *161*
1:7 *161*
1:9 *161*
1:16 *161*
1:17 *161*
1:21 *161*
3:21–26 *159*
5:20 *161*

Ezekiel
7:1–9 *156*
16:49–50 *128*
27:33 *167*
28:2 *167*
28:12–15 *169*
28:16 *167*
28:18 *169*
28:19 *167*
38 – 39 *166*

Daniel
3:4 *166*
3:7 *166*
3:29 *166*
4:1 *166*
4:37 *168*
6:25 *166*

7:14 *166*

Hosea
1:7 *139*
2:14–15 *154*
2:23 *155*
3:1 *154*
4:1–3 *153, 163*
4:14 *153*
6:4 *154*
11:1–11 *154*

Amos
5:21–22 *149*
5:23 *150*
5:24 *150*

Jonah
4:11 *170*

Micah
5:10 *139*
15:40–41 *181*

Nahum
3:1 *167*
3:19 *167*

NEW TESTAMENT

Matthew
4:18–22 *183*
5:13–16 *186*
5:14 *177*
6:12 *178*
6:24 *185*
6:32–34 *178*
10:15 *128*
11:23–24 *128*
27:55–56 *181*

Mark
1:1 *184*
5:1 *178*
5:2–5 *178*
5:9 *178*
5:15 *179*
5:16–17 *179*
5:18–20 *179*
7:9–13 *188*
12:38–40 *188*

14:12–26 *190*
14:50 *190*
15:20 *190*
15:40–41

Luke
3:1–2 *174*
4:18–19 *177*
8:1–3 *181*
13:34–35 *189*
19:8–10 *181*
19:37–44 *189*
23:49 *181*
24:10 *181*
24:13–35 *190*

John
19:15 *189*
20:19 *191*

Acts
2:1–13 *195*
2:9–11 *187*
2:22–24 *228*
2:31–33 *228*
2:42–47 *228*
4:32–37 *228*
7:36 *190*
9:15 *195*
13:17 *190*
17:24–28 *195*
19:9 *194*
19:23 *194*
22:4 *194*
24:14 *194*
24:22 *194*

Romans
1:1–2 *197*
1:4 *227*
1:7 *197*
1:14 *197*
2:16 *202*
5:5 *201*
12:2 *202, 221*
12:3 *199*
12:9–10 *199*
17:1 *208*
17:15–18 *208*

1 Corinthians
15:58 *47, 212*

Galatians
1:15–16 *195*
4:4 *202*

Ephesians
2:14–18 *225*

Colossians
1:15–20 *203*
1:18 *203*

1 Thessalonians
5:3 *203*

Hebrews
11:10 *53*
13:12–14 *191*

James
4:13 *191*
4:13 – 5:6 *204*
5:3 *204*

1 John
2:2 *193*

Revelation
1:9 *207*
1:17–18 *211*
2 – 3 *205*
2:1–7 *205*
2:7 *207*
2:11 *207*
2:17 *207*
3:14–22 *205*
4:1 *206*
5:6–14 *212*
5:9–10 *209*
7:9 *209*
10:9–11 *209*
13:4 *238*
13:14 *238*
17:9 *210*
18 *26*
18:4 *191, 211*
18:9 *210*
18:12–13 *210*
18:13 *211*

21 – 22 *211*

21:4 *39*

21:10–11 *19*

21:22 *214*

21:23 *213*

21:24 *209, 213*

22:1–2 *213*

22:1–5 *82*

22:2 *26, 213*

INDEX OF SUBJECTS

Abram/Abraham 48, 53, 128, 129, 131, 133, 138, 195–196, 209
Abuja, Nigeria 81, 90
acquisitiveness 41, 66, 67, 74, 146
Actium Games 187
activism 42, 227
Adam 19, 64
advertising 91, 207–208
Aeneid 55, 177
affluence 38–39, 42, 156
Africa 31–35, 42, 44–45, 56, 59, 87–89, 97, 99, 136, 210, 224, 230, 233
African Christian theology 32
African Initiated (Independent) Churches 45, 230, 231
agoraphobia 80, 87
AIDS 201
Akkad 127
al-Qaida 101
Alexandria 87
alienation 23, 40, 48, 145, 218
America 93–97, 230, 233
American cities 69, 71, 83–84, 93, 95
Amsterdam 105
Ancient Near East 124, 141

anomie 30, 72
anti-urbanism 19, 21, 22–24, 40–41, 70, 74, 122–123, 181, 200, 217
Antioch 192, 200
Antonine Wall 106
Anxiety (painting by Munch) 66, 73
apartheid 32, 89
Apocalypse (book of Revelation) 68, 192, 206, 212, 239
apocalypticism 91, 94, 216
Approaching A City (painting by Hopper) 73
architecture
  classical 197, 203, 213
  modern 80–81, 83, 86, 93, 95–96, 104, 116–117, 123
Areopagus, Athens 195
Arequipa 88
arms race 220, 221
Ashurbanipal, library of 50, 51
Asia 31, 36, 45, 88, 89, 187, 202, 205, 208, 216, 221, 225, 230
Assyrian Empire 46, 54, 168, 171, 215
Athens 18, 40, 56, 80, 187, 194, 195
Atlanta 84

Babel, Tower of 49, 117, 125–126, 195, 217, 218

Babylon 18, 23, 26, 40, 46, 49, 52, 127, 147, 166, 168, 171–172, 205, 210, 212, 238

'Babylon' (Rome) 205, 210, 212

Babylonian Empire 156, 171

Baghdad 49, 59

Bauhaus 77

Beijing 37, 38

Berlin 66, 76, 138

Bible see Scripture index

bipolar-moralistic model 70, 71

Birmingham 67

Bogota, Columbia 97–98

Bologna 60

Brasilia 81, 90

Bristol 67

Bruges 60

Budapest 105

Buenos Aires 89, 91

bureaucracy 62, 74, 140, 145

Byzantium 58, 59

Caesarea 175

Caesars, cult of 174, 184, 189, 193, 202, 222

Cain and Abel 122

Cairo 59, 99, 100

Calvary see Jesus, death of

Calvinism 62–63, 107, 108, 112

Canaan
    cities of 53, 125, 130–131, 132, 133–140
    Conquest of 133–134, 176

Cape Town 94

capitalism 66–67, 68–69, 70–71, 73, 78, 93, 116

cathedrals 95, 103, 105, 106, 108

catholicity 235–236

Celtic Christianity 106, 233

central business district 69

Charismatics 230

Chartists 204

children, treatment of 76, 86, 100, 137, 159, 160, 189, 200, 220

China 23, 37–38, 87, 93, 97, 233

Chongqing, China 37–38

Christ Event 198, 225, 228, 229

Christendom, medieval 44, 64, 65, 66, 82, 105, 192, 193

church buildings 95, 104, 110–111

churches, suburban 234

cities of refuge 139–140

cities of the South 45, 87, 89, 94, 109

cities of the world 165–170

city
    ambivalence towards 23–25, 127, 169–170
    birth and growth 48–73
    earthly see City of Man
    heavenly see City of God; Heavenly City; new Jerusalem
    meaning of 29, 36, 37, 50, 53–55, 56–58, 68, 75, 103, 105, 115–117, 121–122, 123, 145
    negative views of 23, 29, 30, 40, see also anti-urbanism
    positive views of 23, 29, 40, 74, see also pro-urbanism

City of God 22–24, 32, 40, 58, 69, 149, 165, 211–213

City of Man 32, 40, 66, 75

city skylines 103–106, 108, 111, 113–114, 141

civilization 19–20, 21, 23, 24, 54–55, 59, 76, 145, 164, 174–175, 213, 225

claustrophobia 80

Clyde, River 106, 109, 114, 115, 116

Cologne 60

colonial cities 11, 88–89

colonialism 32, 44, 88

comfort 147, 151, 160–161, 196, 211, 229, 238

commerce 21, 72, 85, 106, 108, 182, 187, 208

community (Christian) 162, 177, 194, 198–199, 203, 205, 222–223, 225, 228, 230, 234–235, 239–240

community (general human) 20, 23, 24, 29–30, 41, 43–45, 57, 60, 69–70, 78, 94, 95, 99, 127, 149, 152, 155, 218

Confucian culture 97

Constantinople (modern Istanbul) 18, 58–59

consumerism 36, 85, 87, 102, 115, 116, 196, 207–208, 216

conversion 236–237

Copperbelt 89

Coptic Church 87

Corinth 192, 203

covenant 46, 130–133, 142–149 passim, 152, 154, 156, 163–164, 166, 172, 178

Covenanters 109

creation 25–26, 39, 54, 125, 162, 184, 203, 213

cross see Jesus, death of

Crucifixion see Jesus, death of

Crystal Palace, London 68
cultural mandate 123, 127
culture 234
Curitiba, Brazil 97–98
Cuzco 88

Damascus 59, 166
Dan 141
death 50, 53, 127, 140, 206, 209, 211, 220,
    227, 240
  of the city 83, 92, 128, 149, 152, 157–158,
    160–162, 169
  covenant with 155–156
  of Jesus see Jesus, death of
debt 24, 132, 175, 175–176, 177–178, 183,
    199, 224
Decapolis 178, 179, 180
Delhi 59
demon possession 178–179
demonic, the 140, 180, 181, 185, 221, 222,
    225–226, 236
disorders 72–73, 81, 86, 100, 183
Djenne 87
Dominicans 60, 61
dualism 184
Dubai 24, 34, 36, 37, 57–58

ecological footprint 18, 162
economic growth, 164, 102, 219–220, 224
economistic culture 207, 219
Eden 19–20, 23, 26, 49, 65, 82, 122, 123,
    169, 213
edge cities 84
Edinburgh 63, 67, 112, 115
Egypt 21, 46, 100, 101, 129–130, 131, 166,
    171
ekklesia 194, 195, 223
  urban 197, 202, 231–235, 236
elderly people, treatment of 86, 92, 165
elites 100, 105, 140, 198, 238, see also global
    elites; political elites
emergent church 44, 234–236
empires 44, 46, 48–49, 54–56, 134, 166–168,
    171–172, 215, see also Assyrian Empire;
    Babylonian Empire; Egypt; Roman
    Empire
Enlightenment 66, 69, 93, 97, 100, 184, 230
Enuma Elish 51–52, 54, 126
Ephesus 192, 205
Epic of Gilgamesh 50, 53
equality 98–99, 102, 132, 152, 221

eschatology 23, 200
ethical challenge 62, 102, 114
Ethiopia 87, 166
ethnic tension and conflict 198, 200, 203,
    226
Euphrates, River 21, 48, 50, 129
Europe 31, 32, 60–61, 94, 103
evangelicals/evangelicalism 43, 96, 97, 111,
    112, 226–227, 231, 233, 234, 235
evil 29, 40, 44, 53, 57, 126–127, 140, 145,
    149, 153, 178, 181, 213, 216, 217, 220,
    225–226
exile, Babylonian 147–148, 160–162, 164,
    165, 167–168, 171, 223, 237–238
existential crises 66, 85–86, 227
exodus from Egypt 54, 130, 135, 140, 142,
    152, 184
exorcism 226
Expressways 83, 162

favellas 45, 90, 136, 215, 216, 229
female followers of Jesus 181–183
feminist critique 86, 95
Fertile Crescent 92–93, 166, 168
fishing industry 182, 183
Florence 61, 64
foundational ethics 42
Franciscans 60
free-market economics 90
freedom 221

Galilee 167, 172–178, 180, 181–182, 188
Galilee, Lake of 173, 175, 183
garden cities 78–79, 82, 213
garden vs city 19–24
Gemeinschaft 70, 71
gendered space 86, 183
genealogy of urban shrines 105
Geneva 62–63
Gentiles 178, 198, 209
Gesellschaft 70, 71
Ghent 60
Glasgow 11, 12, 23, 25, 63, 67, 105–116
  City Chambers 111, 112, 115
  George Square 112–113
  Gorbals 114
  M8 motorway 114
  Merchant City 108
  as Red Clyde 113
  slum clearances 114
global elites 24, 220

Global South 11, 44, 87, 90, 94, 97, 99, 100,
    102, 114, 136, 200, 200–201, 201, 203,
    216, 219, 224, 229, 230–231, 232
global/globalized cities 90, 91, 197, 217, 220
globalization 34, 71, 155, 202, 208, 219,
    223–224, 224, 229, 232, 236
globalized economy 115, 136, 137, 206, 232
God-of-the-gaps 154
Gomorrah 49, 127, 128
good city 55–58, 99
good life 29, 42, 44–45, 58, 102
gospel
    of Caesar 184, 202
    significance of term 184, 197
Great Assize 155, 160, 164
Great Plains, North America 93, 94

Hadrian's Penhellenion 223
Haran 48, 53, 156
Havana 88
Hazor 141
Heavenly City 43, 58, 60, 66, 213, 223
Heliopolis 46
hell 40, 225, 227
Hellenistic cities/culture 194, 213, 223
Hellenization 178, 186
Helsinki 105
Herodian dynasty 173–175, 182, 186, 187,
    210
Herod's Temple 174, 187–188
Highland clearances 109
Hiram, king of Tyre 141, 167
holy commonwealth 63, 107, 112
Holy Russia 59
Hong Kong 38
honour 41, 198, 199
hope 19, 25–26, 38, 40, 45, 46–47, 95, 97, 99,
    101–102, 123, 131–132, 143, 146, 147,
    154–155, 156–158, 160–162, 189–190,
    203, 205, 207–208, 211–212, 216–217,
    221–225, 227, 231, 233, 236, 239–240
horses and chariots 138–139, 164, 220
house-church, Roman 198–199, 200
hubris 82, 94, 140, 164, 167–168, 218
human consciousness, affects on 71–73
hypermarkets *see* shopping malls

iconic buildings 37, 103, 104, 105, 110, 111,
    116, 141, 187, 200, 218
ideologies 71, 128, 137, 151, 167, 220–221
idols/idolatry (biblical and modern) 77, 164,

189, 206, 208, 218, 219–221, 222–223,
    224, 226, 236, 239–240
imagination 40, 46, 47, 55, 123, 151,
    206–207, 207–208, 215, 230, 238–239
    prophetic 160–161, 168, 237
imago Dei 127
imperial cities 45, 46, 103, 129, 180, 190, 198,
    210, 223
imperialism 88
Independent Labour Party 113
individualism 44, 74, 84, 117
Industrial Revolution 20–21, 29, 30, 64–69,
    74, 105, 124
industrialization 21, 23, 39, 43, 44, 75, 107,
    112, 204
inequality 38–39, 97
insulae (Roman tenement blocks) 199
International Style 81, 90
Iranian Revolution (1978–9) 100
Isaiah of Jerusalem 155–156
Islam 59, 87, 88, 99–100, 101, 102, 195, 235
Islamist movements 100–101
Israel, religion of 54

Jeremiah's Confessions 157–158
Jerusalem 25, 40, 132, 147–148, 156, 158,
    161, 186–189, 220
    destruction of 157, 168, 171, 186, 189,
        237
    as Holy Zion 140–146, 148
    Jesus' lament over 189
    negative and positive attitudes towards
        142–146
Jerusalem temple 145, 148–150, 156–157,
    174, 187–188
Jesus
    and the city 172–176, 183, 189
    death of 181, 189–191, 193, 195, 197, 203,
        211, 225–228, 237, 240
    message and ministry 182, 184–185
    methodology 185
    Nazareth 'manifesto' 177, 181
    resurrection of 172, 181, 184, 190, 192,
        193, 195, 212, 227
Jesus movement 181, 182, 188, 192, 194
Joanna 181, 182, 183
Johannesburg 32, 34, 91, 102
Jos, Nigeria 159
Joseph 129–130
Joshua 135–137
jubilee 132

Judah 139, 143, 154, 237
judgment 40, 108, 122, 149, 155–157, 160,
    164–165, 166, 168, 202
justice 24–25, 26, 57, 72, 94, 98–102, 100,
    102, 112, 123, 132–161 *passim*, 169, 175,
    177, 195, 200, 202, 204, 213, 218, 220,
    224–225, 230, 236

Kampala 32, 88
Kano 11, 59
Karachi 99
Katrine, Loch 25, 112
Kenya 18, 89, 109
Khartoum 34
Kibera, Kenya 18
Kilwa 88
kingdom of God 23, 45, 64, 142, 165, 178,
    181, 183–184, 186, 188, 194, 229, 234
Kinshasa 34

Lachish 22, 141
Lagos 11, 32, 34, 81, 88
lament 146, 151, 155–162, 167, 169, 210, 239
    for the city 155–160, 189
Laodicea 205–206
Las Vegas 58
Latin America 45, 88, 89–90, 97, 99, 208,
    216, 230
leaven 185, 186, 204, 223
Leeds 67
legions, Roman 173–174, 178–179
Letchworth 78, 79
liberation 23, 25, 30, 32, 42, 139, 168, 190,
    230, 240
light
    divine 19, 47, 165, 206, 216
    metaphorical 185–186, 193, 204
    physical 80, 82, 85, 90, 138, 213–214
    spiritual 54, 143, 156, 160
Liverpool 67
London 40–41, 60, 61, 67, 68, 73, 76, 101,
    105
love 24–26, 57, 132, 134, 148, 152–156,
    163, 180, 189, 191, 194, 198, 199–201,
    203, 205, 218, 220, 222, 225–226, 231,
    236–237, 240

Madinat al-Harar ('Silk City'), Kuwait 36–37
Madrid 101
Magdala 182
Majority World 224

Mall of America, Minneapolis 85
mammon 77, 181, 220
Manchester 67, 73
Manila 11
Marduk 51–52, 126
market economy 75, 78, 90, 239
market forces 29, 99, 219
marriage and family life 153–154
Marsh Arabs 92–93
Mary of Magdala 181, 183
megacities 89, 94, 98, 99, 114, 136, 231
Memphis 46
merchants/merchant class 61, 62, 106–108,
    198, 210
mercy 218
Mesopotamia 48, 51, 56, 129, 130, 133
Metropolis (movie) 36, 39
Mexico City 88, 89, 90–91
Middle Ages 50, 58, 65
middle classes 73, 84, 110, 111, 113, 116
migrants / migration 34, 36, 37, 84, 90, 109,
    127, 133, 138, 232, 235
military urbanism 220
Milton Keynes 79
modernism 21, 77, 93, 94
modernity 68, 87, 91, 240
modernization 23, 81, 88, 89, 97, 132
Mombasa 59, 87
monarchy, Israel's 131, 140–142, 144, 147, 149
monasteries 60, 67, 95
money 29, 37, 67, 72–73, 77, 107–109,
    116–117, 132, 147, 178, 185, 188, 191,
    229, 234, 294, 299
monuments 103, 104, 105, 107, 110–111, 196
moral absolutes 217
Mosaic Law 133, 156, *see also* Torah
Moscow 59
motor car ownership 83, 84, 95, 96
multi-ethnic church 223
multicultural church 235–236
Mumbai 91, 94
Muslim cities 11, 99, 208, 216, 230
Muslims *see* Islam
Muslims, British 194–195
myth/mythology 51, 53–54, 55, 85, 125, 126,
    130, 151, 167, 184, 186, 196, 208, 219,
    220, 225, 238

Nairobi 18, 32, 88, 94, 101
    Korogocho slum 201, 202
    Mukuru-Kayaba slum 229

Naples 61
nations (the) 26, 43, 113, 127, 138, 143,
        160–171 *passim*, 177, 189, 195–196, 198,
        208–210, 212, 213, 224, 239, *see also*
        Table of Nations
native peoples, treatment of 89, 94, 133
nature 30, 54, 66, 81, 93, 125, 130, 164, 173,
        213
Nazareth 'manifesto' 177, 181
Nestorians 233
networked society 18, 235
New Age 230
New Delhi 89
new Jerusalem 23, 26, 82, 191, 205, 210–214
New Rome 104
New Towns Act (UK, 1946) 79
New Urbanism 95–96
New Year Festival 52, 126
New York 76, 83, 84, 101, 114, 162, 212
Nigeria 159
Nighthawks (painting by Hopper) 73
Nile, River 48, 129
Nineveh 46, 49, 50, 54, 127, 156, 166, 167
non-Pauline literature 203–205
non-places 218
North America 31, 32, 36, 93, 94, 136, 184

Operation Gommorah 137
Orthodox monks 233

Pacific 31
palace(s) 48, 50, 52–53, 103, 131, 141, 183
Palestine 124, 130–131, 134–135
    at time of Jesus 172–175, 180, 186, 197
Palm Jumeirah development, Dubai 24
Pantheon, Paris 104
paradigm shifts 231
Paris 60, 61, 66, 76, 104–105
Parthenon, Athens 80
pathologies, urban 19, 66, 69–73, 74, 80,
        85–87, 152, 216, 227
patriarchs 46, 48, 49, 129
Pauline Christianity 192
Pax Romana 197, 203, 209, 223
peace 24, 26, 55, 60, 82, 134, 138, 140, 145,
        156, 165, 168, 189, 191, 203, 220, 221,
        225, *see also shalom*
Pearl River Delta, China 93
Pentecost 187, 195, 212, 228, 229, 231
Pentecostalism 45, 229–231
Pharaohs 129–130

Philistia 166
pilgrims 60, 106, 148, 175, 187, 195
polis 57–58, 85, 103, 177, 222
post-colonial cities 44, 89
post-colonialism 102
postmodern cities 37, 91, 104, 235
postmodernism 21, 22, 44, 102, 104, 115,
        230
Potosi, Bolivia 88
Poundbury, Dorchester, UK 96
poverty, the poor 38, 43, 44, 73, 89, 110, 112,
        178, 202, 234, *see also* rich–poor division
prayer for the city 128, 146, 159
pre-industrial society 21, 124
pre-patriarchal time 124–128
preaching 216
Presbyterianism 110
Priene, Roman province of Asia 202
primate cities 89
pro-urbanism 23, 123, 127, 217, 222–223,
        224–225
progress 65, 72, 74, 76, 89, 93, 97, 102, 162,
        169, 217, 225
proof-texting 46, 121
propaganda 55, 149
    Babylonian 168
    Roman 177, 184, 207, 211, 238
prophets, prophetic critique 127, 147–148,
        150, 177, 217–218, 221, 237–238,
        239–240
prostitution 68, 153, 200, 201
public health 216
public space 86, 87, 91, 98, 99, 117, 208

Qur'anic Belt 99

Radiant City 80–81, 82, 84
Reformation, Protestant 61–64, 66, 106, 107
Reformers 43, 65, 67
religion, religious critique of urban 148–151
Renaissance 64–65
resurrection *see* Jesus, resurrection of
Revelation, book, of 205–212, 213
rich–poor division 37, 97, 110–111, 178, 198,
        201
Rio de Janeiro 94
Roman Empire 106, 171, 173–174, 175, 177,
        184, 192–197, 203, 206, 209, 210–211,
        215, 221, 223, 238
Roman legions 178–179
Romans, Letter to the 197–202, 206, 222

Rome 18, 24, 55–56, 103, 106, 180, 192, 194, 198, 199, 200–201, 210–211, 225
royal consciousness 151
royal-temple ideology 155
Russia 59, 104, 233

sacred cities 49–55, 82, 106
sacred kings/kingship 54, 129–131, 134, 139, 189, 238
sacred shrines 108
sacred space 50, 68, 103, 150
sacred, the 95, 104–105, 153, 165, 169, 214
Salisbury 32
salt 92–93
salt (spiritual) 185–186, 193, 204, 223
salvation 55, 122, 142, 152, 153, 181, 183, 195, 202, 212, 222, 224, 226, 239
San Francisco 83–84
Saxony 61
Scream, The (painting by Munch) 65–66
secular, the 54, 63, 105, 214
secular shrines 105, 108–109, 111, 112, 113, 116
secularism 229, 240
secularization 41, 45, 104, 112
Sepphoris 174, 176, 177, 188
Sermon on the Mount 178
sex/sexuality 153–154, 155, 234
sexual exploitation 199, 200
shalom 128, 131, 138, 140, 162, 164–165, 189, 190, 220, 232, 236
shame 64, 157, 199
Shanghai 38, 91
shanties 136
Sheffield 67
shopping 86, 95, 216
shopping malls (hypermarkets) 85, 86, 115, 116, 218
slave trade 108
slums 11, 12, 38–39, 42, 44, 45, 71, 90, 94, 112, 200–202, 224, 229, 233
social transformation 62, 101, 136, 137, 201, 218, 231
sociology 49, 66, *see also* urban sociolgy
Sodom 40, 49, 127, 127–128, 128
South America 31, 88
Soviet Union, former 23
Spirit, Holy 228
strangers 60, 71–72
streets 80, 84, 92, 213, 235
Structural Adjustment Programmes 100, 101

suburban sprawl 84, 92, 95, 96
Sudan 87
suffering 42, 44, 50, 53, 91, 94, 98, 100–101, 114, 137, 146–149, 151, 154, 157–159, 161, 164, 179, 186, 191, 193, 207, 216
Susa 46
Susanna 181
sustainability 163
syncretism 144, 188, 230, 240

Table of Nations 49, 127–128, 165–166, 195
technological society 122, 123
Tehran 99
Temple Sermon of Jeremiah 150
temples 48, 50, 52–53, 82, 103, 104, 131, 134, 141, 155, 190, 196, *see also* Jerusalem temple
terrorism 101, 190, 220
theophany 130, 131
throne of God 206
Tiberius 174, 175, 182, 188
Tigris, River 21, 48
Timbuktu 59, 87
tobacco trade 107–108
Torah 131–133, 135, 139, 141–142, 148, 152, 156, 176, 184, 188, 220, 228
tourism 36, 108, 115, 159, 175
tower blocks 81, 94, 114
town halls 104, 105, 111
trade 60, 61, 70, 89, 107, 108, 149, 167, 169, 188
tribal confederacy 135, 142
tribes 30, 71, 132, 176
Tyre 166, 167, 169

Ubuntu 45
United Nations 31, 38, 151
universities 60–61, 103, 106
Ur 48, 53
urban conflicts 159
urban cultures 11, 18, 21, 43, 48, 58–61, 87, 92–93, 107, 225, 235
    biblical views of 123, 126, 142, 167, 169, 174, 175, 181, 183, 185, 188, 191, 192, 197
    hybrid 232, 235
urban elites 37, 125, 127, 130–131, 132, 134, 136, 148, 167, 174, 175–176, 178, 197, 199, 201, 219
urban footprints 18, 162

urban futures 24, 26, 34, 38, 97, 101–102, 229
urban growth 20–21, 29, 31, 38, 49–74, 84, 88, 110–111
urban imagineers 123, 239
urban ministry 11–12, 121, 148, 151, 233–234
urban mission 185–186, 194, 228, 233–234
urban myths 85, 186
urban phobias 66, 79–80, 81, 86, 87, 90
urban regeneration 97–98, 115, 168
urban sociology 18, 69, 73–74
urban spirituality 43, 143, 146, 203, 229
urban theology 41, 42–47, 214, 215–240
urban villages 71, 96
urbanization 19, 43, 88, 215, 218
   in Africa 31–34, 33 Fig 2.2, 35 Fig 2.3
   defined 17–18
   and modernization 89
   recent and projected trends 31 Fig. 2.1
   Reformation 61–64
urbicide 138, 161
Uruk (Ered) 49, 50, 127
utopia 23, 40, 75, 78, 93, 113–114, 138, 210

values 18–20, 32, 37, 77, 78, 97–98, 163, 173, 175, 186, 191, 197, 204, 205, 212, 217, 227, 240
   cultural 67, 116, 199, 218, 219
   ethical 99, 169, 217, 236
   gospel/kingdom 65, 165, 187, 191, 194, 228
Venice 60, 61
Victorian Christianity 77, 213
Victory of God/Christ 191, 193, 211, 225, 226

Vilnius 105
violence 21, 22, 40, 54, 75, 101, 127, 133, 135–140, 144, 151, 157, 159, 166–167, 170, 179, 184, 203, 206, 216, 220, 222
   myth of redemptive 54, 220
virtue 57, 85, 99

wailing 64, 65, 159
walled cities 48, 103, 134, 136
Washington DC 104
Way (of Jesus Christ), The 194, 222, 228, 229
Welwyn Garden City 78
West Asia 31
Westernization 217
will-to-power 226
women, treatment of 86–87, 159, 183
World Christianity 44, 232, 235, 236
world cities 34, 235
World War, First 77, 79, 84
World War, Second 137
worldviews 32, 104, 111, 125, 135, 173, 178, 181, 184, 206, 207, 215, 217, 225, 238–239, 240
worship 41, 43, 95, 97, 115, 130, 134, 142–143, 148–150, 152, 159, 165–166, 168, 170, 177, 185, 188, 193, 213, 220–221, 224, 225, 235, 238–240

Yahweh(ism) 130–135, 139–140, 142–150, 152–155, 160–166, 168, 177, 184, 188, 238–239

ziggurats 49, 126
Zurich 63